FORT UNION AND FORT WILLIAM

Letter Book and Journal, 1833–1835

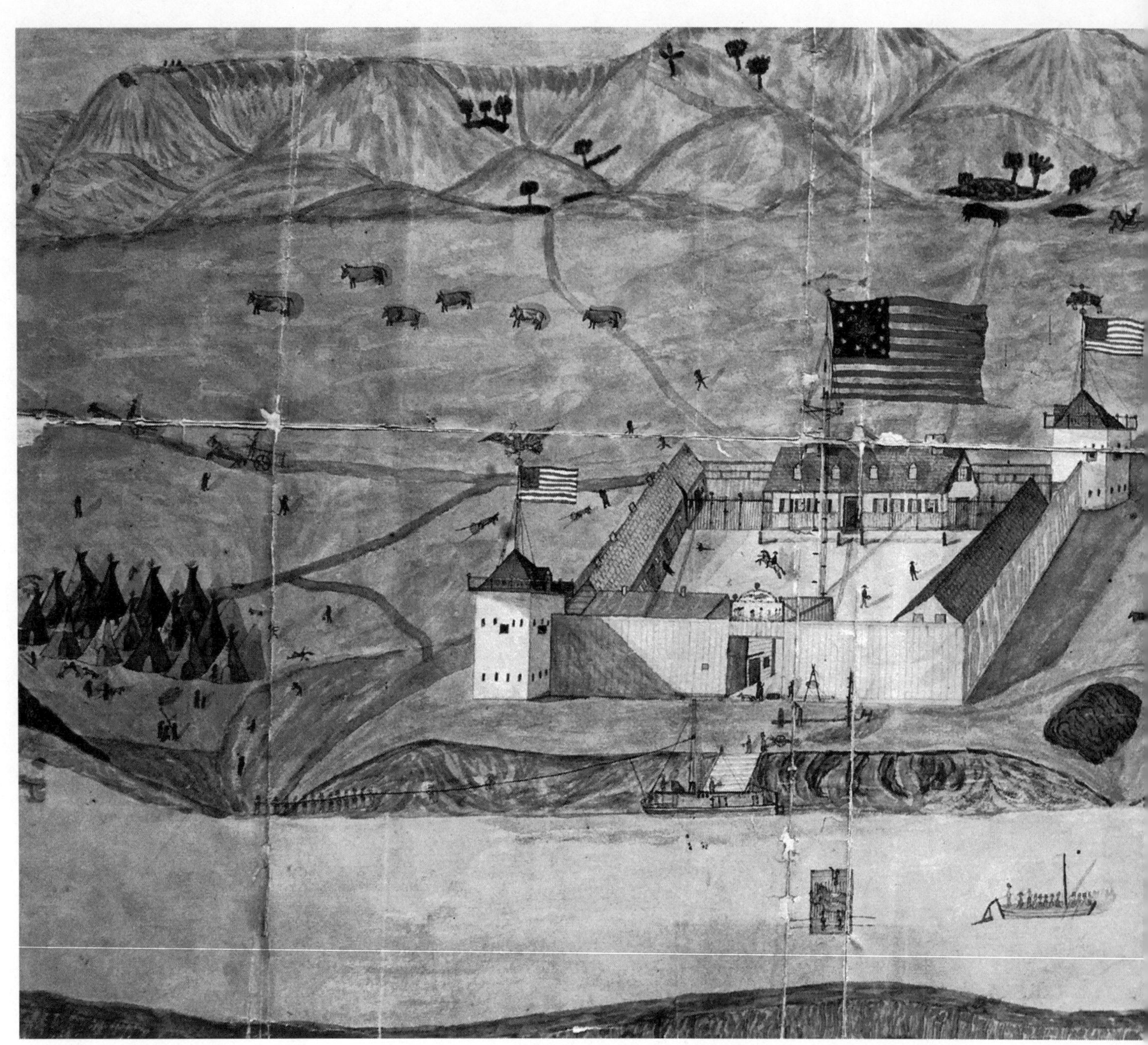

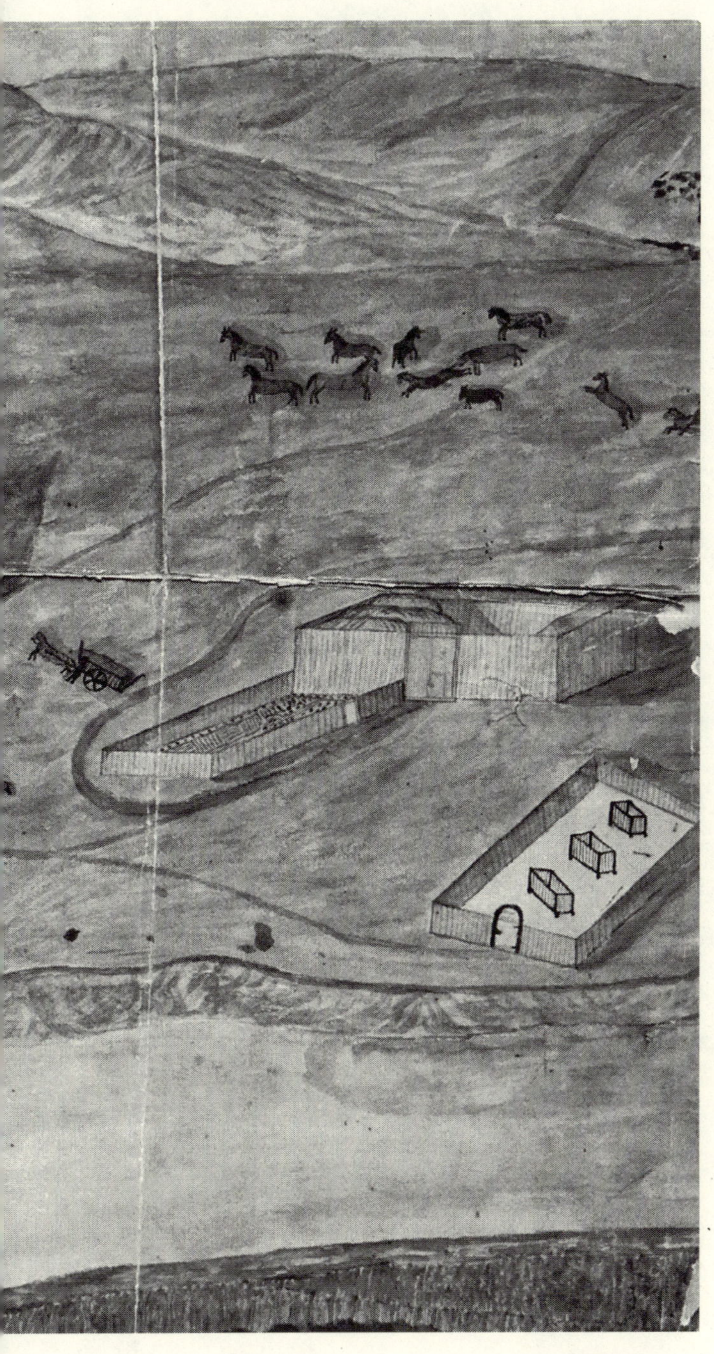

Fort Union and Fort William

Letter Book and Journal, 1833–1835

Transcribed and Annotated by

W. RAYMOND WOOD *and*

MICHAEL M. CASLER

Forward by William J. Hunt, Jr.

SOUTH DAKOTA
HISTORICAL SOCIETY
PRESS Pierre

The South Dakota Historical Society Press gratefully acknowledges Orville and Janelle Loomer and W. Raymond Wood for their help in funding this publication.

The paper in this book meets the guidelines for permanence and durability of the committee on Production Guidelines for Book Longevity of the Council on Library Resources.

Cover image:

Text and cover design by Rich Hendel
Typeset in Miller, Sentinel, and Egiziano by Kim Bryant

Please visit our website at sdhspress.com.

Printed in United States of America

Library of Congress Cataloging-in-Publication Data
is available

Cover image
Jean Baptiste Moncravie depicted Fort Union (left) and Fort William (right) in this painting, c. 1843.
Midwest Jesuit Archives

CONTENTS

Foreword *by William J. Hunt, Jr.* vii

A Note on the Letter Book Transcription xi

Introduction 1

1 FORT UNION LETTER BOOK 7
29 October 1833–10 December 1835
Notes 61

2 THE PRIVATE JOURNAL OF ROBERT CAMPBELL 83
Transcribed and Annotated by George R. Brooks
21 September 1833–31 December 1833
Notes 100

APPENDIX 109
Letters Concerning Fort William, 1833–1834

Bibliography 119

Index 123

FOREWORD

It was 1827, and the richest man in America, John Jacob Astor, was about to obtain his long-sought goal of participation in the fur trade west of the Mississippi River. Astor, who had emigrated from Germany in 1784, built a financial empire through his shrewd business acumen. He created the American Fur Company (AFC), which the New York State Legislature incorporated in 1808, after the Lewis and Clark Expedition reported the great wealth in furs on the upper Missouri.[1] Astor's attempt to expand his fur business to the Pacific from 1810 to 1813 failed, but he subsequently regrouped, creating a fur empire east of the Mississippi and along the Great Lakes.

In 1822, under the direction of Astor's field manager Ramsay Crooks, the AFC established a Western Department at Saint Louis, the acknowledged headquarters of the Rocky Mountain/Missouri River trade. For some time, the powerful Saint Louis trading firms operated by the Chouteau and Pratte families successfully repelled the AFC's repeated efforts to get more than a toehold on the western trade. Nevertheless, after an initial management contract with the Saint Louis firm Stone, Bostwick and Company, Crooks secured an agreement with a major player, Bernard Pratte and Company, to manage the AFC's Western Department in 1827. That same year, the AFC made a similar arrangement with the Columbia Fur Company, the most important trading firm operating on the upper Missouri and west of the Mississippi in what would become Minnesota Territory. The men in this company were seasoned, with experience in the Canadian, Missouri, and Great Lakes trades. The company was not capitalized to the extent that it could control the upper Missouri trade, however, a factor that facilitated its partnership with the AFC.

As part of the articles of agreement, the Columbia Fur Company, now called the Upper Missouri Outfit (UMO), withdrew from trade in the Minnesota/Mississippi region, turning their forts and business over to the AFC's Northern Department. In return, the UMO acquired all trading posts, trade goods, and employees of Bernard Pratte and Company and the AFC on the Missouri River above its confluence with the Big Sioux River. Theoretically, the UMO was under the bureaucratic umbrella of the

Western Department, but it functioned more as an independent enterprise than a subdepartment. The UMO ordered and received its trade goods and sold its furs and robes through the Western Department, which then channeled its orders and products through the AFC in New York. This arrangement allowed the company to combine orders from its various branches and partnerships to purchase trade goods in bulk at greatly reduced prices. The AFC was also able to place a massive volume of furs and robes on the American and European markets each year, giving it an advantage in setting prices for its products.

With the new partnership in place, the UMO refocused on controlling the upper Missouri trade. The UMO's proprietors were William Laidlaw, Daniel Lamont, and Kenneth McKenzie, the latter serving as the president, or agent, of the company. In order to secure the upper Missouri trade, particularly the lucrative trade with the Blackfoot Confederacy, McKenzie and his partners sought to establish a large trading house that would serve as the UMO's administrative headquarters and as a warehouse to hold goods for lesser posts. Doing so would allow the UMO to expand its control over the higher reaches of the river and the mountains to the west. Their chosen location was at the confluence of the Missouri and Yellowstone rivers. From here, all of the drainages to the west, from the upper Platte River in present-day northern Colorado to the United States–Canada border as well as the lucrative, fur-bearing northern Rocky Mountains could be easily accessed by land or by water.

In the fall of 1826, James Kipp took men and equipment to the mouth of the White Earth River and built Fort Floyd on its eastern bank. The fort was either named after Sergeant Charles Floyd of the Lewis and Clark Expedition or his cousin, Virginia congressman John Floyd. The Columbia Fur Company had agreed with the Assiniboine Indians the year before to build a post in their territory.[2] At the time, it was the farthest western expansion of the company. The post came under the control of the UMO the next year and remained operational until the spring of 1830, when Francis Chardon abandoned and burned it.[3]

In October 1828, McKenzie sent a new outfit of men aboard the keelboat *Otter* from the Mandan post near Knife River to the confluence of the Missouri and Yellowstone rivers. The expedition was successful, and despite cold weather and freezing ground, the outfit had raised the palisades of the new Fort Union by 26 December 1828.[4]

For the next four decades, from 1828 through 1867, Fort Union served as the major trade distribution and collection center on the upper Missouri. As headquarters of the UMO, it was the grandest of America's western fur trade establishments. Fort Union was the main staging point from which the AFC and its successors—Bernard Pratte & Company and Pierre Chouteau, Jr., & Company—could easily access the fur and robe trade in the Rocky Mountains and high plains. It was the primary trading post for the Assiniboines on the American side of the border, although much of the trade was also conducted through secondary and smaller wintering posts such as Forts Floyd, Assiniboine, and Kipp, the Dauphin trading houses, and Roulette's Post, among others.[5] Similarly, Fort Union served other American Indian nations by warehousing trade goods and returns for posts that traded with the Crows (Forts Van Buren and Alexander), the Blackfoot Confederacy (Forts Piegan and McKenzie) and to a much lesser degree the Crees and Métis.

During its existence many Euro-American explorers, traders, artists, and travelers visited the fort and recorded their impressions of this "proud citadel in the wilderness."[6] Artists who depicted Fort Union include George Catlin (1832), Karl Bodmer (1833), Rudolph Friederich Kurz (1851–1852), John Mix Stanley (1853), Karl Ferdinand Wimar (1858, 1859), and William de la Montagne Cary (1861). Aside from its economic importance, the post significantly contributed to the history of western exploration, hosting researchers in natural science (John James Audubon in 1843 and Thaddeus Culbertson in 1850) and anthropology (George Catlin in 1832, Prince Maximilian of Wied Neuwied in 1833, and fur trader Edwin Denig from 1837 to 1854). The trading post and its owners also played instrumental roles in transforming western transportation. In 1831, the AFC built the first steamboat, the *Yellow Stone*, designed to ply the upper reaches of the Missouri River.[7] Such vessels largely replaced overland routes and human-powered keel boats, allowing the UMO to haul people and massive amounts of trade goods to the far reaches of the upper Missouri. The post also hosted Governor Isaac I. Stevens's 1853 transcontinental railroad survey expedition.

Finally, Fort Union served as the home of the United States Army from 1864 to 1865, just as its campaigns against American Indian tribes heated up on the northern plains. The soldiers and the fur traders shared the fort and made many physical changes to it during its last years of existence. In 1867, the army purchased the dilapidated old trading post. Soldiers promptly tore down the building and used the materials to construct a new military post, Fort Buford, about two miles downstream at the confluence of the Yellowstone and Missouri rivers. Given all these contributions, Fort Union is not only the longest lasting fur trade post in America but one of the most important frontier sites.

William J. Hunt, Jr.

Notes

1. The incorporation expired in 1834.
2. According to Charles Larpenteur, "the chief of the band of Rocks had desired [McKenzie] to build" there (Larpenteur, *Forty Years a Fur Trader on the Upper Missouri: The Personal Narrative of Charles Larpenteur*, 2 vols., ed. Elliott Coues [New York: Francis P. Harper, 1898], 1:109).
3. Until recently, many confused Fort Floyd, at the mouth of the White Earth, with Fort Union, some arguing that Fort Floyd was the first name for the post at the Yellowstone confluence that later became Fort Union. This error, its history, and correction are described in William J. Hunt, Jr., "'At the Yellowstone.... to Build a Fort': Fort Union Trading Post, 1828–1833," *Fort Union Fur Trade Symposium Proceedings* (Williston, N.Dak.: Friends of Fort Union Trading Post, 1994), pp. 7–23; and "Origins of Fort Union: Archaeology and History," in *Fur Trade Revisited: Selected Papers of the Sixth North American Fur Trade Conference, Mackinac Island, 1991*, ed. Jennifer S. H. Brown, W. J. Eccles, and Donald P. Heldman (East Lansing/Mackinac Island: Michigan State University Press and Mackinac State Historic Parks, 1994), pp. 377–92. Chardon abandoned and burned Fort Floyd sometime after May 1830; he was in charge of Fort Tecumseh by July 1830. Annie H. Abel, ed., *Chardon's Journal at Fort Clark*, by F. A. Chardon (Pierre: South Dakota Department of History, 1932), pp. 229–30n90. *See also* W. Raymond Wood and Michael M. Casler, "A New History of Fort Floyd, North Dakota," *North Dakota History* 80 (Winter 2015): 3–13.
4. Excavations at Fort Union from 1986 to 1988 provided evidence of rushed construction of the palisades, suggesting that the ground froze early. For the sake of expedience, workers sawed planking rather than use split or whole timbers to enclose the north side of the trading post. Hunt, "Origins of Fort Union," pp. 383–84. New documents confirm the 1828 construction: "The people of the Yellow Stone arrived on the 11th Instant [11 May 1829], the returns from that place falls much short of what we expected, only amounting to 270 packs of Buffalo Robes, 29 Rats & 13½ Beaver or say fifteen packages of beaver" (Kenneth McKenzie to Messrs. Laidlaw & Lamont, May 1829, E. V. Papin Collection, Missouri Historical Society Archives, Saint Louis).
5. For descriptions and histories of the western fur trade posts, *see* Robert G. Athearn, *Forts of the Upper Missouri* (Englewood Cliffs, N.J.: Prentice-Hall, 1967); R. G. Robertson, *Competitive Struggle: America's Western Fur Trading Posts, 1764–1965* (Boise, Ida.: Tamarack Books, 2012).
6. Erwin N. Thompson, *Fort Union Trading Post: Fur Trade Empire on the Upper Missouri* (Medora, N.Dak.: Theodore Roosevelt Nature & History Assoc., 1986), p. iii.
7. The steamboat *Yellow Stone* was built in Louisville, Kentucky, in 1830–1831. It was a side-wheel, measuring 130 x 19 x 5.5 feet and weighing 144 tons. Michael M. Casler, *Steamboats of the Fort Union Fur Trade: An Illustrated Listing of Steamboats on the Upper Missouri River, 1831–1867* (Williston, N.Dak.: Fort Union Assoc., 1999), p. 37; Enrollment Papers, *Yellow Stone*, Enrollments 1832–1834, Vol. 7959-C, p. 591, Custom House Records—Port of New Orleans, Records of the Bureau of Marine Inspection and Navigation, Record Group 41, National Archives and Records Administration, Washington, D.C.

A NOTE ON THE LETTER BOOK TRANSCRIPTION

The transcription we offer in this presentation of the Fort Union Letter Book follows contemporary documentary editing standards, clinging as closely as print will allow to the original handwritten text. These standards derive from those Gary E. Moulton employed in *The Journals of the Lewis and Clark Expedition* and the recommendations in Mary-Jo Kline's *A Guide to Documentary Editing*, a study prepared for the Association for Documentary Editing.[1] The resulting product is a literal rendition of the original, though we have made certain concessions to economy and clarity. Robert Campbell's journal, on the other hand, is reprinted as originally published in the *Bulletin of the Missouri Historical Society* in 1963–1964, with notes and an introduction by George R. Brooks.[2]

The original Fort Union Letter Book and Campbell's journal have been reproduced with the permission of the Missouri History Museum in Saint Louis, where the originals are housed. Letter books are clerk's copies of the communications sent by the bourgeois of Fort Union to the owners of the company and to directors and employees of its various sub-posts. Robert Campbell's journal is written in his own hand. A few minor typographical errors that we noted in Brooks's transcription have been silently corrected here.

Andrew W. Hahn, director of the Campbell House Museum in Saint Louis, provided the texts of the eight letters in the appendix. Tom Gronski, the museum's lead researcher and historian, provided us with careful new transcriptions; he corrected many errors from earlier efforts, so these letters vary somewhat from previous versions. Four of the letters (numbers one, five, six, and eight) are reproduced with the permission of the Campbell House Museum; two of them (numbers two and seven) are in the archives of the Missouri History Museum and are published courtesy of director of library and collections Christopher Gordon; and the two Rocky Mountain Letters (numbers three and four) are published as they appeared in *The National Atlas and Tuesday Morning Mail*, 6 Dec. 1836. Brian Austin of Mandan, North Dakota, created the fine map for this book.

All spellings, punctuation, and grammar have been preserved in the letter book. Kenneth

McKenzie was a good writer, and his spelling and grammar are usually excellent, although he spelled French words phonetically. No spelling has been changed to conform to modern usage or practices, except that raised letters at the end of abbreviations or contractions have lowered to the line. Underscored words have been underlined. We have retained those few entries in which words or lines were scored out, which appear struck out in our text, though some words were not legible and have been denoted [word struck out]. Single words or letters added by the editors to clarify the text appear enclosed in brackets. A few of the letter book documents had previously been published. Annie H. Abel's transcriptions of some of the letters in *Chardon's Journal* closely follow modern usage, though the careful reader will note minor and inconsequential differences between our presentations. Kenneth McKenzie's letters relating to Prince Maximilian also have been published.[3]

The Fort Union Letter Book offered an array of problems for transcription. Sentences that ended in commas or periods and dashes have been standardized as periods. Paragraphs sometimes are indicated by indentations, but often a change in content that otherwise would be indented is denoted by a dash. The reader therefore will find that paragraphs have been added when they are not in fact indented. Capitalization follows that in the original, though in the few cases where the author's intent was not clear we have followed modern usage. The original also contains several complex tables that we have reformatted for readability. Readers will note that the headings and closings of the letters have been standardized. Some letters were chronologically out of place, but their position in the letter book has been retained.

The editors are grateful to William J. Hunt, Jr., Nicole St-Onge, and Robert Englebert for use of their employee databases for the American Fur Company/Upper Missouri Outfit. Both the UMO Employee Database and the AFC Voyageur Contracts Database proved extremely useful in helping us identify the workforce of this massive undertaking on the upper Missouri River.

Our annotations in the Fort Union Letter Book generally are confined to noting those persons, places, and events that are necessary to understand the content of the entry. The documents are designed for further scholarly study, for, as Donald Jackson once said, the documentary editor's work is not meant to be exhaustive, but to be plundered.

Notes

1. Gary E. Moulton and Thomas Dunlay, "Editorial Procedures," in *The Journals of the Lewis and Clark Expedition*, Vol. 2: *From the Ohio to the Vermillion*, ed. Moulton and Dunlay (Lincoln: University of Nebraska Press, 1986), pp. 49–54; Mary-Jo Kline, *A Guide to Documentary Editing* (Baltimore, M.d.: Johns Hopkins University Press, 1987).
2. Robert Campbell, "The Private Journal of Robert Campbell," ed. George R. Brooks, *Bulletin of the Missouri Historical Society* 20 (Oct. 1963): 3–24 and (Jan. 1864): 107–18.
3. Michael M. Casler, "Letters from the Fur Trade: Kenneth McKenzie's Letters to Prince Maximilian at Fort Clark, 1833–1834," *Museum of the Fur Trade Quarterly* 41 (Spring 2005): 9–14.

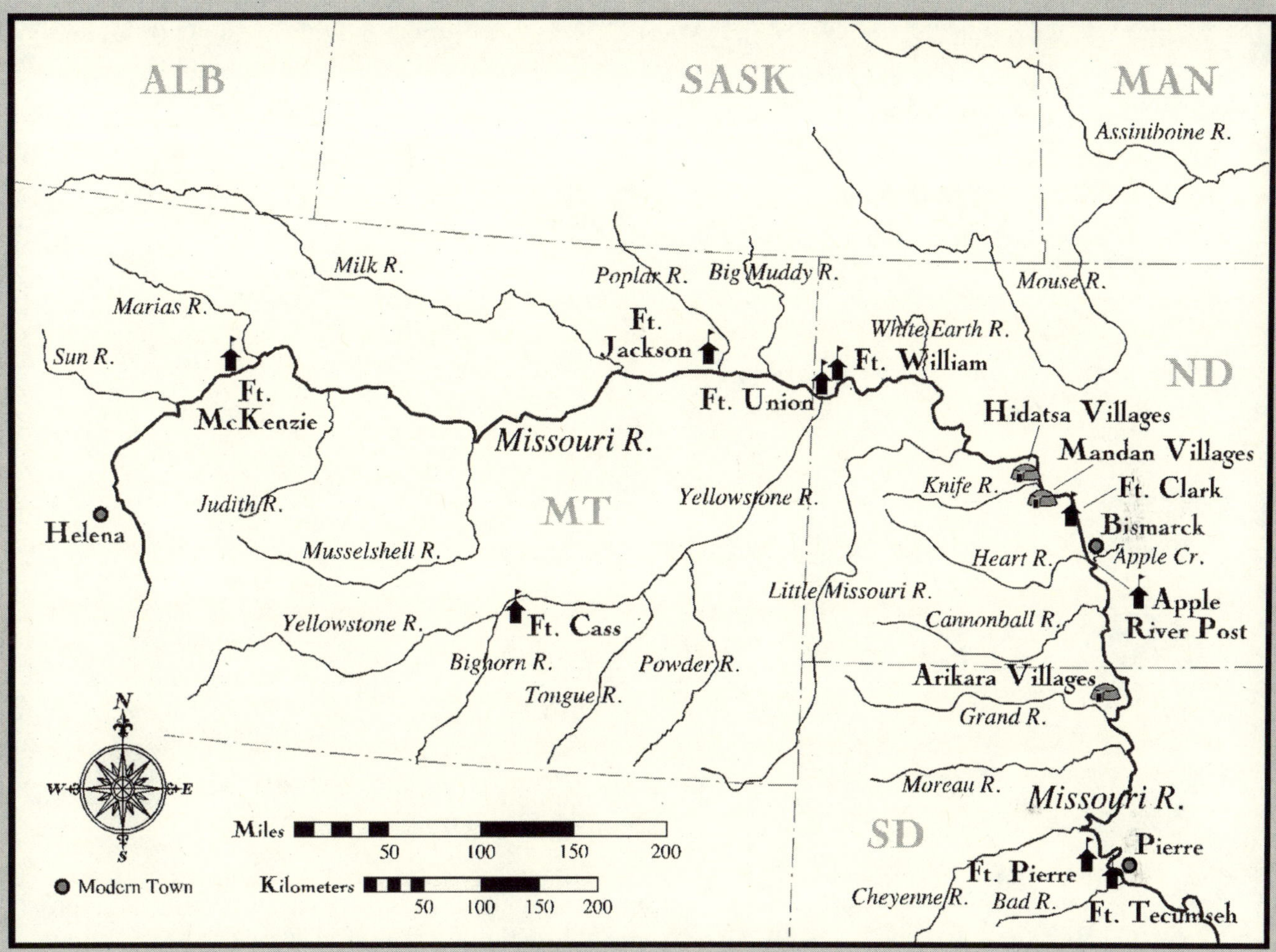

Map by Brian Austin

INTRODUCTION

The 1833–1835 Fort Union Letter Book and the 1833 journal of Robert Campbell provide a rare glimpse into the fur trade at a time when it was undergoing major realignments. Beginning in the early 1830s and continuing throughout the decade, the Upper Missouri Outfit (UMO) transitioned from a trade largely focused on beaver and peltries to one dominated by bison robes. Traders took in rapidly diminishing numbers of beaver pelts throughout the 1830s, as the species had been nearly exterminated in the Rocky Mountain valleys. Trapping was a dangerous and often brutal occupation, fraught with many hardships and the ever-present threat of attack by American Indian tribes, especially the Blackfoot Confederacy, who controlled the prime fur-bearing areas of the Rockies. Further, hat makers had discovered a much cheaper substitute for beaver pelts: the coypu, its fur known as "nutria."[1] As the decade ended, male hat fashions switched from beaver, to nutria, and then to silk, reducing the overall demand for and value of beaver pelts.

With the downturn of peltry prices, the fur trade became dependent on bison robes, a product of seemingly unlimited supply. Whereas white trappers had primarily collected beaver pelts, bison robes were a wholly American Indian product. Women in several tribes produced tanned robes by the thousands, which American factories used as raw material for lap blankets, gloves, and heavy coats for winter travelers.[2] Throughout the decade, traders shipped ever-greater quantities of bison robes from the upper Missouri posts. In 1832, trader James Kipp brought 6,450 pounds of beaver but few bison robes from Fort McKenzie, near the Marias River. Three years later, a trader at the same post shipped fifteen hundred pounds of beaver and nine thousand bison robes weighing forty-five tons to Saint Louis.[3]

Disastrous changes in the markets compounded this monumental change in fur trade products. In 1834, a financial panic that would last the remainder of the decade struck America and Western Europe and had major impacts on the fur trade. The American Fur Company (AFC) had to change in order to survive. That same year, Astor, aging and perhaps seeing the handwriting on the wall regarding the coming turmoil in the trade, decided to sell his interest in the AFC. He sold the Western Department, known as Bernard Pratte and Company when the original partnership was established, to Pratte, Chouteau and Company of Saint Louis, which a few years later became Pierre Chouteau, Jr. and Company. The Upper Missouri Outfit remained an element of each of these reorganizations of the Western Department. Ramsey Crooks acquired the eastern branch of the business, retaining the name "American Fur Company" and applying it to the AFC's former Northern Department. Nevertheless, the general public referred to all of the company's former branches as the American Fur Company.[4]

As business practices and products shifted, Fort Union also underwent physical changes. Archaeological excavations in the mid-1980s demonstrated that the original post, built in 1828, was rather hastily constructed. It was of average size, 178 feet wide and 198 feet deep. The pickets, or palisades, of the fort walls were set in trenches, and the buildings inside the fort either sat directly on the ground or slightly raised on log footers. This kind of construction was not intended to provide a permanent facility, for the soft cottonwood used to build the post could not last much more than ten years.[5]

Kenneth McKenzie, who had become a man of great wealth and power, initiated construction of a new and much more impressive trading post in 1833, when the Fort Union Letter Book and Robert Campbell's journal begin. References to construction events appear many times throughout both documents. Whereas the first post went up in months, its replacement took three years to complete. The new fort had more internal capacity than its predecessor, adding thirty-two feet in width and forty-two feet in depth. Rather than placing elements of structures in trenches or the ground's surface, the builders set all structures on stone quarried from the hills to the north, including the palisades, which increased in height from fifteen to eighteen feet.[6] In the process, two of the unsupported walls blew down during one of North Dakota's "gentle zephyrs," an event remarked upon by Robert Campbell in his journal on 15 December 1833: "Last night two sides of McKenzie's new fort was leveled with the ground. He had built a stone and lime foundation and raised his pickets thereon but as it appears something more substantial is required in this country to brave the winds."[7]

Builders corrected this structural deficiency by placing a massive bracing system on the post's interior to support the palisade walls. A stonemason traveled from Saint Louis to construct elaborate new stone blockhouses at the southwest and northeast corners, among the last structures to be built. They were almost finished by the time James Archdale Hamilton observed, "The bastions are completed with the exception of laying down the floors" in a letter to McKenzie on 29 March 1835.[8] Workers then whitewashed Fort Union's palisades and buildings, making them visible from many miles away, and gaily adorned McKenzie's house with green and red trim.

Reading the letter book is somewhat like listening to someone's telephone conversation. You only hear one side of the dialogue so, without some context, it is often difficult to understand what is going on. Yet, these compilations of outgoing letters were common items at upper Missouri fur trade posts. They document the movement of men and trade goods and capture how company managers directed their employees in the field. While the responses to these messages have rarely been preserved, the reader can often infer whether the recipient followed instructions by reading ahead. These letters also introduce us to some of the most famous fur trade personalities of the day. The voice of the "King of the Upper Missouri," Kenneth McKenzie, is prominent during the first couple of years of dispatches from Fort Union. His letters reveal plenty of ego, hubris, and a tinge of ruthlessness, while hinting at much intrigue. James Archdale Hamilton, who often signs letters as "JAH," reveals himself a capable head clerk. Yet, he apparently disliked being forced into the role of acting agent after McKenzie embarked on a forced European "vacation" in 1834 to avoid legal troubles. Another notable figure mentioned in the letters is "the fort builder," James Kipp, an "old man" in his forties with much experience in the Canadian and American fur trades.[9]

Several other prominent characters in the American fur trade appear in the letters, among them Francis Chardon, Honoré Picotte, Pierre Didier Papin, Johnson Gardner, Joshua Pilcher,

William Laidlaw, Pierre Chouteau, Jr., Ramsey Crooks, John J. Astor, and Alexander Culbertson. Virtually every person with a prominent hand in the upper Missouri trade in the early 1830s is either mentioned or sent a communiqué from this post. The document is indeed important and instructive, one of the last unpublished sets of papers associated with Fort Union. Until now, the Fort Union Letter Book has largely languished in obscurity. Annie Heloise Abel included some of its letters in her edition of *Chardon's Journal*, and the entire document has been available on microfilm in the original handwritten form through the Missouri History Museum, but only a few fur trade scholars have examined it.[10] With this publication, the entire letter book appears for the first time in an accessible and easy-to-read format, making it available to a broad audience.

Another important document in this publication is Robert Campbell's 1833 journal, first published in the *Bulletin of the Missouri Historical Society* in 1963–1964. Its inclusion here supplements the letter book by providing the other side of the story, so to speak. In contrast to the letter book, whose documents are formal in tone and addressed outward to other individuals, Robert Campbell's journal is personal, revealing the author's innermost thoughts and emotions. It offers a detailed glimpse into the daily activities of one of the UMO's "opponents," the Missouri Fur Company, at Fort William, a few miles downstream from Fort Union. Campbell clearly had a hard time at the confluence, in part due to his being left to run his company's business without the assistance of his partner William Sublette. The machinations of "the King," however, largely caused his misery. Campbell admits as much on the final day of December 1833: "I can safely say as unhappy a time as this I have never before passed during my life. What is worst our prospects are not good for McKenzie has hired our interpreters and bribed them whilst they were here to betray us."[11] Interestingly, after the AFC purchased the properties and goods of the Missouri Fur Company, they dismantled Fort William and transported it piece-by-piece to a site about two hundred yards east of Fort Union. Once re-erected, it provided housing for UMO employees and their families, hay storage in the winter, and protection for the fort's cattle and horses from storms and thieves.

The Fort Union Letter Book and Robert Campbell's journal—in addition to the eight newly-transcribed letters from Robert Campbell and William Sublette that appear as an appendix—provide interesting windows into the fur and bison robe trade on the Northern Great Plains in the early 1830s. They complement one another in viewpoint and in detail, illustrating the hardships and loneliness traders endured, while making clear the amount of business acumen they needed to succeed. Together, these sources add another small but important piece to our understanding of this chapter of American history.

Notes

1. In 1832, John Jacob Astor's son William wrote to Pierre Chouteau, "An excellent good looking Hat, when napped with Nutria, can be sold for $4.50 and yield more profit to the manufacturer than one made of beaver at double the price" (Quoted in David S. Lavender, *The Fist in the Wilderness* [New York: Doubleday & Co., 1964], p. 412).
2. The American Fur Company briefly attempted to trade bison robes on the European markets. The robes could not compete with cheap German blankets, and the experiment failed. The greater share of the company's business turned from the foreign to the domestic market, as robes were a profitable commodity throughout the eastern United States and Canada. Andrew B. Chamberlain, *Historic Furnishings Report: Indian Trade House and Strong Room, Fort Union Trading Post National Historic Site, Williston, North Dakota* (Harpers Ferry, W.V.: National Park Service, 1993), p. 23; Michael M. Casler, "Drayage Included: Steamboat Operations of the American Fur Company at St. Louis," in *Indians & Traders: Entrepreneurs of the Upper Missouri—Fort Union Fur Trade Symposium 2000 Proceedings* (Williston, N.Dak.: Fort Union Association, 2001), p. 121.
3. Lavender, *Fist in the Wilderness*, p. 412.
4. The incorporation of the American Fur Company expired in 1834. From 1834 until his death in 1848, Astor focused on investments, lending money, and real estate. At his death, he was the wealthiest man in America. Hiram M. Chittenden, *A History of the American Fur Trade in the Far West*, 3 vols. (New York: Francis P. Harper, 1902), 1: 364–67.

5. Lynelle Peterson and William J. Hunt, Jr., *The 1987 Investigations at Fort Union Trading Post: Archeology and Architecture* (Lincoln, Nebr.: National Park Service, Midwest Archeological Center, 1990), p. 109.
6. Erwin N. Thompson, *Fort Union Trading Post: Fur Trade Empire on the Upper Missouri* (Medora, N.Dak.: Theodore Roosevelt Nature and History Assoc., 1986), p. 15.
7. "The Private Journal of Robert Campbell," herein.
8. "Fort Union Letter Book," herein.
9. By leaving so abruptly, Kenneth McKenzie failed to sign the new 1834 Articles of Agreement between the Upper Missouri Outfit and the Western Department. The original four-year contract, signed in 1827 at the creation of the UMO and renewed again in August 1830, lapsed, and the UMO ceased operating as a quasi-independent company and became more of an accounting entry. Michael M. Casler and W. Raymond Wood, "The Rise and Fall of the Columbia Fur Company: Rethinking the Fur Trade on the Northern Great Plains," paper delivered at the 2018 National Fur Trade Symposium, 26–29 Sept. 2018, Bismarck, N.Dak.
10. Annie Heloise Abel, ed., *Chardon's Journal at Fort Clark, 1834–1839*, by F. A. Chardon (Pierre: South Dakota Department of History, 1932), pp. 353–83; William R. Swagerty, ed., *Papers of the St. Louis Fur Trade, Part 1: The Chouteau Collection, 1752–1925* (Bethesda, M.d.: University Publication of America for the Missouri Historical Society, 1991), microfilm ed., reel 22.
11. "The Private Journal of Robert Campbell," herein.

1

FORT UNION LETTER BOOK

29 October 1833–10 December 1835

Fort Union 29 Oct 1833
Mr Jas Kipp[1] [Fort Clark]
Dear Sir

You were doubtless apprized by Mr McKenzie that it was very probable the Baron Braunsberg with Messrs. Bordman & Drydopple[2] would pass the winter at your fort, this will be handed you by the Baron & I am satisfied he will receive every attention in your power to render him. I have endeavored to persuade him to pass the winter here but he is so anxious to gain full information relative to the Mandan's[3] & Gros Ventres[4] thro' your means that he cannot wait for it until Spring. If Mr McKenzie[5] on his way hither before this reaches you allows me to request you will make such arrangements for the Baron's comfort as the nature of your establishment will allow, he will require men to conduct him down stream in the Spring but hereon you will receive instructions during the winter. Hugron Beaugard & Beauchamp[6] will remain with you until further orders & you can no doubt find them work to do, the latter has generally attended on the Baron to make his fire carry water &c. H[enr]y Morrin & L Vachard[7] you will send back after a day or two rest unless you are expecting dispatches from below & wish to keep them to [be] the bearers thereof for a few days longer.

I send you the statement of the Men's a/c's, if Morrin or Vachard take any thing at Ft. C. charge it to this post handing me particulars on their return. Mr Chardon[8] Comp[limen]ts. I beg to assure you of my best wishes & am &c.

[Signed] JAH.[9]

The Baron is charged in a/c with the boat; will you have it looked after during the winter that it may serve him in the Spring.[10] I send you lists of prices to be charged Baron B. other things in like proportion on his departure send copy of his a/c to Ft. Pierre handing him duplicate. Make any purchases you can in accordance with his wishes of the Indians & charge him a reasonable price. ~~that~~ please supply him with what he applies for if you can.

[Signed] JAH.

Fort Union 30 Oct 1833
K. McKenzie Esqr.
Dear Sir

On 5th Inst. I wrote you by Dubreuille,[11] & sent letters from Mr Mitchell & Mr Tulloch[12] if they reached you ~~you~~ in course, you will be prepared to find Baron B. at Ft. Clark. The Baron looks to you to find men to take him to St Louis in Spring he paying their wages as also from Ft. McK. to Fort Clark.

I have no portion of Morrin's engagement; Mr M. relies on his being back with him & Vachard also. I send Hugron to accommodate the Baron as he complained much of his first crew also Beauchamp who acts as servant & Beaugard a simple harmless fellow who is terribly haunted with fear of dying without confession & being buried in unconsecrated ground. I have furnished a fresh boat. I send you duplicate of the Baron's a/c. M. Gravelle & the Deschamps[13] are returned from hunting we have only 100 lb Beaver from them: Mr. Campbell[14] has engaged the 3 Deschamps for one year at $1500 salary. Le Vache Blanche Le fils des Gros Français le Jamb blesse & L'Ours have been here but nothing to trade they have crossed the river to hunt. Le Brechu's band with Gens de Canot are on head of White Earth r[iver]. Le Manguer d'homme on R au tremble & have cattle. Le Gauche[15] is gone to the north with 100 lodges. Le Sonnant ["The Rattle"] came in to beg dogs & horses he has two lodges with him, no peltries. On 10th Ins. Duchaine deserted with Durocher[16] who arrived the preceding day. On 14th Miller[17] deserted he had tried for 10 days to persuade Maloney & Holmes[18] to go with him. The work progresses tolerably well but having lost the boat the supply of stores is very scant. Hunters have killed cows once only since you left. A copy of mens a/c is enclosed to Mr Kipp, you will of course direct the men whether to remain or return here. Yours truly

[Signed] JAH

Fort Union Wednesday Nov 13. 1833
Robt. Campbell Esqr [Fort William]
Dear Sir,

On visiting you yesterday I was under the impression that you were disposed to negotiate with me for the transfer on equitable terms of your several establishments Mdse. stock &c. I listened to your proposition & after due reflection thereon am constrained to say our views differ so widely that as any offer I could make might to you have the appearance of under-rating the value of your property & decline submitting any proposal to your notice and remain Dr Sir Yours truly

Sent by J.B. Moncrevier.[19]

(Signed) K. McKenzie

Fort Union Dec 17 [1833]

M Jas. Kipp [Fort Clark]

Dear Sir

Hy. Morrin & the men under his charge made a long trip not arriving here until 29 Nov, being so long absent I was fearing some accident had happened to them. I was glad to get your letter of the 15 Nov although much disappointed that the long looked for express[20] from St. Louis was not forth coming however before breakfast on the 9 Dec the express arrived. ~~The express arrived~~. I thank you for your promptitude in forwarding it and now very particularly request that not an hours unavoidable delay may interfere with the progress of my packet for Fort Pierre & St. Louis, every hour is of consequence and after all with every exertion I fear my letters will not reach St Louis in time for my proposes but I rely on every effort being made to effect my wishes.

The extraordinary state of the weather (for even the river here, flows smoothly on like Spring) preventing my compliance with your wishes in sending Mdze & Stores, so soon as trains can travel I will endeavor to supply all your wants not forgetting the bitters for your Stomach's sake. I have not Sugar to supply my table until Spring but I will spare you a little.

I shall write to Baron Braunsberg and though I cannot let him have Hy Morrin I will arrange to supply him with men in time for his descending the river. I am very sensible that a good deal of trouble is laid on your shoulders by the Baron's arrangement to winter with you, as you observe he is a fine old gentleman and I much regret that I have not his company for the winter myself.

I arrived here safe & well on the 8 Nov.[21] and have experienced a continued succession of fine weather since that day: on the 13 Nov Mr Chardon started with a snug equipment & 20 men in boat to build and winter near la rivière au tremble,[22] he writes me that he has a comfortable fort abt 80 ft. square called by him Fort Jackson, the Indians are visiting him regularly and giving him abundance of provisions, his prospect of making robes is far more cheering than mine: Cattle are far off [&] it takes my hunters 6 or 7 days to send in a supply of fresh meat and the Assiniboins[23] are poor, poor, beyond any thing ever known on this river, horses they have none, their dogs they have eaten[24] & a large portion of the Indians have not killed cattle sufficient for their own clothing.

Our opponents are not idle, they have opened a house near Mr Chardon.[25] Deschamp's three hopeful sons are in their employ, and are very active, they have sent Glenday & a Mr Vasquez[26] to the Crows,[27] they are giving a blanket for a robe, and have already partially dressed several Indians. You know that I have hitherto abstained from this procedure but I suppose I shall be driven to it in my own defence and if I begin I will do it well. I expect a good many Crees to trade here this winter, M Gravell is engaged as interpreter. Should cattle even yet visit us in numbers as they once did there are Indians enough on the river for me to make a respectable quantity of robes notwithstanding the opposition I have to compete with.

I am well pleased that Pecotte [Picotte] kept Ortubise[28] to winter with Crawford and hope they will do well.

I would wish Bellehumer[29] to be at one of the Indian villages for even with the utmost industry & exertion on our part our opponents contrive to get both beaver & robes that should come to us: I am informed that Durand[30] has a pack of beaver & a great many robes, if true, 'tis pity, that with his small means he should do so much

You astonish me by one observation in your last letter, "The interest of the Company suffering by your not having Sct, Chfs [Chiefs] Coats & Gr Blkts [Green Blankets]." you know they are waiting for you at Apple River[31] & even if you had no horse both you & I remember the time when two men could carry on their backs as many Chiefs Coats & blankets as would supply your immediate wants. I cannot bear to hear or read the word "impossible" applied to business affairs especially when of so easy accomplishment.

You inform me that Bapte. Deguire[32] is employed

by you, having passed an engagement with Mr. Pecotte; when he left Fort Cass[33] in Sept last, he was indebted to A.F.Co. $205.04 & engaged to deliver two horses he had ~~with~~ to bring him down on his arrival here, however, he sold his horses to Subletts[34] Co for $80 and never shewed himself here at all, keep your eye on him.

Our opponents are almost without horses & are offering such unusual prices to the Indians even for horses they know to have been stolen from the Mandans or Gros Ventres that I wish you to keep your Indians on their guard for in consequence of the opposition my power of restraining the ~~Indians~~ Assiniboins is at an end and as soon as Winter sets in they ~~Assiniboines~~ will endeavor to make a haul.

I do not expect our opponents will make any considerable number of robes at Fort William[35] as was to be expected the Assiniboins rushed towards them at first but having spied out the nakedness of the land they have nearly all returned to their old allegiance.

You know the sorrel horse, white face, which I rode up, called Steam boat, he is a pleasant riding horse, & has already proved himself one of the best buffalo horses I have, I am told he is 9 or 10 yrs old, and though I should very unwillingly part with him, if Bellehumer cannot get an American horse to suit him at Fort Pierre where they have a good collection or if he prefers said Steam boat he shall have him in the Spring at $120.

Please send me acct. of advances to L'Anje Guerir[36] who came up with Hy Morrin.

A few days after my arrival Mr Campbell called upon me to ascertain if I was disposed to buy their company out, but as he could not sell the Sioux outfit in which Leclerc[37] had a share until Spring, moreover being unwilling that Leclerc should [words struck out] prior thereto be privy to any transaction we might enter into and more especially as it was your opinion made in which all my old respected clerks on the river concurred, that it was not good policy to buy out opposition, rather work them out by extra industry & assiduity, I was somewhat indifferent to Mr Campbells proposition & after two interviews the negotiation broke off. [Word struck out] I trust I am not unreasonable in expecting that all my experienced & faithful clerks will justify by the results of the Spring the correctness of their opinion.

Our opponents must get some robes but it is my wish that it should be on such terms as to leave them no profit.

I have been very unfortunate with my dogs this Summer and am unable to procure a single one from the poor Assiniboins. I must look to you to secure me a few trains by the time I send down.

I send you a little Calomel and hope when obliged to be used it may always be efficacious.

Fr. Croteau[38] an engageé is privileged to accompany the express to St Louis, on his arrival there he will be free & on paying his debt to the A.F.Co. of $107.

(Signed) K. McK.

Fort Union Dec 15 1833
M. Baron de Braunsberg [Fort Clark]
Sir

I beg to acknowledge the receipt of your letter by Hy Morrin bearing date Nov 15th and assure you it has been cause of great regret to me that our travelling arrangements so clashed as to prevent our meeting had I been so fortunate as to have arrived here before your departure I think I should have prevailed on you to have given me your company for the winter and although at any place in this wild country you must have suffered some privations I would have endeavoured to have made them less sensible than at any post not under my immediate personal control. If the fates have so ordained that we do not meet again in the Missouri territory I do hope Sir at no distant day to renew the acquaintance in your Country for I shall ever cherish the most agreeable reminiscences of our last Summer's intercourse.

With respect to your arrangements for the Spring [two words struck out] I will find you men to convey your boat down stream but I cannot promise you Hy Morrin as he is about to make the voyage to Fort McKenzie and cannot be down in time to answer your purpose, but I trust you will be fully satisfied with such men as I shall appoint to conduct you. Although the winter has not yet commenced, no snow having fallen, for a month past not a single gale of wind, & the river flowing as smoothly in front of the fort as in the month of May, yet though it tarry it will come. I shall then renew this pleasure and in accordance with your request will furnish you my bill of charges. I have no prospect of visiting Fort Clark this winter but Mr Hamilton tells me he invited you hither if you find the voyage practicable and to me there appears no insurmountable difficulty, allow me to assure you of a hearty welcome and that your visit will be considered an honor conferred on

Sir
Your very obedient Servant
(Signed) K. McKenzie

Fort Union Dec 15 1833
Mr Hr Picotte[39] [Apple River Post]
Dear Sir

The express which I had long waited for with so much anxiety reached me on the 9th Inst. just one month after my arrival; for the promptness with which you accelerated its progress accept my thanks. The tin Smith arrived here Nov 29, he is a good workman I shall find him a ~~valuable~~ most useful artisan.

It was some cause of regret that adverse winds had prevented you reaching Apple river at the time I passed but the detail of your arrangements and the result of your exertions since your arrival are so satisfactory that it is evident no additional remarks from me were necessary as a spur to your laudable efforts if the interests of the A.F.C. are as well looked after at every other post as yours the Opposition of Messrs. Sublette & Co. will not be very detrimental to our interests. On my arrival Mr Campbell called on me proposing to sell out their interest on Missouri river at all the posts above the Sioux but Leclerc having ~~an interest~~ a share in the Sioux outfit ~~they~~ he could not sell the interest therein until Spring

I have so much confidence in the support I receive from my old & tried clerks that I was very indifferent to Mr Campbells proposition & after two or three interviews the negotiations ~~ceased~~ terminated [words struck out] if we are to be opposed on the river it will be more honorable to break up a formidable Company like our present Opponents by dint of extra industry & long tried experience ~~in the trade~~ than for them to abandon the trade from other circumstances at this ~~place~~ station which they call Fort William they have a heavy outfit, more ammunition & tobacco than I have alcohol and wine & an expensive establishment of clerks & men. They have sent a small equipment to the Crow Camp & another to oppose Mr Chardon who is stationed at Fort Jackson a five day journey above this place, the Indians naturally visited their establishment at the outset but hitherto they have had nothing to trade and I believe I shall lose very few of my old friends. My trade at this post I fear will be very limited but Sublett & Co. shall have much less, if health & vigour be spared me.

Since my arrival there has been a continued succession of fine clear weather and the river still remains open but when the winter commences & the ground is well covered with snow I will contrive to send you some whiskey.

With respect to your visiting St Louis in the Spring. I do not at this moment ~~say yea or nay, but~~ see any insuperable objection thereto and you well know that I would suffer some personal inconvenience to comply to the ~~reasonable~~ requests of those who [several words struck out] do their utmost for my interest, ~~on this subject you shall hear from me by next~~ [several words struck out] but as unforeseen circumstances may arise between this and the Spring I am sure you will excuse my not promising absolutely but you shall however hear from or see me in time for you to make your arrangements.

~~I rely on your making every exertion to forward the express to Fort Pierre for I much fear the letters will reach St. Louis too late for my purposes~~.

With respect to the boat to convey your peltries you shall also hear from me with full instructions. Will you ascertain from your Indians if they are desirous to have a permanent fort, if so I will build a good fort near the old Mandan Villages & will do all I can to please them, inform me fully hereon. You will please write to me by every opportunity, as you have hitherto done giving me all the information which reaches you of our opponents mighty deeds!! as well as your own proceedings with your Indians relative to Soldiers & endeavors to get robes I prescribe no limit but your own discretion my object as you know is to prevent the robes going past us. I am convinced all you do will be done to the best of your judgement.

B. Deguire whom I understand you engaged is indebted to A.F.C. $205.04, he ~~engaged to~~ promised Mr. Tulloch at Fort Cass to deliver his two horses on his arrival here, but he sold them to Sublett Co for $80 & pocketted the money, and [word struck out] came not to Ft. Union.[40] I rely on your using every exertion to forward the express without delay to Fort Pierre for I much fear the St Louis letters will not reach their destination in time for my purposes.

[Unsigned] [Kenneth McKenzie]

Fort Union Dec 1833
Mr P. D. Papin[41]
Onkpapa post[42]
Dear Sir

The express which reached me on the 9th Inst brought me your letter for which I thank you. On every occasion which presents itself it is very pleasant to me to receive communications from my confidential clerks traders and at this time more especially when our opponents are doing their utmost and as you justly observe by their possessing Alcohol they have a great advantage over us which can only be met by such extra experience as you possess & the extra exertion I know you will use. ~~My confidence in my old and true clerks prevented me agreeing~~ On my arrival I declined negotiating with Sublett on their proposition to me to buy them ~~On my arrival here as they wished [some words not decipherable] to do~~ out, judging it better that ~~they should withdraw of their own accord finding they their chances of success on the river to be hopeless & that~~ the unanimous opinion of all my old & tried friends should be justified by what I consider my self will be the result of our combined exertions to compel them to withdraw on finding their chances of success to be hopeless: they are very active here but hitherto with no better results than at the other stations on the river and they will find what few robes they do ~~robes they and~~ trade will cost them dear: they have sent an equipment to the Crow Village & another to oppose Mr Chardon who is stationed at Fort Jackson about three days march above me, they have abundance of Mdze. & a long list of clerks & men.

Hitherto the trade here has been inconsiderable but I have confidence in my Indians and if cattle can be found I shall have robes.

I hope it will not be long before I have another of your letters to acknowledge and please to bear in mind that all information about your own trade or the proceedings of your opponents will be very acceptable.

My express for St Louis is ~~too~~ I fear is too late in leaving this place, spare no exertion to accelerate its progress on its reaching you.

[Unsigned] [Kenneth McKenzie]

Fort Union 16 Dec 1833
Mr Joshua Pilcher[43]
Council Bluffs[44]
Dear Sir

You will long ere this have heard of my visiting Fort Pierre in the month Sept where for several weeks I anxiously awaited the arrival of Mr Lamont[45] with my letters & Invoices &c from St Louis. My patience being exhausted & having the fear of a winter voyage before me, I directed my course hither leaving Fort Pierre Oct 24 and arriving here Nov 8 the long looked for letters consigned to Mr Lamonts care did not reach me until the 9th Ins. and I much fear unless extraordinary attention is paid by my people on the river my present express for St. Louis will not reach its destination in time to answer my purpose. I know Sir I can rely on your diligence when it reaches your post to forward it [word struck out] by trusty men in the most expeditious manner, it is of very great importance that it reach Mr Chouteau[46] with the least possible delay.

I have been very busily but very unprofitably occupied with Indians since my arrival here, very few of my old friends will leave me but my opponents are not wanting in exertion, they have a large assortment of Mdze abundance of Alcohol in barrels which came up the Missouri independent of what came via the Mountains & down the Ye[llow] Stone and wine highly charged with spirits no lack. That the partiality or laxity of the Government officers should allow them to pass an unlimited quantity of Alcohol for they have abundance at all their Sioux posts and by their extreme rigor carry away every drop over which we had control not leaving us enough to moisten a hair of our heads, will surely justify me in making a complaint: be the laws good or bad they were enforced against the A.F.C. and ought in like manner to be enforced against others engaged in the same trade & at or near the same stations. Could I hope for the pleasure of a visit from you I could regale you with a glass of genuine Fort Union wine;[47] it is such as you would not sneeze at.

Notwithstanding the great pretensions and formidable preparations of our opponents I think I can say with great truth there may be great cry but very little wool at their station near me they must lose money and my information from every other post tends to the same conclusion. Mr Campbell proposed to sell out to me. I prefer that they should try their powers & finding their chance of success hopeless be compelled to withdraw.

You know the nature of opposition & that Indians will try new traders but all that are worth having ~~have~~ will [word struck out] ~~to the interest~~ stick to their old friends, saying the new people are only come for a day and [one line illegible]. I give a blanket for a robe and other things in like ratio.

There has hitherto been no cold weather here, nor any fall of snow, & the Missouri is still open, in consequence thereof Buffalo Keep so far out in the plains that though Indians are numerous, as they have neither horses or dogs, robes will be very scarce.

The Baron Braunsberg spent a month in the Black feet[48] country, passed some weeks here on his return and is now at Fort Clark where he will pass the winter he has made ~~an~~ a valuable & interesting collection of objects in Natural history & Mr Bordman has been very industrious in making drawings of the ~~most~~ peculiarly interesting scenery of the upper country with a great number of Indian portraits, the Baron expresses himself greatly <u>interested</u> with his voyage, he expects to reach your post early in May if not before.

I shall expect a long letter from you by the upward express,[49] and I trust we shall meet again next Summer.

I hope you will be able to furnish me with a good supply of corn in the Spring or my ~~corn~~ wine vats will be idle. I beg Dear Sir to assure you of the esteem of

Yours truly
(Signed) K. McKenzie

Fort Union Dec 16th 1833
M. Laidlaw[50] Esqr [Fort Pierre Chouteau]
Dear Sir

Letters explanatory of a/cs. accompanying them bearing date 18 Oct & 14 Nov were received here on Dec 9: with respect to the mens ac/s ~~it is evident Mr Denig~~ I cannot understand why some of the Manger de lard's of 1832[51] should have credit given them for their three years service & others for only one, the circumstance has mainly tended to confuse the accts. rendered here when the men came up in Steam boat. ~~and~~ Some further information is still necessary.

Chas. Trudelle[52] is stated as being engaged for 3 yr at $116.50 pr an[num]. his a/c comes to me with charge of advances on leaving Fort Pierre $148.61 & $100 placed to his credit said to be for services ending Sumr 1833, ~~I cannot understand~~ this requires explanation. Jacques Berger,[53] J.B. Moncrevier, & A. Harvey[54] each say their accts. are wrong, let me have them in total.

Invoice of Mdze ~~paid~~ forwarded from Ft. Pierre pr S.B. Assiboine[55] varies very materially from the packing a/c sent therewith & with which the goods recd corresponded. I send you particulars of Mdze which came to hand:

So soon as the Ft. Union & Ft. Clark Invoices of Mdze & Steam B. Assiniboin are examined & copied they shall be sent to you.

I send you acct of sundry men who have deserted & others who may appear at your posts. Fr. Croteau is allowed to accompany express to St Louis free on his arrival there on paying his debt.

Mr Chardon particularly requests you will entrust his woman & child to be at your fort in readiness to come up hither by Steam boat in Spring.

[Unsigned] [Kenneth McKenzie]
Invoices of Mdze &c which came by S. Boat
a/c of Duchemain[56] 240.70
Durocher 100.00
Miller 172.55
Leguire[57] 25.04

Delorme 311.50
Stapin[58] 140
F Croteau 107

Fort Union Dec 16 1833
P. Chouteau Jr Esqr [Saint Louis]
Dear Sir

My last letter from ~~this place dated 17 Sept and supplementary thereto from~~ Fort Pierre entrusted to care of Mr. E.L. Patton,[59] I ~~trust~~ presume reached you ~~safely~~ in due course. I remained at Ft. Pierre anxiously awaiting the arrival of Mr. Lamont until 24 Oct: when the rapidly advancing season compelled me to commence my journey hither. I arrived here Nov 8. and three days afterwards sent a boat with good equipment up Stream under charge of Mr Chardon to establish a trading post as near to mouth of ~~Milk R~~ R au Lait[60] as the ice then running fast in the river would permit him to proceed, after 10 days heavy work he came to anchor on this side La R. au Tremble[61] where he has built a ~~fort & called~~ fort & named it Fort Jackson ~~& is to this time doing a better trade than at this~~

I ~~found~~ considered it ~~peculiarly~~ desirable to establish a wintering post [three words struck out] west of this post for the convenience of the Indians who frequent that section of the country ~~and who have often complained that in coming hither from their hunting grounds they had to pass several successive nights without wood this season~~ and in this region, no Buffalo can be found in any other ~~direction~~ quarter there was good prospect of securing more robes [three words struck out] but principally with a view of ~~annoying~~ compelling our opponents to divide their forces and the principle of divide & conquer has often been verified; they have sent up a small equipment under Mr Geness[62] to try their powers against Mr Chardon but hitherto without any success.

A few days after my arrival Mr Campbell visited me to make a proposition to sell out to the A.F.Co. all the interest of Sublett & Co. in each and every trading post established by them from the Sioux upwards with the exception of their stock of Alcohol Brandy & other spirituous liquors: Leclerc having a share in the Sioux outfit Mr Campbell could not negotiate for the sale thereof until next Spring. I deliberated one night on the terms submitted by Mr Campbell which were too preposterous to have been acceded to under any circumstances and especially ~~considering~~ contemplating the advantage our standing in the Country ought to give us with the Indians, some consideration being also made for our hard earned experience in the Indian trade and further the inclination I felt to try the spirit & tax the exertions of our expensive establishment of clerks & traders who were unanimously of opinion that they could drive ~~them~~ our opponents from the field, determined me to ~~abandon~~ decline making an offer to Mr. Campbell even on terms that might have served our purpose. Nor do I regret having so ~~determined~~ resolved for altho' as was natural, the Indians flocked at first to the New house all who are valuable have returned to their old allegiance and if cattle are killed and robes dressed I shall have my full share: I am prepared and expect to pay a good price for them but I am no prophet if Mr Campbell does not find in the Spring his returns very unequal to the amount of his expenditure: the statements I have received from the Onkpapa, Yanctona[63] & Mandan posts are very gratifying inasmuch as the exertions of Messrs. Papin & Picott at the former have more than counterbalanced the advantage our opponents possessed in being abundantly supplied with Alcohol, and at the latter ~~post~~ the Indians are all for us: ~~Old Charbonneau cannot~~ The Gros Ventres[64] are very much scattered this winter but they express themselves so delighted by some unlooked for kindness shown a large war-party (comprising their principal men) who visited this fort last Summer that we have secured their interest.

I have no news from Crow or Black feet posts since my last: The Crows are wintering on Wind river, I have a trader with them; Mr Campbell has also sent out an equipment there & I hear Fitzpatrick & Co[65] were to winter in that country: The Baron Braunsberg arrived at Ft. Union a few days after my departure for Ft. Pierre & moved forward again down stream a few days prior to my return: he will pass the winter at Fort Clark, and take the earliest opportunity in the Spring to proceed to St Louis. I will send you the bill of charges against him to the time of his leaving Fort Clark, any subsequent expences incurred by him at the lower posts will be handed you from thence.

I much regret that circumstances prevented my further intercourse with so interesting a companion. I understand the Baron is highly gratified with his visit to this country and I trust the public will some day [two words struck out] have an opportunity of judging how judicious and indefatigable his researches have been [word struck out] relative to the manners & customs of the natives, in procuring an extensive collection of objects in Natural history hitherto unknown or undescribed, a vast number of new plants & a ponderous cargo of mineralogical specimens & a portfolio rich in Indian portraits and the peculiar and unrivalled scenery of the Upper Missouri.

I send you herewith, an order for Mdze &c requisite for Fort Clark to be packed & Invoiced as before, also a copy of the order I sent by Mr. Patton for Mdze &c for this post & a supplementary Order for further articles absolutely necessary; as to the trade here has not commenced it is impossible to say what my expenditure may be, but as I am determined to have the robes I know it will take a great quantity of Ammn. Tobacco &c.

I will give explicit instructions for the Inventories to be rendered from Fort Pierre in the mode you desire. I congratulate Mr Cabanné on the amicable arrangement of Leclerc's affairs and hope he will not suffer much in pocket how much soever he may have been annoyed in mind pending the transactions.[66]

The returns of this year ~~will~~ I hope and have reason to expect will be [three words struck out] larger in quantity & better in quality than last season.

With respect to the Mountain affairs upon the present arrangements I cannot look for profit; last Spring Mr Fontenelle[67] was empowered by me to make certain propositions to Milton G. Sublett & Co.[68] William Sublett is no longer a partner and communicate the result to me here.

I received a letter from Mr. Fontenelle but he was wholly silent on the subject: Mr. M. G. Sublett[69] arrived here, had seen Mr. Fontenelle but nothing new passed on this point, [three words struck out] I have good reason to believe he would willingly have entered into some arrangements with me, but it was as necessary for him to consult his partners as for me to know if Mr Fontenelle had abandoned the views suggested & recommended to him in the Spring, thus a chance has been lost of relieving ourselves of a dead weight or perhaps of turning the scale in our favor.

My thanks are poor payment for your care & attention to my interest relative to my buildings. I have nought else to render you. I pray you accept them, they are sincere.

The Invoices and accts. have only received a cursory glance, but I beg to make one or two observations: N. W. Guns[70] in packing a/c are priced 19/ Per charged in Invoice 21/6. Flint in like manner marked 6/6. Invoiced 7/3 2 doz. 12 in half round files & 2 doz 8 in smooth files are charged in Invoice 4 doz 8 in smooth files recd. as 12 in half round. 2 [doz] brass cocks,[71] charged as packed in box #43. None recd. 1 ps blk linen charged 33 yd it is stamped & measures 20 yd & 33 inc[hes] wide 200 Blue Barley corn beads charged, only 196 Beads recd 231 [Blue] Black [Barley corn beads charged, only] 216 [Beads recd] ~~All the butter charged to this fort~~ one bag of coffee & 230 lb Sugar & 129 lb Butter were taken for the use of the Steam Boat Assiniboin from the outfit charged to this post.

In the a/c Cur[ren]t. there is a charge on the 22 Apl of $24.75 I think [four words struck out] must be a mistake.

Mr. Chardon is very anxious to get information about his Osage boy,[72] can you obtain it and if it is practicable for him to be conveyed hither by Steam boat, please let it be done.

~~The sum~~ I could not with any propriety send off my winter express until I received the long looked for letters by Mr Lamont and though late in the season, having urged extraordinary dispatch at all the posts I hope it will reach you in due time, my order is large but I cannot prudently reduce it, and some of the articles I fear I may yet be short. To the supplementary order I have appended some remarks which I beg may be regarded.

Mr Hamilton desires his respectful remembrances. Accept Dear Sir the assurances of respect and esteem of

Your friend and Sert.

(Signed) K. McK.

[P.S.] Do not load Steam boat too much as I must have 2 or 300 bush corn from C Bluffs. Ft. U. & Ft. C. goods must be first placed on board the S. B. Goods for Sioux post if not too weighty must remain in part to follow in Keel boat which will be time enough for lower trade. Our manufactory flourishes, we only want corn enough to be able to supply all our wants the quality is fine but the yield from Mandan corn is small. You will surely contrive to send Alcohol to Bluff for Sioux trade; it is hard that people with so limited means should have an advantage over us. Campbell has not traded of every kind of 5 packs. Fitzpatrick, Capt. Stewart[73] robbed by Crows.[74]

Fort Union 16 Dec 1833
W.B. Astor[75] Esqr. [New York]
Presdt Amn Fur Co.
Dear Sir

I have the honor to receive your polite & friendly letter of the 26 Apl last, on my arrival at Ft. Pierre on the 28 Sept. In consequence of the formidable appearance our opponents presented at their various stations on the river and particularly near the mouth of the Yellow Stone two miles below this place I judged it prudent to visit our various posts this fall that by my personal instructions & advice I might in some degree counteract the plans of Mr Sublett & his partners and inspire our several clerks and traders with ~~fresh Spirit &~~ zeal & energy to drive them from the field.

Dr McKenney[76] accompanied ~~hither~~ me on my return to this place we arrived ~~here~~ on the 8th Novr. and much as I am inclined to respect him as a man and value him as a companion candor compels me to say that I fear it is beyond my power to convert him into a good Indian trader, his walk in life, his knowledge of the world, his pursuits & habits and the bent of his mind & inclinations appear to me calculated to disqualify him for the petty detail of our trade which although en masse it may some seasons present a favorable an[d] imposing appearance on paper, is made up of so many trifling transactions as tend to disgust all who are not at a comparatively early age initiated into its mysteries. There is no scope here nor at any post on the river for the fair exercise of his talents, and the drudgery of an inferior clerk would ill comport with his character & appearances views neither could I in consonance with my own feelings see him in such a situation he seems by nature formed to command though I do not question at the same time his willingness to obey: In his medical capacity ~~hitherto~~ such has been hitherto the salubrity of this climate, no one post could furnish him on the average a patient a month: Salts, castor oil, & essence of peppermint are our usual specifics and it requires but little skill in administering them: in cases arising from amatory passions the remedies are equally simple & in ~~almost~~ all cases not too long neglected are efficacious. I am thus explicit that no disappointment may be felt if after a fair trial of this western wild Dr. McKenney should find his own expectations were raised too high. Rest assured I will do all in my power to promote his views that personal respect, regard to your recommendation and the high estimation in which I hold your father and the late Superintendent of Indian affairs[77] can unitedly present to ~~my~~ claim my attention, and the result we must leave to time & circumstances.

With regard to the trade of the Upper Missouri I have reason to expect that our returns will somewhat exceed in quantity those of last year, but they will cost us dear, our opponents are well supplied at all their trading posts with Alcohol & wines highly charged with Spirit, whereas our Steam boat was minutely searched & every drop taken from her, and we have only to depend on the extra exertions of our traders the ~~footing~~ standing we have with the Indians & our hardly earned experience to countervail the decided advantage liquor ~~would otherwise~~ gives our opponents, hitherto I am happy to say our success has fully equalled my expectations.

In reply to your kind enquiries after my health and progress I beg to say that I have been happily free from sickness except of a slight nature, that ~~I left St. Louis aft when Ind~~ I had an agreeable journey to St. Louis and after remaining there 110 days placed my self on board the Assiniboin on the 10 April but in consequence of the unprecedented low stage of water did not arrive here until June 26.

Though tardy in my acknowledgements of the very many polite attentions I received from you in New York I feel afraid you will not ~~doubt~~ question the sincerity with which I now tender the respect & friendly reminiscences of Dear Sir

Yours very obediently
(Signed) K. McKenzie

17 Dec 1833

To Mr Jas Kipp [Fort Clark]

After filling one sheet some fresh ideas occur to me on commencing a second: the fact is I want much to see you and consult you about some matters that I cannot well put on paper & it strikes me you could at this season make the trip in a short time & be hardly missed from home, Belhumer I presume you may safely place in charge.

I send you down one extra man P Gaboleau[78] to return with you & you will bring two more men with dogs & trains to supply yourself with Mdze & stores such as you want & I can spare in addition to the dogs necessary to carry down your goods you must contrive to bring me at least 6 more or all you can. Every day after Jany, 1 I shall be looking for your arrival. Could it be practicable for you to pass New Years day with me it would afford me much pleasure, at all events the sooner I see you the more agreeable.

Mr Hamilton desires his respects & will be happy to greet your arrival in conjunction with your friend & well wishes & who always has pleasure in subscribing himself

Yours very truly

(Signed) K McKenzie[79]

Acct. Le Brun, Denoyer, J. Papin, Fr Delorme[80] & Calomel $1

To Mr Chouteau Dec. 17. 1833

[Page Blank]

Fort Union 16 Dec 1833

Ramsay Crooks Esqr [New York]

My Dear Sir,

If the perusal of a letter from a friend can afford you as much pleasure when every day and almost every post contributed to your enjoyment without satiating your desire, you will perhaps admit that my gratification on the arrival of a packet must be ~~seen~~ of a degree somewhat proportioned to its scarcity. The last express from the lower posts brought me on the 9th your [word?] very acceptable letter of 23 Aug: it was a long time making the voyage. Mr Halsey[81] tarried for Mr Lamont in St Louis & Messrs. Lamont & Halsey were so late before they commenced their journey, that they were subjected to great inconvenience & detention en route by some severe weather in Oct. I waited their arrival at Fort Pierre whither I had gone to note how matters were stirring in our adversaries camp until my patience was worn out, when I directed my course homewards if this can be called a home after the comforts and conveniences you so often made me witness in New York at all events it is the best I have.

Dr McKenney who had presented me with your favor of Apl. 26 at Fort Pierre accompanied me hither we arrived here Nov 27th, and since that day I have been busily though not very profitably employed. Talks with Indians every day and all day long is very wearying when they have nothing to trade, but I have some satisfaction in feeling that the promises presents and extravagantly low prices of our opponents have ~~failed~~ not succeeded in attaching any of my old friends to their establishments.

Sublett & Co. have a large & expensive establishment two miles below me, but hitherto they have ~~not~~ traded comparatively nothing they have a post above me ~~to oppose~~ some few days march, where I have a small fort built this season & there they are doing nothing at the Gros Ventres Mandans Yanctonas &c &c we have every advantage that experience of the Indian trade & knowledge of the Indians can give us but at the lower posts they have abundance of Alcohol & we are destitute and you well know how fond some Indians are of strong water. For this post I have established a manufactory of Strong water, it succeeds admirably. I have a good corn mill a very respectable distillery.[82] I can produce a fine liquor as need be drunk: I believe no law of the U.S. is hereby broken though perhaps one may be made to break up my distillery but liquor I must have or quit. If my pretentions to trade at this post, especially while our opponents can get any quantity passes up the Mo [Missouri] or introduced it as they have done by another route: On my arrival here Messrs. Sublett &Co. proposed to sell out to the A.F.C. all their interest on the river from the Sioux post upward. I did not approve their terms nor the principle of buying out opposition. I would rather drive or shove them out: it is impossible for rival companies to make money on the Mo river & as

Sublett &Co. have been induced to try their strength with the A.F.C. they shall gain neither honor nor money ~~if~~ while I have health & vigour, and they must [two words struck out] meet with more good fortune than falls to the lot of most men if they do not lose some few dollars: what robes are made by the Indians I am determined to have. I know they will cost me dear but 'tis my business. I have reason to expect the returns will be larger than last season but it will be a sorry balance.

I have provided medals to some [word struck out] Indians ~~they say~~ I never ~~break~~ forfeit my word to an Indian if it can be avoided. Can 15 or 20 Silver Astor medals be struck of[f] and sent to me; the size & thickness of Government medals would be most approved.[83] I leave this matter in your hand do what you can for me. The German full stock Guns you may recollect we bought 60 of at $50 ea[ch] the fellow cheated us sending one half to sample the other half rubbish, old half & looked shabby mean things as ever were looked at.[84]

In these stirring times cheap goods are needful, if you meet with cloth or blankets remarkably low buy them for this outfit for it is satisfying to give an Indian a good article for almost nothing when an inferior one would please him as well. & [two words struck out]

Dr McKenney what shall I do with him, he is too good for an inferior clerks place & he cannot sustain the situation of a Superior: Indian trading is not learnt in a month or a year it as much requires an apprenticeship as any of the handy craft trades of the civilized world.

I have written fully to Mr Astor on this subject I will not therefore weary you therewith Let me rather turn to a more interesting subject the pleasure you give me by sending such good tidings from Mr. Crooks & your family commend me much kindly to them. Forget not to present me to Mr. Whetton[85] who has laid our order to many obligations -- & other friends who have claims on my friendly remembrance

(Signed) K McK

Fort Union 18 Jany 1834
Mr H Pecotte [Apple River]
Dear Sir

You know of Mr Kipp's intention to pay me a visit he arrived 15th Ins. but having lost his best dogs in a snow storm. I have no means of sending liquor but finding you are destitute of Coffee & Sugar I send you a small supply which pass to Cr of Ft Pierre.

When your trade is over in the Spring it is my desire that Mr Crawford[86] take down his peltries in skin canoes to Ft. Pierre leaving you as many men as can be done with prudence & propriety. I presume Mr C & Ortabise[87] will do the Steering part, and it is my wish that with as little delay as possible you will move up to Ft. C. with your furs robes &c and the Mdze reserved for this post for which purpose Mr Kipp will lend you all his hands, by that time I will have a crew for you at Ft. C. & you will bring on the boat here laden with as much corn as Mr Kipp can furnish, making up your load with such Mdze as can be best stowed; the lead & Iron I am less in want of than other things, if wind & water favor you I shall see you early in the Spring & will not detain you long here.

I am much pleased with our proceedings, go on & prosper & do, as I am happy to say has thus far been done here, get all the furs & peltries that our opponents may in the Spring cry over their Mdze rather than laugh over their peltries of the season I am fully assured, every thing that can be done for my interest by your own exertions & judicious management will be effected.

Believe me
Truly Yours
K. McK.

Fort Union 21 Jany 1834
Mr. A. Culbertson[88] [Fort McKenzie]
Dr. Sir

I received your letter of Sept 4 on the eve of my starting for the Little Missouri.[89] I took charge of your letters for the States. No early opportunity has presented itself to allow of my reply to the subject submitted to my consideration. I fear you will think it long in reaching you. As it respects a reduction of prices in the articles furnished you from the Store it is not in my power to make it and surely you have been long enough engaged in the Indian trade to know the general terms on which Mdze is sold at the various trading posts in the Indian Country & I think on reflection you will admit that my prices at Fort McKenzie are [three words struck out] only proportionally higher than on the St Peters taking, the risk & difficulty of getting them there into consideration.[90]

You ask if there is any instance of a reduction made to clerks on the river in reply I beg to say there is one & only one case when a stipulated allowance is made to a trader who has been 15 years in the Company's service [word struck out] ~~at a~~ & most of the time at a very low salary [two words struck out] & a few years since on renewing an engagement for a term of years the said allowance was agreed upon in lieu of advance of Salary.

To the second point in your letter I beg to say that from the entire confidence I know I might repose in you & from the result of our conversation previous to your departure it was my desire & expectation that you should take charge of Fort McKenzie for the ensuing summer on Mr Mitchell's coming down with the returns; surely you are too diffident of your own powers, for without considering the gentlemen whom Mr Mitchell left in charge last year I think your experience to be fully equal to his with respect to Indian trade & the charge of an establishment such as Fort McKenzie: with respect to the risk you speak of I cannot at this distance be ~~on~~ perhaps a competent judge but from all I can learn I think you imagine it to be much greater than it really is. It is as remote from my principle as any practice, to press an irksome duty on any gentleman in my employ, a willing service is always the most pleasant & generally the most profitable to all parties concerned, but at the present moment I do not see my way clear to relieve you so early ~~in the Spring~~ as I could desire [several words struck out] In consequence of the opposition I have to contend with this year I have been compelled to establish several outposts, & I ~~am left alone with~~ now [have] only Mr Hamilton with me.

The Summer boat will start at the earliest possible day by which time I will endeavour to make arrangements for your Relief unless as I confidently hope circumstances may have given a new aspect to affairs & your own views, [word struck out] for the few intervening months I must leave you & Mr Mitchell to [word struck out] act as shall appear for the best convinced that you will not allow the interests of the A.F.C. to suffer.*

I am happy to inform you that my opponents have lost all heart from this fort down to Fort Pierre. My traders have so judiciously availed themselves of their hard earned experience & influence with the Indians that they have hitherto traded so nearly all the beaver & robes that at one fort Sublett Co. have only 2 packs robes & 8 Beaver, at another under 1 pack & at all their posts in this district under 15 packs robes & no beaver.

I send you letters which I have no doubt will be acceptable to you, ~~You will~~ from the newspapers you will learn that the Cholera[91] has made dreadful ravages again during the last Summer in St Louis & all the Western States, it is truly a terrible scourge.

For further news I refer you to Mr Mitchell & with best wishes for your health & prosperity

I am Dr Sir

Truly Yours

(Signed) K. McKenzie

*That your situation is less comfortable than you expected & than I wished it to be, is source of ~~gr~~ regret to me; such is my confidence in & respect for you that at some personal inconvenience I will endeavour to remedy the evils complained of you [word struck out] shall you fail to find me [two words struck out] just and as liberal as my situation will admit.

Fort Union Jany 21 1834

Mr D D Mitchell [Fort McKenzie]

My Dear Sir

Since the departure of the final express I have had no opportunity of addressing you and sometimes I have inferred from the Tenor of your letters that I might expect further information from you on subjects left open by you for future comment, before you would look for letters from me and again I feared you would defer sending until my express [word struck out] intended to be entrusted to Hy. Morrin reached you. I have at length resolved to start. Morrin & Vachard & Almanza[92] tomorrow morning and altho' the latter is to you an objectionable man the others asked my permission for him to accompany them & knowing Morrin's ~~cautious engaging~~ timidity, his willing hand would in case of difficulty over-rule the objections of the third, moreover he can come down by first boat & need not annoy you long.

Your letters by Mr Patton of 13 & 16 Aug I recd Aug 23. I regret the loss of Mr. Patton's services, he remained with me a month & improved upon acquaintance; he was firmly resolved on visiting his brother &c in Alabama & has almost promised to return next Spring but I fear he will not, we went down river together as far as Fort Pierre leaving this place 19 Sept & he took charge of the mountain beaver from thence 60 packs: I remained at Fort Pierre until 23 Oct waiting Mr Lamont's arrival but he came not & I returned hither without letters or Invoices & accts so anxiously looked for from below: the latter part of my visit at Fort Pierre was rendered uncomfortable by a fortnights duration of cold stormy weather, rain & snow driving thro' every crevice there was no possibility of keeping oneself warm: In the mean while, equipments were sent to the different wintering grounds: Campbell at the Chiaens: Papin near river Moreau Crawford at la River Castor Picotte at Apple R. and various others at accustomed stations, and arrived here Nov 8 & from that day until Dec 23 had one continued series of fair weather unprecedented in this Country; the river did not close here until Dec. 20.

Mr Lamont & Mr Halsey arrived at Fort Pierre Nov 12. Left St. Louis Sep 22, nearly lost in a Snow storm before they reached C. Bluffs, letters by him are forwarded for yourself & others at your post, they bring sad news of the continued ravages of the Cholera in all the Western states, from the small Supply of Newspapers sent me you will glean some information I send you all I can.

L. Cerré[93] Capt. Bonnevilles factotum[94] arrived here Aug 26 ~~if he is to behind~~, he says he traded with the Contannaha;[95] beaver in May & June last if that be that be true your expedition would turn out all for this season, however I hope better things and trust all your reasonable expectations will be realized.[96]

A Capt. Wythe[97] also paid me a visit he was on his return from an exploring excursion to the Columbia, he is a man of many schemes & considerable talent but in return for my civilities & furnishing him with a boat to go down to St Louis, on his arrival at Cantn. Leavenworth I hear he made some tremendous strong affidavits about my new manufactory.

Poor John Dougherty, sincerely do I regret him, how soon he has followed his friend Tom Dickson & that promising youth C Rose to the place appointed for all living.[98]

I was pleased to hear of your prosperous voyage & the friendly conduct of the Gros Ventres. It seems to me that there was as much design as accident in poor Martin's death.[99]

Your beaver trade has certainly fallen very short of my expectations but I will give you the credit of getting every skin that ~~any one in your Situation~~ could be obtained, respecting the course you pursued when the fort was attacked. I look to the motives which prompted you they were noble & evinced the purest & strongest devotedness to my interest, what the eventual result may be time only can determine but it's more than probable had I been in your situation I should have done as you did.

We can only regret that the Leviathan company of the North[100] have means so extensive & good so cheap but they will not drive me from my purpose, industry & perseverance will overcome many obstacles, and if your Indians are faithful another season may be more profitable than the present. Opposition from the South is the next point of consideration. Sublett & Campbell arrived here Aug 29 & soon fixed on a site to their fort which they have built two miles below me & called Ft. William. They came up in great force with a very large outfit & abundance of alcohol! & wines highly charged with Spirits. They engaged the three young Deschamps[101] as Interpreters at Salaries of $500 pr annum, & Tom Kipland[102] at $600 they had moreover a full complement of clerks and seemed prepared to carry all before them, nothing doubting but they would secure at least one half the trade of the country. Aft[er] they abandoned the idea of sending to the Black feet this season, they started a small equipment on horses to the Crow village on Wind River, they were expected to return early in Decr but have not yet been heard of. Mr Winter & J Beckwith[103] passed the fall in the Crow camp & traded all their beaver While Mr Winter was with the Crows, Mr Fitzpatrick of R. & F. Co. (my friend Capt. Stewart was with him) arrived with 30 men 100 horses & mules, Mdze &c &c & encamped near the village; ~~during the night all his horses~~ he had not long been there before a large party paid him a visit and pillaged every thing he had taking even the watch from his pocket & the capot from his back also driving off all his horses: this has been a severe blow on Sublett &Co. and although on their first start here they made great show & grand promise, to the Indians & even among the men nothing was talked about but the New Company; they have now at the Sign of "The case is altered."

Their interpreters have quarelled & left them and are now working here for me, the Indians find their promises mere empty words & their men are continually ~~taking employment~~ applying to me to engage them: They have a post near la Riv au Tremble in opposition to Chardon, where they are doing literally nothing, Chardon has it all his own way: they have another post on the Y. Stone in opposition to Pellot & Barzeau[104] & there they get no robes altho' they offer a blanket of scarlet for a robe.

You must be aware that I have not been asleep this fall, it has cost me something to secure the Indians to me, but being determined to get the peltries nothing has been neglected that would ~~secure~~ carry my point

My opponents cannot by any means get peltries sufficient this season to pay the wages of their men. At the Gros Ventres & Mandans they have not even robes to sleep on at the Yanctones, my last asst states that Picotte has 80 packs R[obes]. 500 Beaver the opposition 2 packs R[obes] 8 beaver and I hope things are equally promising lower down. On my return from Ft. Pierre Mr Campbell called on me (Mr Sublett had previously gone down ~~to Ft~~ Stream ~~I had on~~ on his way to St Louis) and proposed to sell out to me all their interest on the river. I listened to his terms but was by no means disposed to buy out opposition when all my old ~~faithful~~ experiences & faithful clerks & traders felt so certain of driving them out, especially on my giving them a carte blanche with respect to trade at their respective posts of course to be used with discretion but with their condition that all the peltries must be secured for A.F.Co. and thus far I have no reason to complain, the New Co is now in bad odour & must sink. Mr Campbell told Mr H-- the other day that he did not expect to make many robes this year! Which year does he expect to do it?

While on this subject as I am looking forward to what ~~they~~ my opponents may attempt next year. I am desirous you should re-engage Mr. Berjen[105] & all the men who ~~have gained knowledge~~ can talk sufficient Black foot to do us harm if offered to us ~~to remain at the F~~ to continue at the Fort, in fact you will engage all you think desirable. I send you Berjen's engagement written by you last Summer by which you can see an equipment was promised although the equipment ~~&~~ fixes his term at only two months & for which he was to receive 800 cents,[106] but I remember it was done in a hurry & bustle & the mistake is very pardonable; the Spirit not the letter is to be observed.

Though I am anxious your returns should be large I want them to appear small for such things are always talked about, please have all your beaver therefore made up in packs of 100 lb ea. ~~it will not sound~~ they will not make too great a swell.

I received 8 horses & Deschamp you charged 9 he says you gave him a mare in charge, he had two of his own & one of J Papin's[107] gave out on the way.

I have written to Mr Culbertson and though [three words struck out] he might be of more special service to the Co at a Sioux post, I have so much confidence in his doing his utmost for the interest of the Co wherever he may be placed that as he is now with you and ~~or~~ much inconvenience would be received by ~~his~~ my ~~sending~~ removing him to another post and as I hope by this time the mountains of last fall have dwindled into mole-hills, he will I trust reconcile himself to [six words struck out] ~~until the arrival of the~~ [two words struck out] his present situation, you see how I am inconvenienced, I have only Mr Hamilton with me, if you had the means of conforming to Mr. Cs wishes, I shall say do so & arrange as shall to you seem best, my ~~desire &~~ object in sending him was that in addition to assistance rendered you he should succeed you in the charge on your coming down with the returns; and I shall be glad to find he enters upon it with cheerfulness & good will and who can tell but you may resume your command for one little year more? Your letter of 14 Sept sent by the Baron Braunsberg I received on my return from the lower posts. The Baron I did not see much to my regret, he had started for the Mandans a few days before I arrived here. Morrin steered him down & he would gladly have kept him to conduct him to St Louis.

I hear you have fixed on a fine situation for the new fort. I hope you may have been able to make good progress with it but I must have Saucier[108] down in the Spring & send some one also to finish it. I presume he will not be unwilling to return to Fort Union.

You may rely on it the Gros Ventres & Blk feet meet with no favor at Fort Cass, ~~I am sure~~ they recd. my present there & no preference in trade. Mr Tulloch's tariff is the same as yours ~~with~~ & would give your Indians an arrangement to trade with him; moreover on the 3rd Dec an attack was made on his men who were cutting wood near the fort by a party of Blk feet or Gros Ventres & two of seven were killed on the spot. Mr Tulloch is very indignant against the Blk feet having last Summer paved the way for a peace between them & the Crows & as he says having on one occasion saved the lives of 7 on another 20 on a third 8 & on a 4th 13 & on a 5th 32, all their lives he says were "at his discretion" he worked hard to save them & now to come and kill his men at his post gates is very hard:

It is true Durocher[109] who deserted from him killed a Blkfoot but every recompense possible was made by paying for the body[110] & if the man can be found I will deliver him up to the nation to be dealt with as they think fit.

~~The~~ I wish you to bring down all the meat & grease your post can spare: they have been starving all fall at the Mandans & would eagerly give robes for meat.

Mr Kipp has paid me a visit ~~recently~~ & desires his respect to you he started yesterday on his return, he only remained here four days.

Gardeau[111] sold his or rather my beaver to the sutler at Cantonment Leavenworth at 350 pr lb and has retd. to Indian country with 40 horses & 15 men.

Papin is free & hunting with old Delorme Valandre has joined Legris[112] again on a beaver hunt. Vortefeuille & son[113] are hunting for opposition in the lower country. Old Deschamp and his sons are with Mr Chardon and working well for me. I have reason to be much pleased with their energy & exertion.

My distillery was progressing admirably a very excellent article was manufactured when early in Decr my man John was attacked with inflammatory rheumatism succeeded by a pleuresy & though now convalesced he is confined to his room & it will be long before he can resume his duties.

Urban Boldeu, & Thibeau gave up their guns on arrival. Beauchamp[114] also had a gun which I claimed he says it was sold him, was it included in his acct? Guion[115] was engaged for $250 receiving no equipment, there is no ac/ charged to him.

It will be desirable to bring down the books in the Spring, transferring the acct. as you did last year.

I send you some blank engagements & various letters. Your men will take a ball [word?] from Fort Jackson (Mr Chardon's fort) who this year gave the whole hog. I send also 1 doz good gun locks. Mr C: will furnish the men with dogs & train.

I would recommend your bringing me 3 or 4 first rate Buffalo horses down in keel boat they would not take up much room mid-ship. & I want them if to be had on good terms.

My best compliments to Mr Harvey & Mons. Berger In which I am joined by Mr. Hamilton.

My best wishes will ever attend you

Yours very sincerely

(Signed) K. McK.

[Ft. Union 6 Mar. 1834]

Mr. J. Berger [Fort McKenzie]

Sir

In reply to your request made through Mr Mitchell, I consent to allow you interest at the rate of 5% pr ann. for such sum or sums of money due to you remaining in my hands

Yours obediently

(Signed) K. McKenzie

Ft. Union 6 Mar. 1834 Agt. UMO

Fort Union 8 Mar 1834

Mr D. D. Mitchell [Fort McKenzie]

My Dear Sir

On 21 Jany I sent Morrin away with letters for you he & Vachard recd. 8 Feby leaving Almanza above Milk river to proceed alone. I send you copy of letters sent by him, so many of your enquiries are satisfied. I have but little more to say. Delighted to hear of your health & welfare, I detail reports relative to defeat of your fort.

With regard to attack of Assin. upon you they admit they were very wrong & are this year behaving with exemplary propriety.[116]

As it respects the preliminary arrangements to your start for F.U. you will engage Berger on the same terms as before for two or more years if he is willing to engage for more than one, & I am sure he can never do better for himself. I send the letter he requests not in fulfilment of any promise but as evidence of my desire to please him.

Sandoval[117] you will engage on the best terms you can. Harvey, arrange with as you think best but act for me as if it was your own case.

Mr Culbertson will remain in charge and my letters in the Summer will instruct him with regard to the future, assure him of my respect, & confidence that under his management nothing will be left undone which ought to be done & which he has the means to effect.

I wish you to leave as strong a force as possible to protect the property during the Summer & impress on Mr C. the importance of the adage "An ounce of prevention is worth a pound of cure." I trust I shall be able to send up very early this year especially as you say only a small equipt. will be required.

My present views regarding your forts are that it is best to remain tranquil & not strive to push the trade farther west until mutual confidence is established between A.F.Co. & Indians Cootenasha [Kootenai] trade will not pay risk & expense attending it. I prefer [word?] to court the good opinion of Indians around you for any seriously disastrous occurrence arising from too much risk or too little caution may destroy in a moment what I have been years building up.

Your fort arrangements please me quite as well; as your building a new one on fresh ground tho' it be now almost impregnable to Indians from without, it will be very necessary during the Summer to avoid the admission of many within at one time.

I have said secure me some [Blackfoot] Peigan runners if they can be brought down with convenience in the mode I suggested. You remark that all the men who came down are deeply in debt except Joe Howard[118] how has he paid his debt of $205 when he deserted last year? the silly fool & worthless rascal has been passing all this morning at Campbell's fort allowing himself to be pumped of or voluntarily giving all the information in his power & no doubt clandestinely offering his services if he [was] worth the trouble I would put him in Irons & take him to St Louis but he may be useful in mak[in]g the present voyage to you & it depends on the nature of your arrangements with him whether or not it would be better for him to come down with you in the Spring & then be subject to such plans as I may think proper to adopt with him. Hamille gave up rifle & horses, J Marchand the Gun, rifle is back to Marchand.[119]

I have no provisions, no dry meat in Store & know not how to feed so many additional mouths as will be here in the Spring. A Sautieux[120] [Ojibway] Indian apprized me in Nov last of poor Douartte's death.[121]

Will you bring down any good dogs you may have, they will get accustomed to the fort during the Summer & useful to me next year:

Do not forget to bring down what books you have of mine; the books of accts. must not be forgotten with a complete Inventory of every thing left behind.

May a bright sun shine on your progress down & a fair stage of water facilitate your voyage with how much gladness shall I greet your arrival.

Your men arrived here on the 5th with 8 horses I have since recovered 1 more: other 5 are left so far off I fear I shall never see them. I sent Mr Morrin & others back without delay. I have no fresh papers or letters to send you. My Compts. to Mr A.C. J.B. & A.H.

I could not in conscience load your men with 18 Gun locks, much fearing you would never get them. Believe me ever at all times

Your friend.

[Signed] K. McK.

Fort Union 8 Jany 1834

Mr S. P. Winter [Fort Cass]

Dear Sir

Having written fully to Mr Tulloch I refer you to him for general news but I avail myself of the opportunity to convey my "best wishes" for your health & happiness. I thank you for the care of a/ct for which I value too much to send the whole thereof to the Baron. In these times of opportunity when every energy should be called into [word?] to countervail the movements of the enemy I should have been pleased to find that you had remained in the Crow camp for the winter, even had you done nothing more than mark their proceedings & encouraged them to make peltries to trade at Ft. Cass in the Spring: it would have been [a] source of high gratification to me to have heard that Sublett Co. sent to the village & did nothing & had you continued on the spot such I flatter myself would have been the result. Should you on your travels meet with some various specimens of minerals ~~mineralology~~ any thing collected by you would be very acceptable to me.

I am Dr. Sir

Truly Yours

[Signed] K. McK.

Fort Union 8 Jany 1834

Mr. Saml. Tulloch [Fort Cass]

Dear Sir

Your letter of 10 Aug introduced to me Mr. G. Sublett[122] who passed some days here before his brother arrived. I found him a plain straight forward man I was pleased with him. I asked him if he had any proposition to make to me but he only offered to sell his own interest in the mountain trade, in the absence of his partner he could offer no terms upon which we could agree. I offer to supply Mdze to R. M. & Co at any place between Lit Mo & Ft. Cass on terms Mr. G.S admitted to be very reasonable & I knew to be less than any other person could.

Mr W.S.[123] arrived 29 Aug, he soon fixed on a spot for building his place is called Ft. William it is about two miles below me on this side of the river, the brothers went down then together in keel boat 24 Sept. I paid your note of $9.00.

Your letter of 21 Aug pr Moncrevier I also recd. Beaver & peltries arrived safe on Mr Campbells arrival I was certainly surprised to find my old servant Tom Kipland engaged to him, he has been ashamed to see me & is the only man I regret having lost. Let me know what traps &c he rendered you. As I have before said I want no more from J Beckwith there is justly due from him to Am. Fur Co: if the a/c I sent by you was erroneous it was just as I recd. it from Little Mo, as part of the debt was contracted here. I believe the surpluses arises from some transactions at the Aricara fort, if he has no knowledge thereof or says it is not just I will at once strike it off the book as I know him to be honest; I think you did well to engage him altho' his Salary is high.

Your letter of 24 Sept was delivered by Diabreuille[124] during my absence at L[ittle] Mo for which place I started with Mr Patton Sept 18 & returned here Nov 8th. Deguire would not come to the Fort having sold his horses for $80 to Vasquez recd. an order for [two words?] Mr R. Campbell to whom notice was given not to keep the money which he handed out. I am vexed & disappointed at the conduct of the hunters you equipped. I am sorry you did not take Deguires horses especially looking at the rest of his debt they proved of partial service to Mr V. indeed without them he could not have got on.

Your report about getting more large red beads, I sent you all I had & have indeed a fresh supply for next season. J Beaugard arrived here on 28 Sept. What advances have you made him? Your letter of 14 Oct. was brot by Legris &Co. Mr Campbell offered him a high price for their beaver; they sold it all to me, Mr C claimed the last portion, they would not give it up.

Your letter of Dec 8 was delivered by Lamont & others on the 17 Dec the intelligence is distressing; on further evidence of the faithlessness of Indians to the many former on record. Durocher arrived here in the evening of 9 Oct & decamped during the night, persuading one of my men to go off with him; they stole a canoe & went down stream but have not since been heard of. I have sent instructions to all places on the river to have him secured if possible. I have no recent news from Blk feet but propose sending there in a few days one of my men A. Martin[125] was killed in the fort by a Blk.foot in Sept & a grand attack was made on the [Blackfoot] Peigans encamped near the fort by a party of 6 or 700 Assiniboins; several Peigans were killed, remains took shelter in the fort, when a general attack was made on the fort; on some of the men being wounded Mr Mitchell gave orders to fire, the enemy quickly withdrew & were followed for some miles by the Whites & Indians; there you see you do not monopolize all the war.

I thought Mr Winter & J Beckwith went out to

winter with the Crows what reason do they give for acting contrary to your orders, & in these times of strong opposition it is somewhat extraordinary that Mr Winter should come away & leave by his own admission 30 beaver in a Crow Camp. They should not have left the Crows while one beaver remained & come when they had traded all for the day more might have come in the days following:

I consider your instructions should have been as completely obeyed as if they had come direct from me & it is a grievous reflection to think that two or three men & a few pack horses should get an advantage while I have been at so much expence to secure, moreover it was of paramount importance that when my opponents were in the villages my people should be there also to see what was doing & be ready to answer & satisfy the Indians on all points & statements made, as no doubt many would be tending to the disadvantage of A.F.Co. & endeavouring to possess the Crows favorably toward the New Co. My object and resolve was & is to secure the Crows to the A.F.Co. they shall be supplied with such articles as they want & approve, on reasonable terms & I would make almost any sacrifice even to sell goods at cost rather than let my opponents get a skin.

Further what object could Messrs. W. & J B have in returning to Ft Cass there were no Indians there or prospect thereof & by wintering with them, they would have encouraged them to make robes during the winter & hunt well in the Spring as you were well prepared to supply all their wants when they came to trade.

The 43 B. skins traded, marked R. M. & Co. I would in the present instance give up if Mr Fitzpatrick wishes to have them, on his paying the price the articles traded for them were worth on their arrival in the Crow village & the expense of bringing the beaver in & securing it. My goods are brought into the country to trade, and I would as willingly dispose of them to Mr F. as any one else; for beaver or beavers worth if I get my price: I make this proposal as a favor not as a matter of right for I consider the Indians entitled to trade any beaver in their possession to me or any other trader.

On my arrival here from little Mo Mr Campbell called on me & offered to sell out Sublett &Co. interest in the various posts established by them to the A.F.Co. I entered into no treaty with him, not approving the principle of buying out opposition: I much prefer driving them out by dint of exertion & the advantage the A.F.C. ought to possess in their influence with the Indians from their long standing in the Country & to the liberal conduct they have adopted toward them.

Mr C. is becoming much dissatisfied he finds he has brought his pigs to a bad market & I hear he has given orders to his people at a post established on the Y Stone & another near Poplar River two days march above this on the Mo where I also have trading houses (Mr Chardon in charge of the latter) to get robes at any sacrifice. I fancy I can beat him at any game he chooses to play in the Indian trade & hitherto he has traded comparatively nothing, his liquor is surely done tho Indians will not drink his wine & here as trade can be carried on without whiskey.

I shall depend on you in making your arrangements to pay me a visit in the Spring entrusting the charge of your post to whom you deem worthy & competent: we have many things to talk over, & I shall moreover be very happy to see you.

I hope your affairs in the States may not absolutely require your presence the coming Summer, if there is any thing in my power to do or arrange for you there, it shall be done, but when we meet your own feelings shall be consulted & complied with as far as in me lies, at the period

I should be sorry the A.F.C should lose some valuable services even for a month.

I thank you for the robe & shirt, should any thing good & curious come in your way during the Spring please secure it for me. At all events I am in want of two more good Indian dresses.

If Mr. Fitzpatrick pays you a visit this winter I am in hopes Capt. Stewart will accompany him, render him any attention in your power & help him on his journey hither, he is a valued friend of mine, I much wish to have him here.

I am so burdened with Assiniboins, pieces of lodge, & mean wolf skins, I must restrict you in the trade of these articles I cannot convert them to any useful purpose, they will bring nothing in St Louis. dressed Cow skins should be traded only on very low terms. I have some thousand by me: Elk skins

Beaver skins & robes you cannot get too many of: Calf skins of which you had a large number last season are of very little value.

I send back Laderoutes[126] a/c with a statement of how it stands here, please explain the difference.

I understand Mr J. Gardner sold the bison in his possession last Spring to the Sutler at Cantonment Leavenworth at $50 pr lb where he got equipped with goods suitable for mountain trappers he was seen on Ponca Creek[127] the latter end of Aug with 40 horses & abt 156 men, some freemen, he said he was going to the Crow country where he would trade if he had a chance: he owes the A F Co. $930.10 making advances at Ft. Cass, unlikely things do happen, you may possibly by some means be able to recover part hereof.

I am sorry you sent down 4 men as I fear you will want them in the Spring to bring down your returns & three of them being in debt & do much fear, if I started them on a return voyage I am afraid you would never see them; however I can employ them. C. Coe, Keen & Close[128] have not been heard of at any of the lower forts I fear they fell sacrifice to the Aricaras.

I am informed that one of the New dragoon regts. Commanded by Genl Dodge[129] will be up here Next Summer & range from hence to the Rocky Mountains.

The Cholera has been very fatal again this past Summer in the Western States. You were very right in telling the Crows you would give them as much for peltries as the opposition & with care & industry I hope you may secure all they have to trade. In establishing a post in their country I hoped they would have been induced to winter in its vicinity; if they continue for so long a beaver as far away as Wind River it is impossible they can make robes enough to support the expenses of a fort; I will not however abandon them without a fair trial; the permanency of any establishment in their country depends entirely on themselves; I say this much that you may talk with the principal men on the subject in the Spring. I leave you to make your own arrangements for bringing down the Spring returns, if needful to leave any part behind let it be the inferior articles only. I am anxious to get my Beaver & robes to market as early as possible. I send you the best supply of Medicine my means will afford. In the Spring I shall have the pleasure of introducing you to my friend Dr. McKenney a physician of some experience who accompanied me hither from Lit Mo to pass the winter in this country. I send you tea and Sugar for your own use, I wish I could send more; last summer my outposts were too liberally supplied in proportion to my means & I have not now sufficient to last until the arrival of a Steam boat,[130] but I would cheerfully go without myself rather than an invalid like yourself should be deprived of it. Wine I would send with pleasure, but it would freeze, lose its virtues, & be valueless. I recd. 5 horses and 3 dogs by your men.

Pitch[131] is placed to your credit also 6 wood bowls altho' it is mysterious what became of them. Perhaps Mr Hunter[132] does not know the risk he runs in going with the Crows to war, if taken hold of by the In. Agt. or Govm troops he could be severely dealt with.

I do not send list of prices for Mr T. Mr G Sublett told me he should write him, & appearing well pleased with my terms, if Mr G. has any desire to transact business with me he will write or perhaps pay me a visit, I should be glad to see him & in one interview we should understand ourselves better than if 6 letters passed between us.

I have no half breed boat men with families, they could not conveniently transport them to you, or with satisfaction leave them behind. I send you Beauchamp free 1835 in debt, in these times of opposition the best & almost only hold we have on our men is by keeping them out of debt, if money is coming to them they are more diligent & faithful.

Laderoute I have ordered to join company at Y.S. fort, I cannot send his a/c not knowing what he has taken there but am sure it is very trifling. I wish you to re-engage Labonnharde[133] before you come down. I prefer his continuing at your fort.

If you can bring me a large rough long hair Crow dog I shall be obliged to you, also a young [word?] of the largest kind for breeding. Should you have a good Buffalo horse & can conveniently spare him he would be a valuable acquisition to my Stock. You have heard of my new building & mill for grinding corn & operations carried on, every thing was progressing in fair order an excellent article was manufactured & approved by all men of taste until a month ago my head man was attacked by inflammatory rheumatism & pleuresy; the work stopped & the poor fellow is still in a dangerous state. I much fear his services are lost to me for ever. I have good reason to believe that Sublett Co. will not establish a permanent post in Crow country even if they continue another year in this district as they think they do better by following the Crow Camp & trading there

Legrie Carriera & Valandré[134] leave me to finish in partnership on their own a/c if they need any thing you will supply as heretofore. Accept my best wishes for your health & prosperity & believe me to be

Dear Sir
Yours truly
(Signed) K. McKenzie

Fort Union March 11 1834
Mr Saml. Tulloch [Fort Cass]
Dear Sir

T Louette[135] arrived here on 26 Feby I have engaged him for one year. I recd your letter some days earlier on the 9 Jany I started Beauchamp & Laderoute with letters & Mdze for your post in company with Carriera Legrie & Valandré. Beauchamp not here 26 Jany, Laderoute continued on with the others. I hear they met Mr Vasquez who recited a tale of horrors abt. J. & McK & the forts of my people there. I am happy to inform you there was not the least foundation for the report Mr. D M.[136] writes me on the 9 Feby "all's well." Mr V. brought with him 300 Beaver skins which I hear he traded from the Crows. I would give no credence to his having so obtained them, until Losett[137] informed me that my people last fall traded only with Le Borgne's band leaving Rotten Belly's for the opposition. I may have been deceived in their information, but if true I must say it is very shameful.

There is no doubt Vasquez had that number of B. Skins wherever he may have got them & I am told he saw a white man en route: he started again Feby 27 with 16 horses or Mules laden, to meet the Crows. It is very strange if with the Crows only; of all the Indian tribes, Sublett Co. should successfully compete with A.F.Co. I can safely say at every other place we have thus far beaten them ten to one & I should indeed be mortified to find your Indians the only faithless ones. Where you have opportunity you must push the trade & not let your opponents do any thing if possible, you have full liberty to outbid them in every thing.

At very great inconvenience I send up Latress Hainelle Diagneau & Girard[138] to help bring down your peltries: (they are all in debt deep debt you will not make them advances) you proposed making skin canoes for 80 packs in ea[ch], at all events leave only trash behind if you have not means to bring down all. An Inventory of what remains in Good peltries utensils &c must be furnished with the books of a/c transferring the balances of persons remaining at Ft Cass into the new book.

With your accustomed consideration you give me the option of availing myself of your services until return of boat which will take up your Summer equipment; I thank you for this for this foretheight [foresight] it is a considerable relief to me & I hope your visiting the States in the Fall may answer your own purposes equally well; should you decide otherwise you will apprize me that I may arrange accordingly. I should certainly be gratified by your consenting to remain one more season before you go down, perhaps you may so determine. I presume you will send Mr Winter in charge of Canoes, tho [the] only men with you whose time will be up this Summer are Arguistte Sibeau & Labombarde,[139] the two former I expect will prefer coming down tho [the] latter you may find it desirable to re-engage Luiss[140] a good lad & I have no doubt will be glad to remain with you. Such additional hands as are necessary & you can best spare you will send, if Costy or any other freeman offer their services to assist in the boats provided you need them it may be well to secure them. 9 or 10 men with Grosclaude Beckwith[141] & your occasional visitors I should suppose would be sufficient for you during the Summer especially as the Gros Ventres of Fort de Prairie[142] say they are fully revenged now both on Whites & Crows, I suggest these arrangements to you but have you full exercise of your own judgement to alter or amend in any way you think best.

In my last I alluded to J Beckwiths a/c you state that all he admits due is his note to Papin Co. $225 & a/c at Ft. Clark not $6.00 but signed in the books by McKnight[143] on ball [balance] agreed as $68.17

in all $293.17. The a/c originally rendered you as ball. agreed was $499.54 I have deducted as charged in error or allowance 206.37 leaving Balance due 31 Mar 1831 $293.17 You report advance in May 1833 566.03 859.20 Cr Sept 1833 Salary horses &c 150.00 Ball. On 19 May 1833 $209.20 instead of $415.51 as then stated, you will therefore adjust your books accordingly. If W. & B.[144] had conformed to our instructions last fall even had they not traded another skin it would have been for the Co. interest, as their presence alone would have compelled to opposition to pay dear for what they got, your arrangements were good, if disregarded it was no fault of yours.

Give me outline of articles required for next season. Command me if any thing can be done for you in the States. Mr. Campbell charges A.F.Co. as instigators of Crows to pillage. Mr. Fitzpatrick he read me a letter from him on the subject. I scouted the idea & laughed at his infamous imputations, it is now worth enquiring who instigated the Crows to pillage the trappers. I equipped from this place on[e] who has been equipped by you? but disappointed men must look out for some back to bear the burden which to them is irksome, though by shifting the saddle they Seldom place it on the right horse. Mr C. at Ft. Jackson & Mr Brayeu[145] on YS. have driven our opponents from the field & afterward traded at their case FA.C 259 packs.

Yours truly,
(Signed) K. McKenzie

Fort Union 20 Mar [18]34
Mr Baron de Bransberg [Fort Clark]
Sir

I had the honor to receive your letter of 10 Feby. & regret that I could not avail myself of your instructions relative to Le Gros corne &c.[146]

I am so particular circumstanced this season & my men are so dispersed it is not without difficulty that I have selected trusty men to conduct you down [the] Mo: I have no men here whose term of service expires earlier than 26 Sep. next & they have of course a claim on me for wages until that day. I have explained this matter in my letter to Mr Laidlaw & requested him to furnish you with men whose engagements will expire in July in order that the charge may be lessened, in either case I ask no more from you than I have actually to pay.

I have learnt with much pain how poorly you have fared at the Mandans & again express my regret that I had not the pleasure to entertain you at my own table during the past winter. I trust your health has not suffered,[147] in which case on your arrival in the land of plenty you can look back on your privations without pain or regret.

It would be very pleasant to me could I utter orally my Adieus! on your leaving this inhospitable clime but I must content myself with assuring you of my best wishes that you may be blessed with health & a prosperous voyage to your Father-land.

I enclose the accts. as requested, Mr. Laidlaw will make such additions as appertain to his department & your final arrangement will be made with Mr. Chouteau in St. Louis.

Mr. Hamilton begs I will present his Compts. nor would he forget Mr. Bordman to whom also I wish to be remembered. I have the honor to remain

Sir
Yours Very Obediently
(Signed) K. McKenzie

Fort Union April [1834]
M. Baron de Braunsberg [Fort Clark]
Sir

Very much have I been annoyed at the surprise & anxiety you have doubtlessly suffered from the non arrival of the men I promised to conduct you to St Louis. I have no power over the wind & water, this season the ice has been unusually obstinate and would not move & previous to the breaking up of the river it was impossible to transport my men with their baggage to Fort Clark. My principal object has been to furnish you a good steersman, & at considerable inconvenience I send you James Filteau[148] a steady trustworthy man whom I have no doubt will do his duty to your satisfaction the other three men are J. Maloney J. Beaugard, & Martin Facts,[149] the latter an European, honest & worthy, on their arrival in St Louis they will report themselves at the Am. F.C. office & I trust they will deport themselves during the voyage in every way conversant with your wishes.

My letter of 20 Mar. & one from Mr Hamilton

25 Mar. implied that the men I should send you would conduct you as far only as Fort Pierre[150] but considering the uncertainty of Mr Laidlaw's having suitable men to proceed & conceiving it would be more agreeable to yourself that the hands who started with you should continue onto St Louis. I have to arrange it.

I send you from my own limited means a little sugar & coffee[151] to help you on to Fort Pierre where I believe you have some store & wishing you a prosperous voyage. I have he honor to be

Sir
Yours Most obediently
(Signed) K. McKenzie

Fort Union March 17 1834
Wm Laidlaw Esqr [Fort Pierre Chouteau]
Dear Sir

By a/c from St. Louis in Nov last & list of articles furnished Dr. McKinney are given amt. $23.13½ also to C Morrin[152] $12.35 In Decr. another a/c is recd. charged first $31.00 the other $15.00 & no detail or explanation of the difference, please give it in your next.

You ask for St Louis book of a/c 1833; I placed it in the office last Sept. & now send the books of 1831 & 1832 Groschaude's & Laderoutes a/c were correctly stated, advances on Flora were charged as from the post $60.99 is allowed J Beckwith making his a/c on 1 July $209.00.

Gardners a/c, Mr Chouteau writes can be only recd $13.21 you state the recd. at $1371.00 refer to St Louis a/c Curt. & see which figure is legible Manta;[153] debt of $39 ¼ was forgiven him in St Louis.

It is strange as statement of B Marchands[154] old debt should be sent me until two years after his new engagement had commenced, I had no means of Knowing that he was indebted to A.F.C in 1832 excepting his advances in St Louis nor can I make him understand it please explain how balance of $126.76 due Oct 1831 has arisen.

When C. Vachard left this place last Summer his advances were stated as on St Louis book $165.62 but a remark was also made that Mr Halsey reported his advances as $190.12 but having no date here to a/c for the variance in the two a/c's I left you to adjust it with Vachard, it would appear that he is still indebted to the Co $45:

In a/c Curt. I have not entered wages & being incomplete many hands are engaged at Ft. Cass & Ft. McKenzie whose wages I am ignorant of. Charge for equipments I have altered to $207.62 striking out Holmes Montaignis Wilson & Sicanze[155] Inform me abt. charge of exps of Manger de Lards of $51.14, was the expense per toto as this post has only 2 years service from the men it should pay only 2/3. You enter as credit no list of advances sent from this post for you guidance & information, of freemen & runaways, partial entries of this kind tend to confuse the a/c. Invoice of Mdze & cargo will be entered on arrival I gave Mr Kipp ~~copy of~~ Invoice of Mdze & S. Boat charging 5% Insurance. I send you copy, also Invoices of Mdze in one case recd. & not charged: you can regulate the Invoice on your new principle at your leisure.

I send you copy of the Baron Braunsberg's a/c Mr Kipp will furnish you with par[ticu]lars of advances at Ft. Clark you will please inform Mr Chouteau of the amt due from the Baron on his leaving Fort Pierre. I pledged myself to furnish men to take him down. I do it at a very great inconvenience & I am under the necessity of giving useful men who have yet a considerable time to serve.

I have no reason to ~~consider~~ suppose the B. will deem any of my charges unreasonable; if I have erred at all, I do not think it is by charging too much as you will perceive by looking over the a/c. In one of my letters to the Baron I intimated that you could possibly supply him with men whose time would expire in July & thereby reduce the charge. I have since thought it best to send men from hence for the whole voyage & make a moderate charge that no room can be left for complaint or deduction.

Believe me as always
Yours truly
(Signed) K McKenzie

I think you have charged F. K.[156] for horses furnished Dr. McKenney, which was only an exchange, please examine & rectify.

Fort Union March 18 1834
Pierre Chouteau Jr Esqr [St. Louis]
Dear Sir

If I were conscious of having infringed the laws of the U.S. I would at once acknowledge my error & admit the propriety of your censure.[157] you seem to have lent a willing ear to a marvellous tale of discrepancy in my conduct & proceedings, and admitted as facts, statements which had existence only in the narrators imagination: "Hear both sides" is no less the duty than the practice of all impartial men.

The facts are simply as follow:

An old acquaintance of mine in the Red River, Mr J P Bourke[158] addressed me last Spring while in St Louis a letter (of which I annex you an attested copy) in consequence whereof I purchased a still in St Louis & bought it hither & last fall he apprized me of his intention to come or send for it in April next (the coming month). While here it may have been seen by a person styling himself Capt Wythe, as under that name a stranger introduced himself to me last Summer, & received the accustomed hospitalities of this place.

Le Ceré was here at the same time & may also have seen the Still, though it is exceedingly improbable that it should have been seen by either of them, nor is it in the nature of things possible for them to prove a single allegation they have made. They both applied to me to sell them liquor. I could not do it, but offered them wine which they declined purchasing & appeared mortified & displeased: independent whereof, the character of the former & the wounded self love of the latter in being deemed unworthy of an engagement from the A.F.Co. would in my mind account for their unwarranted proceeding.

They have lied gratuitously, I content myself with simply denying the truth of their allegations. I am

Dear Sir

Yours very truly

(Signed) K McKenzie

here follows copy of letter from J. P. Bourke & afterward

I Geo. W. McKenney, have compared the above copy of letter, with the original letter from J P Bourke to Kh. McKenzie & hereby declare it to be a true copy thereof

(Signed) Geo. W. McKenney

Ft. Union 18 Mar 1834

Fort Union 20 Mar 1834

Pierre Chouteau Jr. Esqr. [St. Louis]

Dear Sir

After 20 years experience in the Indian trade I can safely declare that an entire prohibition of liquor if rigidly enforced would be an almost incalculable relief to the trader, but you well Know that the Indians of this district from their proximity to the trading establishments of the H.B.C. have always been accustomed to the use of liquor, & it is by no means extraordinary that they should ~~be~~ seek to be supplied therewith when making their trade on this side the lines. I am well convinced that if I had liquor I could extend the trade very considerably but having none I do the best I can.

You very much surprise me by a string of charges in your letter of Decr last, to which in reply, I beg to say, that it is very true that I brought up a Still last season, as I would do any other article of Mdze by the sale whereof I expected to realize a profit & I send you copy of a letter from J P Mr Bourke by whose instructions I acted / This is the Mr Bourke who visited the States last Spring to purchase sheep for Red River Colony. It is also true that while the Still remained at this place until an opportunity of Sending it to Mr Bourke offered which was not expected to occur before Apl next (1834) an American citizen who chanced to be at this fort proposed to make some experiments therewith on the fruits of this country which the past season were tolerably abundant, he entered into the speculation on his own account & certainly succeeded in making a very palatable article but not a single gallon of liquor has been manufactured since last fall & Mr Bourke has apprized me he will send or come for the still next month. If herein I have erred or infringed the laws of the U.S. in Spirit or in letter, I acknowledge my error, but it has been done so innocently.

It is true that Mr L Ceré[159] & a person who introduced himself to me as a Capt Wythe were at Fort Union in August last, they were both very earnest in their application to purchase liquor of me. I had none to sell them but offered them wine which they declined buying altho' they drank freely of it at my table during their stay; notwithstanding which I am informed the said Capt Wythe was beastly drunk during his voyage down the Mo, & mortified at my refusing him liquor, & being moreover a man of such dissipated habits, it seems to me that any statement of his should be listened to with extreme caution. Neither does it surprise me that L Ceré who was judged unworthy of being engaged by A.F.Co. (his brother[160] also being dismissed from their employ) should under the feelings of mortified self love make any statements that he thought calculated to injure the A.F.C. But it does surprise me that a just & liberal Government such as Gt of U.S. is declared to be should listen with such eagerness to whatever allegations may be made from any quarter how despicable so ever against the Am Fur C & viewing thru the distorted medium of pre-conceived prejudices a statement of facts which have existence only in the imagination of the narrators, should also proceed to an ex parte judgement. I am not aware that the Am Fur C have ever received any favors from U. S. Gt. but surely they are entitled to impartial justice.

I am Dear Sir
very truly Yours
(Signed) K McKenzie

Fort Union Mar 17th 1834
Mr Jas Kipp [Fort Clark]
Dear Sir

Your letter & [word?] was recd 19 Feby. the rest sent by him are compared & adjusted our books will more agree. I return your a/c Curt [current]. with a few additions it correspond with F. K. ledger. Invoice of Mdze belonging to the ~~fort~~ outfit I send you invoices of entered on the new principle established at Ft. Pierre. In Inv. furnished you of this years outfit there are some errors say 43 bun[dle]. Cut glass bead it $20\frac{1}{10}$ called 6.88 should be pr. 4 5 pr. Scarlet S. list $111\frac{1}{4}$ $153\frac{9}{10}$ [called] 170 45 [should be] 170.85 3 doz Smooth files $347\frac{7}{8}$ [called] 11.44 [should be] 10.44

The amt. of Invoice will be 5517.44 not 5516.28 In the additional Invoice of 3 bar blue cloth &c there is a natural error 2 ft Green cloth $50\frac{1}{4}$ at 193 called 47.95 should be 97.95 the amt. of Invoice should be $362.67

Believe me to remain
Yours very Truly for K. McKenzie
[Signed] J A Hamilton

Fort Union Apl 7 1834
P. Chouteau Jr Esqr [St. Louis]
Dear Sir

The ice has been very obstinate this season & would not move, take as it is, this is the earliest day a Canoe could make progress & daily expecting the river would break up, it ~~was~~ would be folly at this period of the year to start men by land for the lower posts. I have supplied Baron B. with 4 men to conduct him to St Louis & altho' their terms lf service will not have expired I have agreed they shall be free on arrrival. I [word?] stand on leaving this post. I presume a duplicate will be furnished from Ft. Pierre. I think I have been very moderate in my bill of charges to the Baron & believe he will be well satisfied therewith. Passage to Marias, from St Louis wages of men back to St Louis. Board & attendance & sundry Mdze his bill here amts. to $1789.62.[161] Mr Laidlaw will apprize you of further advances at Ft. Clarke & Ft Pierre.

For your guidance allow me to observe that Maloney is wholly unworthy of a new engagement with the A.F.C. J Killeans is willing to but is too old for this country. Mr Facts begged to be let free that he might return to Europe. Beaugard a harmless lad but so tormented with the dread of dying without confession & absolution as to be of very little value: he is a Manger du Lard of 1832 & prayed permission to go to a place where there were priests & Masses, he is a good boy & merits re-engagement should he seek it.

J Beaugard	Ball [Balance] due him	20
M Fecto	" " "	62
J Filteau	Due to AFC	43
J Maloney	" " "	100

I am Dr Sir
Yours very truly
(Signed) K. McK.

Fort Union Apl 7 1834
Mr Jas Kipp [Fort Clark]
Dear Sir

Bellhumeur & Hugron[162] made a good trip but have been compelled to remain here a tedious while I have selected 4 good & useful men to conduct Baron B. to St Louis. Faltreau Steersman Maloney

Facts Beaugard assuming Facts is the only one who has money & he is the least likely to seek advances from you. I place $150 to credit of your post as share of Baron's board. I charge your fort with advances to Hugron, (his wages this fort will pay your post Sucrie's) in stating his a/c to Ft. Pierre do it this July 1833, To Bal. 34.63 July 1834, By wages due salaries $220.

Oct 30 [to balance] a/c Ft Union 149.62

[to balance] charged Ft. C. 104.62

June 1834 [to balance] a/c Fort Clark.*

*here you will include advances made him here in Jany & Apl. Belhumeur wanted shawl for Charbonneau[163] I have sent 3 that he may have a choice. I send 2 pipes &c. Send me all the corn you can spare for we are reduced to corn & grease. I am in hopes Mr M. will bring a good supply in which case you may depend on a portion of it. As corn is so scarce with you I suppose I must be content with 500 bushels & what beans you can send, but recollect you must reserve corn & beans to provision my boats down in the Spring.

Any excess of Mdze you may have to spare you can send up by the boat. I particularly want some middle size Iron wire if you have it. Let the Canoes and skiff be hauled up high & dry unless H. P. [Henry Picotte] brings the skiff back.

Ever yours truly

(Signed) K. McKenzie

J. Brulle[164] is willing to engage for this fort I should like to have him. I want a good sawyer, you know the wages I give here let him come up in the boat

April 7 1834

H Picotte [Apple River]

Dear Sir

Your letter of Feb 6 I read Feb 17 yours of 27 Feby I recd 8 Mar. I thank you for your full & lucid statements, in no other quarter are my wishes in this particular so well complied with. I have no objection to L Freniere's[165] going to Ft. Pierre. Having no sail I send materials to repair yours, you will put such cargos on board at Ft. Clark as will admit you Make I trust a good & safe trip. If you chance to be wind bound your men would be well employed in cutting Steam boat wood, but this no doubt would have occurred to you. I shall be glad to welcome your arrival & I am Dear Sir

Truly Yours

(Signed) K McKenzie

Fort Union Apl 7 1834

Mr J Kipp [Fort Clark]

Dear Sir

I have been compelled to send men to Ft. Cass to bring down returns from there, this day I have started a Keel Bt. With 13 men for Mr Chardon's returns,[166] & sending also for the Baron & Picottes I am left almost with an empty fort. I shall require A. Hugron to come up with H Picotte to make up his complement of hands, please send a/c of advances made to him by you distinct from his a/c here in a/c & advances to him here in Jany & April & your fort shall be credited with all charges made to it on his a/c

Yours

K. McK

Ft. Union 16 Apl [18]34

R Campbell Esqr. [Fort William]

Dear Sir

One of my men deserted from my fort last night. I have reason to suppose he had taken refuge with you, his name Joe Howard, he wintered with Mr Mitchell who will present this note to you & bring back my man if at your fort.

I do not claim him for his work, for he is utterly worthless, a complete vagabond, but he is my hired servant & I am satisfied you will present no obstacle to my recovering him.

I am Dear Sir

Yours Truly

(Signed) K McKenzie

Ft. Union 22 Apl 1834

Mr S. Tulloch [Fort Cass]

Dear Sir

Yours of 16th arrived to day. I send off your order without delay, the energy you display & the marked interest you take in promoting the views of the Co. demands & receive my warmest acknowledgements

& tho' I have in common with yourself I have often wished that I could in these times of opposition to be in 2 or 3 places at once, my anxiety has never led me to wish myself transported to the spot where you were individually prosecuting your successful measures, except for the pleasure of witnessing your triumph. It gratifies me that your prospect of a favorable trade are so promising. I know from experience that in opposn. peltries cannot be obtained without paying a good price, but you know my grand object is at all costs to get the robes & beaver as the most effectual means to put down Opposn.

I would have preferred all your boats should have started together for mutual protection & assistance but am satisfied you did as you thought for the best.

Blkfoot returns arrived 16th Ins. all well, Indians gone off well satisfied from Fort McK. at least so I hear. I know your influence with your Indians & have full confidence you will content them, if in power of white men to do it. Peigans & Gros Ventres say they are fully revenged on the Crows & are ~~full~~ very proud of their late coups.

I look for long letters from you & will pay strict attention to ~~your~~ any instructions you may give me. From all I hear Sublett Co. will not make 10 packs robes. I am sure they will not if you can help it & tho' they made a coup last fall we must hope to wipe off the effects of the neglect which gave them such an opening.

I send you 4 good men to assist in bringing out your returns I shall depend on your using every exertion to send down all your returns at least all your convertible peltries that I may dispatch them for St Louis & Steam Boat.

There are no Assiniboins at the present time near me, when any of the principal men come in, I will report the wishes & feelings of the Crows toward them & communicate the results to you. I have no doubt they will receive the friendly proposals of the Crows in good favor. Rest assured that my best wishes will ever attend you.

I am Dear Sir
Very Truly Yours
(Signed) K. McKenzie

Fort Union June 30th 1834
Pierre Chouteau Junr Esqr: [Saint Louis]
Agent Amer. Fur Co.
Saint Louis
Dear Sir

This will be handed you by John Morgan[167] who I send down in charge of a Keel boat, and Batteau laden with Robes &c. shipped to your address, for particulars of which I refer you to the Memorandum herewith.

After much difficulty the Assiniboins[168] reached here on the 26th. Inst. The June rise has not yet made its appearance, but we are now in daily expectation of it; indeed if it does not come soon, I shall begin to despair of it altogether.

The Crow returns fell short 200 packs of what I wrote you in the winter I expected would be made there; this arises from my having been wrongly informed on the subject by the clerk at that post.

I scarcely expect to be able to go down in the Steam Boat, and it is quite doubtful whether I will be able to leave this place at all, till I can find some person to take my place; my presence here this year is more required than it ever was before.

Inclosed you will receive a statement of the accounts of the men now going down. Some advantages may perhaps be made them at Fort Pierre; if so Mr. Papin[169] (who is in charge there) has instructions to notify you on the subject. I send back two men sent up in the Assiniboine, as they are perfectly useless to me, and have done little or nothing on board the boat since she left Saint Louis. Their names are Louis Flourant and Jules Traca.[170] Jean Letup[171] is indebted to the Co. $157.50. I send you his note for that amount which perhaps you will be able to Collect.

I have nothing more to communicate at the present moment, and will close with my best wishes for your health and happiness.

Believe Me Ever
Yours Most Truly
(Sign'd) K. McKenzie

Fort Union July 7th 1834
Mr J Groselaude [Fort Cass]
Sir

Having bought out Sublett & Co. and understanding they have some articles of merchandize in cache near your fort, I hereby instruct you to receive the same on my acct from Mr Andrew Sublett or such other agent as Messrs. Sublett & Co. may appoint to deliver them to you at Ft. Cass. Let them all be carefully examined and if any imperfection appears mark it on the Inventory you will take thereof of which let there be two copies with exact weights marks numbers lengths &c you will sign them both and deliver one to Mr A Sublett and retain the other, packing up or keeping the entire parcel of merchandize apart untill Mr Tulloch's arrival who will have further instructions from me respecting them.

I am Sir
Yours [word struck out]
[Signed] K. McKenzie
Agt. U.M.O

Fort Union July 8th 1834
Mr A Culbertson [Fort McKenzie]
Dear Sir

In the Spring I had the pleasure to receive your letter for Mr Mitchell and much wish an early arrival of the Steam Boat had enabled me to give you a more prompt reply, but this year we have had more difficulties to contend with than any former season and I much fear she will be compelled to remain here[172]

Your precautionary measures respecting the Fort were very judicious in this country it is always requisite to be on the alert, for danger or disaster comes when least expected. Mr Kipp has charge of your trunk or Box from the Lower Country. Mr Mitchell having returned on visiting old Virginia, in consequence of your mistrust of your powers, I have been compelled to take Mr Kipp from the Mandan post to assume the charge of For McKenzie: you saw but little of him when passing Fort Clark but I feel convinced you will pass your winter very agreeably with him, he is moreover acquainted with most of the leading Indians in your district, and well known and respected by the men in the Company's employ and should the Indians throng you the coming season as you are sanguine enough to hope and expect, you will find great relief in the main burden's resting on older Shoulders, while I am confident you will render every possible and very efficient aid.

I thank you for your forethought in apprizing me of the probability of the Gens du Sang wintering with you and have regulated the equipment accordingly, the men made the trip in nine days.

In reply to your inquiry respecting horses kept by Clerks or men in the Company's employ, my rule has been hitherto to permit them so to keep them on condition of my using them to aid in supplying the Fort with meat, and should any person possessing a horse object thereto I should not hesitate in making a charge for the guard and care of him. Hoping to hear of your welfare at your earliest convenience

I am Dear Sir
Very Truly Yours
(Signed) K McKenzie

Fort Union July 26 1834
Mr John Carlisle[173] [S.B. Assiniboine]
Sir

I have three Boats laden and in an hour or two I start for St Louis. I leave things to be handed to you by Mr Crawford; In my anxiety to make the most prudent and judicious management to protect the Steam boat during the winter, as there is every probability she will be compelled to remain at her present moorings, I made my arrangements to build a fort near her station, and very naturally calculated that the men under your charge would assist me in so doing, satisfied that their comfort would be essentially promoted thereby. I also proposed using the Fort when completed as a trading house for the Indians of that district: but I am informed your men are resolved to be independent of me, to take care of the boat without any aid from me to build a fort and house for themselves, and at all events to render no assistance to my people. Now I wish you to state candidly and fairly the real facts in a letter to Mr Hamilton whom I leave in charge of this place and whose proceedings will be guided by the information you give at the same time I wish you to understand that I have no desire to establish a trading post near the boat, but if any of my people are there I must provide them with the means of trading with the Indians; if your men persist in their present plans and think they are right in so doing, I will have nothing to do with them. Perhaps I am misinformed I hope such will prove to be the case.

Believe me yours truly
(Signed) K. McKenzie
Agt. U.M.O.

Fort Union 17th Sept. 1834
Kenneth McKenzie Esqr.
Dear Sir

Two days since I had scarcely given my instructions to Francis to have the boat in readiness to start for St Louis, not deeming it prudent to wait longer for the young men from Fort McKenzie, when a packet of Letters was handed me from Mr Kipp I send you a copy herewith: prospects of trade there gloomy in the extreme, Peigans & Bloods at war to the hilt, the summer hunt only produced Seven packs of beaver!!

Mr. Culbertson's letter will show how the Crows have compelled himself and people to live on cords Parfleche for 15 days.[174] Mr Brazeau's name not mentioned, I presume he remains with Mr Kipp for the winter. Mr Crawford has finished his fort on a more eligible spot than the one you fixed on, his equipment is made up and in part sent off.[175] I send you a copy of a letter from Mr Tulloch: both he and Mr Kipp made their voyages in less time than might have been expected from the stage of water. Mr Tulloch had seen some of the Crow nation at the time of his meeting and could hazard no opinion regarding the trade. Rotten Belly[176] was killed this Summer by the Blackfeet. The works at this place have progressed pretty regularly, the last load of hay will be brought home to day. Manta says considerably more in quantity than last year though a good stack has been burnt, for ten days the prairies, West, North & East were burning furiously. One bastion is roofed & shingled & pointed, the other built up as high as the pickets. Luteman has made his arrangements for the Kitchen and has erected & shingled five apartments under the intended gallery.[177] Cattle are far away and the consumption of meat is I fancy greater that ever. I had some difficulty in starting the Deschamps party on their hunt, they are very sanguine in their expectations. Le Enfant du fer has paid us a visit Seven days march from his camp of 80 Lodges, they will all be here to trade this winter: Le Sonant Laroche & La Bras cassé[178] are gone to the North and tried to persuade him to go but he declined. A few hours after you had left this place Fr. Deschamp & Pellot arrived the latter hoped to have been permitted to accompany you to St Louis, he is undecided about wintering here. Halcrow[179] has hitherto conducted himself fully to my satisfaction. Mr Rocque[180] was not able to start untill Aug 28. and even then in so dismal a state of fear he will never reach Red River. I have packed up a white cow skin very carefully and addressed it to you at Fort Clark. I have traded very little except 20 beaver skins, in fact the Indians have nothing. The evening of your departure the young Gauché Le petit Soldat Le Chef qui parle, Le Capot Bleu[181] and many others arrived to see Mr Sandford[182] the two latter started a few days afterwards for the Crow Village and have not since been heard of, it is supposed they are killed. Genl. Jackson[183] is gone thither in search of them prepared for peace or war, some young men who accompanied Le Chef qui parle stole five horses from Mr Tulloch. The young Gauché, regretted he had not redeemed his pledge by bringing a large party to trade here on his return last spring they had all gone to the north he will not promise again but he will do all he can: he said it went hard with him not to get his dram as heretofore on arrival. I sent him away with a glad heart but without tasting Liquor wine. Almost every day small parties of Indians have visited us, some to [word?], others to beg, and many engaged in war or hunting.

On the 29th Aug there were encamped near the Fort 170 Lodges of the [Assiniboine] Gens de Canot 40 Lodges of Les Gens des filles & above 20 Lodges with the General, his father and Lajambe blessé with him: Le Grand Soldat La Souris qui marches & Le chien fou are together near la Lake du Sable; they remained here some days but I had less trouble with them than I feared; they are very reluctant members of the temperance society. Michel has got 300 barrels of coal housed this last kiln is now nearly ready to draw. Bearing in mind your conversation with Capt Bennett[184] regarding supplies of provisions &c for the use of the boat, I was much surprised to receive his order (written subsequent to your conversation) handed by Mr

Carlisle requiring 6 Brls bread, 2 brls. Flour, 2 brls corn and for Sugar & coffee in proportion. I could not comply therewith but gave as much as I could spare. M. Gravelle did not like Fort Cass quarters for his wife and has sent her back here, Jack Ram's family will in a few days number fourteen!!!. Were you not terribly oppressed with the heat on the voyage down? from July 29th to Aug 7 the thermometer rose each day upwards of 100° & some days 105° We have had some furious gales since but scarcely a drop of rain: The Missouri is terribly low, dogs walk across with the exception of the narrow channel on the opposite shore. Francis will not undertake charge of a loaded boat I can send therefore only so many packs as there is a reasonable prospect of making head with, for particulars I refer you to the Bill of Lading. It is said cattle are plenty from La R. au Tremble to Les Montagnes des bois.[185] a Duplicate hereof therefore I address to you at Fort Pierre. Anxiously hoping you will make a prosperous Voyage and have favourable weather for your return believe me ever to be

Dear Sir
Very faithfully Yours
(Signed) J. Archibald Hamilton

P.S. The new Fort Assiniboine[186] Mr Crawford says is 100 feet square the buildings 138 feet front by 18 depth.

Fort Union Sept. 15th 1834
Kenneth McKenzie Esquire
Dear Sir

A. Bourbonnet[187] came down with other men whose term of service expires this fall and was very anxious to engage for this post or Fort Cass untill Spring (you recollect Mr Kipp's instructions were to make no new engagements to terminate sooner than Spring 1836) but knowing your dependance on men from hence to take out remains of last seasons returns from Fort Pierre, though so good a man I will not keep him; he requests me to express his wish of obtaining an engagement for the mountains next spring. I cannot say more than that I consider him a deserving young man.

Ever yours truly
(Signed) J. Archdale Hamilton

Fort Union Sept. 17th 1834
Mr. F.A. Chardon [Fort Clark]
Dear Sir

I entrust this with my best wishes for your health and comfort to your old friend Francis who has charge of boat for St Louis, 15 men with him. Our larder is empty and having in all cases of need found you ready and willing to render assistance, I request you will furnish them with 16 bushls corn which with the grease thy will have will carry them down. The men from the Crow & Blackfoot country have so much news to communicate Since not put much to paper. Mr Kipp had a safe trip of 32 days. The Crows had previous to his arrival stolen every horse from the fort. Rotten Belly was killed near the Fort: The Assiniboines have recently stolen five horses from Mr Tulloch, and the last time we sent out for meat, Pellot blond was stolen and two horses of the companys. I have none of your favors to acknowledge the receipt of but trust I may ere long.

Believe me
faithfully Yours
(Signed) J. A. Hamilton

Fort Union 17th Sept 1834
To Mr McKenzie Esqr
Dear Sir

For the supply of the upper posts next Spring I beg leave to observe that we have neither blue nor white pound Beads and for Fort Cass red & black pound will also be required, nor are there any red cock feathers. In the article of soap please double the St Louis order, there is not enough to last untill spring. Trunk Locks & 4 qar augers are also wanted for this place. Michel is vexed at having refused the screw plate you shewed him. There is not half enough tar in St Louis order, and there is not enough here for more than a months work, the consumption of Iron wire is very large. Chiefs Coats can be made here in sufficient quantity if you can bring little more lace the large round Buttons add much to the appearance of the coats and costs but little more than the other, will you procure a few gross 60 or 100 feet of rod iron for lightning rod I think you should send up.

Believe me
Your Very Your's
(Signed) J Archdale Hamilton

Fort Union Sept 17th 1834
Mr J. Halsey [Fort Pierre Chouteau]
Dear Sir

You doubtless have been many days expecting to receive letters from me, but Mr Kipp having waited 26 days after his arrival at Fort McKenzie before he started the men for this place I could not send Francis away one moment earlier. I hope he will reach Fort Pierre in reasonable time but the river is unprecedently low here he will not take charge of a loaded boat I am compelled therefore to retain a portion of last years returns. The 15 Men have agreed their Accts. The letter addressed to Mr McKenzie, Fort Pierre, you will please retain untill his arrival, one addressed to him at St Louis you will send on up Frances. I shall be much obliged by your forwarding the enclosed letters for England to your friend Mr Hunt, the postage to New York I will pass to on a Dit of acct. Mr Kipp & Mr Tulloch arrived in safety at their respective posts but the prospect of trade is very bad at each of them. This fort has been thronged with Indians since Mr McKenzie's departure but they have nothing to trade and are too lazy to hunt and are grumbling sadly at Liquor being stopped. Mr Crawford paid me a visit a few days since, he says he had built a very neat snug fort 100 feet square plenty of accommodations for Robes & wives. Pray send me any newspapers &c you can spare by the first opportunity and believe to be Dear Sir

Very Truly Yours
(Signed) J. Archdale Hamilton

Fort Union 27 Sep 1834
Mr L Crawford [Fort Assiniboine]
Dear Sir

Sundry articles are packed in Trunk of which A. Kennedy[188] has the key. I propose starting the accts on Monday. Of dye stuffs a small portion sells for $1. rifle Ball & meat (475 lb) arrived safe more meat & return carts would be acceptable: J Ram's son will bring your spare cart & A K ride your extra horse. I can spare A K for a few months or the winter if you wish to have him. I know Asiniboins are great beggars but the merest trifle will often content them tho' at first they ask great things.

We know not where Jackson's camp is, can you inform us? Francis started 17 Sept. A note for Mr Carlisle is enclosed, I regret to hear he has adopted a line of conduct so disagreeable to you & dishonorable to himself, as he shows his card this early you will regulate your play accordingly. Give him a acct for Stores he delivers up.

Your request for any thing I can supply shall always receive my careful attention. You have my best wishes

Truly Yours
[Signed] JAH

Fort Union 27 Sept 1834
Mr J Carlisle [S.B. Assiniboine]
Sir

Such portion of stores sent up in the Yawl Aug 4. last as remain on hand, you will please transfer to Mr Crawford who is deputed by Mr McKenzie to the charge of Ft Assiniboin. You will take Mr Crawford acc for the same.

I am Sir
Your obediently & prs. K McKenzie
[Signed] J Archdale Hamilton

❖ ❖ ❖

29 Sep [1834]
L. Crawford [Fort Assiniboine]
Dr Sir

I send Deschamps a/c they are no better than they should be Keep your eye on them & settle with them amicably. Traps & Saddles to be allowed for if complete & in good order or depreciation charged. My instructions are for Sumr. for 300 Fall 350 Spring 400 inspect this carefully I conceive it can only rate as Summer. Old Deschamp owes $170 & 8 traps & 2 saddles lent & Gun lent in 1833.

[Signed] JAH

7 Oct. [1834]
L. Crawford [Fort Assiniboine]
Dr. Sir

I send F. Deschamp Senr. & his son François will come down here, names of chiefs of Assin. & Crees.[189] I hope you may make something of Mr Kennedy.

[Unsigned] [JAH]

Fort Union 7 Oct 1834

Mr F. A. Chardon [Fort Clark]

Dr Sir

I give this to Legris who has beaver & will sell it to you as it is not yet in order. Manta has left me sans permission & may give you a call. Cattle plenty.

Yours truly Mr F.A.C.

9 Oct

I write per Miller to say Alls well, he has an a/c to show what is due to him should he want any thing. Welsh & Ebert[190] have beaver try to buy it

Yours JAH

9 Oct [1834]

Mr Laidlaw Esqr [Fort Pierre Chouteau]

Dear Sir

Miller has $217.32 due to him for which you will please give him voucher on St Louis. Welch & Co have beaver they ask $5 my limits are $50. Manta left me without permission he owes $30 his time was up this fall but he agreed to stay & pay his debt & his wages were $15 per mo.

I enclose note of Croteau $107.

Yours truly

[Signed] JAH

9 Oct [1834]

K. McKenzie Esqr

Dear Sir

Miller has finished the bastions & starts today for St Louis I offered him $300 he asked $450. for a year. His work is inferior in finish to Pow[de]r Mag[azine] but in other respects I think it is according to contract. Legris Co are gone to Ft. Clark. Welch Co. have beaver but ask $5 pr lb. Deschamp brot nearly 4 packs, the old man is engaged I have sent him to Ft. A. & expect his son here daily. Mr Crawford & Carlisle have had some sparring I have engaged Pelot.

Manta declined engaging but proposed to stay & pay his debts if I would furnish provisns. for voyage when his time expired, knowing it would then be too late for him to go down I considered he merely wanted a salve to his conscience to save his word you may imagine my surprise at his coming after 10 days & contending that his time was up. I have not seen him since 1 Oct but hear he is gone down with Legris.

We have traded no meat. Jackson Gauché's son & Little Dusk are the only Indians who have come in since I wrote. Cattle abundant above. Jackson brot 3 horses recovered from Gens de Canot. Young Gauché says he will return horses stolen from Mr T. all well at Ft. Cass 3 Sep. Yellow Belly chief of Crows. Things move on much in the old way but I cannot get work enough done.

You desire me to send express 1 Dec till when believe me &c

[Signed] JAH

Fort Union 18 Oct 1834

Mr Jas Kipp [Fort McKenzie]

Dear Sir

On the 15 Sept I had the pleasure to receive letters from you the lamentable falling off in Beaver is very discouraging. I regret you did not state what sort of trade. Isidore [Sandoval] made during the summer & your omitting to set forth in letter by Mr Harvey what furs and peltries you have on hand that is the first thing Mr McK will want to know on his arrival.

If you have so engaged Baria Prennard & Marchal & Carisalle[191] let me know the terms. Mr Harvey is so anxious to return saying you expect him, tho' you are silent on the subject as he proposes to start alone. I offer no obstacle he being engaged for your fort but I tell him it is my wish he should stay till Mr McK arrives or until I have occasion to send to you for which purpose I detain the three men who came with him 16 horses & 1 Mule. I have recd. 2 horses were left on the way.

J Dupuis[192] arrived 9th Ins. he pd. $166 in beaver $34 ball I presume he paid you by services rendered.

Sandovals a/c ball due to him in March 52.75 as charge for squaw or Peirot's[193] lost time & $12 differences in traps only now entered viz Nages horses & $385 difference $320.25. dift. traps $12 Bal due 52.75 regarding his new engagement it is strange Mr M. [Mitchell] should tell him one thing & write another but I am sure Mr McKenzie will not exact or expect more services than he has engaged to render, when I write next Mr McK will be here & this matter of difference as also the similar cases of Alacompt & Carpentier[194] shall be satisfactorily settled. Rondin's[195] a/c when re-engaged he owed $40.75 this was allowed him in lieu of equipment, subsequent thereto & before the boat started to embark Sundries amount $11. Harveys a/c Ball agreed $20 exchange of horse $20, amount 10.75.

I have no news other than the Steam boat remains where you last saw her, a fort is built near Mr Crawford in charge & Mr McK Capt. B. & Mr. Sanford started 26 July for St Louis. I expect Mr McK early in Dec. he will be anxious for your promised letter in Jany. My Compts. to the gentlemen of your fort & believe me to be Dear Sir very Truly Yours

[Signed] JAH

Fort Union Nov 3 1834

Mr L Crawford [Fort Assiniboine]

Dear Sir

My opinion is that you should act wholly independent of Mr Carlisle if he wants any assistance from you & asks it in the proper way, you will not refuse any thing that should be rendered; if he does not choose to mess at your table let him go elsewhere but he need not look to you for supplies nor would you be justified in furnishing them.

Is he not a hired servant of the Company? I presume he has sense enough to know that if he fails in his duty he must meet the consequences. I am pleased to find the other officers of the boat exercise more discretion. All this necessary for the working hands is to give them the food of the country they may ask & expect their fare but no law would award them more.

So Mr C. says "there is no law in this country" let him commit any felonious act such as he has threatened to do & he will find the laws of the U.S. to be his master. I refer him to Art 3. Sec 2. clause 3 of Constitution of U.S. & to 2nd clause in schedule following 13 Articles of Constitution of Missouri & he will find the criminal laws in this, the territory of Mo in as full force now as before the state of Mo was constituted. I think you are justified in protecting the property of the Co. on board the boat from being abused, with respect to the management of the boat neither you nor I have any thing to do except in case of Mr Carlisle's wilful neglect or absence from his post.

I send you horse harness & cart, keep as long as you need them. I have tallow enough for "home" consumption. I will send for more meat if you wish it out of your way tho Canoe was 7 days coming down. Return what books you have read by first safe by first conveyance. I have no N W Guns under 12s sell the German at 6. I will trade wine for robes [word struck out] in any quantity. If Mr K kept a list of Indians who trade robes with you as far as practicable Mr. K would be pleased therewith. I shall expect T.D.[196] in a week. Grey foxes only bring 12 ½ cts. Red foxes & wolves from 40 to 50 cts. Trade them as well as you can not buying too dear. I would not willingly give another horse for white robe but as they are rare it is not likely you or I will be tempted. I send Amn.

Write & convey affct.

Very truly Yours,

[Signed] JAH

Ft Union Nov. 15 1834

F.A. Chardon [Fort Clark]

Dear Sir

I send Joe H & P.B [word?] for Mr McK who I expect will arrive at your post abt. this time. Should Mr McK have already passed on hither, which is not probable you will please address the packet to Mr Lou. causing it to be sent from post to post without delay you will also adopt the same course should you receive information from below stating that Mr McK is detained & will not be up this winter but if as such communication has been made to you, retrain the packet & man until you receive such tidings or see Mr McK in progress because if Mr McK has already passed let the men return without delay: the men are in debt what you find necessary to advance them charge this fort & send acct by [name?]

Very truly Yours
[Signed] JAH

Fort Union Nov 15 1834
Kenneth McKenzie Esqr
Dear Sir

I propose starting men tomorrow with boat to wait your arrival at Ft. Clark. My last was of 9 Ult. pr Miller. I enclose copy of last from Mr Kipp recd 11 Oct & Harvey he ret 19 Ult. Good trade in meat at Ft. A. and robes are now coming in daily.

Many Crees and Montn des Bois, McKay only 2 days march from there. Liquor plenty, Mdze low. L'Enfant in for le Bras Capé La Roche & Le Sonant coming here. Jackson Le Maitre du Parc & Le petit Dorion have packed 120 robes for wine. I shall be disappointed if robe trade does not far exceed your first season here. L. Co. writes if S. boat is in a very dangerous situation exposed to the whole force of the current from all I can learn J. Carlisle has not conducted himself properly he is entirely governed by his mistress the Mulatto woman. Having no food for horses, I sent Pallot to camp on YS. with 46 horses he sends in fresh meat regularly by means of 5 carts who come easily in one day. With regard to orders for next year forget not 6 6 in knob locks. I send abstract of mens engagements

	Sum [18]35	fall 35	Sum 36		[total]
Ft. U.	14	16	12	=	42
Ft. Cass	4	13	3		20
Ft. Clark	30	16	6		52
Ft A.	4	—	—		4
	52	45	21	=	118

20 of the 52 will no doubt re-engage.

20 Warriors arrived last night to meet La Lancer who it is said is coming with 80 men to proceed in force agst. the Gros Ventres he may change his mind. Mr Crawford has traded a white cow Skin & F Deschamp has a fine white calf skin. Le frire & Hugise each arrived with 12 robes Le Brechu coming with 60 robes

Yours truly
[Signed] JAH

Nov 27 1834
Mr L. Crawford [Fort Assiniboine]
Dear Sir

The horses you waited for are at Camp, Gaboleau will go for them directly. I enclose an order. I cannot alter your tariffs, though [as] a necessary guide it is sometimes policy to deviate from it to please a good Indian & an opportunity will not be wanting to re-imburse yourself for a sacrifice occasionally made, with respect to the Crees who have been to McKay if they come to you to trade sell the articles you have at his prices & make up the difference out of them on other things as soon as Saucier can travel on your sending to me you shall have some new N W Guns to sell at 8 m & at Cost, to sell at 6 or 7.

By every opportunity let me Know how this robe trade gets on & such inform. as you can rely on from the camps men. I have no smoothing iron.[197] F.D.[198] claims the little horse & contends he was sent here at his wish with a promise he should be kept in stable all winter. I laugh at his statement after what you wrote me when the horse came down

Yours truly
[Signed] JAH

Fort Union Oct 23rd 1834
Mr J. Halsey [Fort Pierre]
Dear Sir

I want some further explanation of Sandovals a/c by the a/cs rendered me you make him a Cr Oct 10 1831 $126.76 he disputes this, & I have no [word?] to shew how it is composed when B Marchand left this place with Mr Sandford on Septr. 1831 his a/c was or ought to have been ~~stated~~ as follows being a copy of the Balls [balance] here

To advances		By 1 years Wage (unknown)	
1831 Sepr. 1 at F. Union	106.25	June 1831	
1830 Decr " " " F. Clark	33.75	Sepr " " " "	$40.00
1831 May 21 " order on " St Louis	50.00	" Transf. F. Tecumseh "	150.00
	$190.00		$190.00

His Accts therefore be stated somewhat in this way

1830 June To advances in St Louis	1831 June By Wages		
Novr. " " at Ft Tecumseh	Sepr. " " Extra		$40.00
Decr 1831 " " F. Clark	33.75		
May 21 " [?] in St Louis	50.00		
Sepr. " Advances at F. Union	106.25		

[No Signature] [JAH]

Fort Union January 12th 1835
Mr A. Harvey [Fort McKenzie]
Dr. Sir

I am glad to hear of your safe arrival at Fort McKenzie, you tell me you saw nothing in the shape of a man on your voyage but you neglected to say whether or no you saw any thing in the shape of the two Horses left at the Muscle Shell. So you have abandoned your grand Scheme of a trip to the Cootrunable [Kootenai Indian] country and are required to commence hunting again. I know of no obstacle thereto and Mr Kipp will be instructed to set you free and furnish you with such things as you may require for your hunt.

I am Dear Sir
Yours obediently
(Signed) J Archdale Hamilton

Fort Union January 12th 1835
Mr J E Brazeau[199] [Fort McKenzie]
Dr. Sir

In reply to your letter of 23rd Decr last I beg to apprize you that Mr Lamont who is now here during Mr McKenzie's absence in Europe, was especially requested by your friends in St Louis last fall, to urge your visiting them the approaching Summer, nor is he willing to present any obstacle to your so doing, but as you say Mr Kipp requests you to pass the summer with Mr Culbertson he will avail himself of your willingness to remain at Fort McKenzie untill the arrival of the summer boat which it is expected will be with you at the latest by the 15th June and will afford you ample time to come down here & accompany me to St Louis early in July.
I refer you to Mr Kipp for further particulars & instructions a copy of your a/c is enclosed which I believe you will find correct. The horses were placed to your credit at the time you made the claim to Mr McKenzie at the dates & prices as by him directed.
I hope you will pass an agreeable spring and have plenty of good buffalo Meat.

I am
Your Obediently
(Signed) J. A. Hamilton

Fort Union January 12th 1835
Mr J Berger [Fort McKenzie]
Dr Sir

I received your letter of the 24th Decr. last in due course, and in reply assure you that I fully approve of your proposal to open the trade with the Cootamahas [Kootenais] and as you so well succeeded in opening the trade with the Blackfeet bands four years ago. I hope the like success will attend your efforts on this expedition. I enclose you a List of prices of the leading articles, and will instruct Mr Kipp to further your arrangements by every means in his power. My best wishes attend you.

I am Dear Sir
Yours Obediently
(Signed) [J. A. Hamilton]

Fort Union January 12th 1835
Mr A Culbertson [Fort McKenzie]
Dear Sir

I have collected all the newspapers over which I had control to furnish you amusement for the ensuing spring & have instructed Mr Crawford to make up an extra packet for you as the men pass Ft Assiniboin

The Bank Question engrossed nearly the whole attention of Congress during last session. The house of representatives support the President, the Senate many powerfully opposed to his views. Commercial distress has been almost unprecedented in the states and no city has suffered more than Cincinnati, real property was freely offered there for sale from one fifth to one tenth of its original cost. Accept my best wishes for your health & happiness and believe me to be

Dear Sir
Your's Truly
(Signed) J Archdale Hamilton

Fort Union January 12th 1835
Mr A. Culbertson [Fort McKenzie]
Dear Sir

Your Letters of the 4th September & 25th Decr Inst were only received. Mr McKenzie is not expected here untill next summer. I am sure he would not have neglected an opportunity of declaring his satisfaction respecting your conduct when the rascally Crows so annoyed you, yet had you punished them as severely as they merited, they would be less likely to return to you, for they are terribly afraid of your big guns. You impart blame to Mr Mitchell for leaving you almost without provisions; in his mind that last spring he blamed you for keeping ~~back~~ the meat he had salted and processed with so much care. I much regret the expectations you so reasonably entertained in June last with respect to a much extended trade with the Northern Indians was not realized. The promises of red skins cannot be much relied on. I fully accord with you regarding presents made to Indians, it is a custom more honored in the breach than the observance it has increased alarmingly & ought to be abolished. I trust Mr Kipp will be able to adjust the grievances under which you state some of the men labor, for the want of sufficient explicitness when re-engaged last spring.

My arrangements for the ensuing summer are fully detailed in my letter to Mr Kipp and I feel assured I may fully calculate on your best exertions to give them effect, confident that on your assuming the charge of Fort McKenzie the interest of the Company will be considered & promoted to the utmost of your power; barring accidents the summer supplies will be with you by the first week in June. I shall by that opportunity address you more at length, in the mean time

I am Dear Sir

Yours Obediently

(Signed) [J. A. Hamilton]

Fort Union January 13th 1835

Mr James Kipp [Fort McKenzie]

Dear Sir

Our efforts hitherto to open a trade with the Cootamahas have been fruitless. I have received a letter from J Berger proposing to make another attempt if goods are allowed him to the extent of $1000 at a reasonable price. I have written to him agreeing to his proposition and included a list of prices of which I send you a copy, at the same time not confining you strictly for as I consider this by far the most eligible plan for the company to accept I would not let it pass for the value of a few cents in the place of goods.

A man may be furnished to J. Berger at the price of the transportation of his wages & equipment but the Company are not responsible for advances J Berger may make to him. Horses &c if required to be charged a reasonable price. Mdze horses &c to be charged to the acct. of J. Berger and when delivered to him to be at his risk, prices of furs & peltries I have annexed to the List of Mdze. Let it be understood fully that these things are furnished to J. Berger for trade with the Cootamahas and should the trade with Peigans or other Bands accustomed to trade at the Fort he will be charged retail store prices for all the articles taken by him. It is probable that J. Berger may not be able to prevail on the Cootamahas to come to the Fort to trade even for the season after the coming one, but if a place of rendezvous be agreed on an outfit could be sent from the Fort at a time agreed upon.

At all events it is very desirable that a trade should be opened with the Cootamahas. I shall hope to find in the spring that you have arranged matters with J Berger to your mutual satisfaction. A. Harvey says he wishes to be set free I have no objection thereto, he is free 3rd June 1835 and obliged to go to St Louis should the company require him so to do. (see a copy of his engagement) I am willing however to give up that part of it. His Account as adjusted here in October last made Dr to the Company $20

All thereto for exchange of horse 20

40

And Sundry Merchandize to amount of $10.75

50.75

Salary due June 3 1835 $400.

Deduct 50.75

349.25 from this you will further deduct the portion of his time you gave up to him and the same proportion of the sum you allowed him for a suit of clothes to which he says he was entitled although by the agreement he stipulated for one suit for two years. Whereas he has had allowances for two suits, you will further deduct such advances as you may have made since his return from hence, and you may supply him with such things as he may require for his hunt.

This much for the present I shall write you on other subjects tomorrow and I am

Dear Sir

Yours truly

(Signed) [J. A. Hamilton]

Mr James Kipp [Fort McKenzie] Fort Union January 9th 1835

Dear Sir

I wrote you a long letter by Mr Havey of 18 Octr. in reply to your letters by him but it is evident you cannot have received it from the tenor of your letter of 26 Decr. received to day. I therefore send you a copy of it and request your reply or rather the documents when you come down relative to the engagements of Baria Pencenneau and others. By the a/c sent by Mr Culbertson he states L Marchals a/c thus: Decr 25 advances at Fort McKenzie $302.25 should it not stand thus:

1834

March 23 Ft. Balance 36

Decr 25 Advances 266.25

$302.25

By the bye how is it so large a sum has been advanced to him in ~~nine months~~ nine months, & how small a sum has he left to spend for the next 18 months should he live so long & do his duty. Our mutual friend F.A. Chardon by his letter of the 9th Decr. requests that I will inform you that your house is in good order and that your lady's Family are all well, he also wishes to purchase your spy Glass if you are disposed to sell it, or if you leave this country in the Spring with the intention of returning he will take good care of it during your absence. Mr. Lamont will inform you of Mr McKenzie's trip to the old country and give you all the news. I have therefore only to assure you of my best wishes for your health & prosperity and believe me I am

Dear Sir

Very Truly Yours

(Signed) J Archdale Hamilton

Fort Union January 14th 1835

Mr James Kipp [Fort McKenzie]

Dear Sir

When your winter trade is over, the river clear of ice, your packs are bound, your booty and all things ready for a start, you will transfer your best at Ft. McKenzie & appurtenances therein to belonging to Mr Culbertson, leaving Mr Brazeau with him & 22 men, selecting those whose term of service does not expire untill next summer & including the Blacksmith & Carpenter. I shall be looking out for you after the first week in April and should fortune's fair favour you, that you have more packs than your Keel & 2 Mackinac boats can conveniently bring leave them in Store to be brought down in Summer. My present determination is to start a Keel Boat with the Summer supplies for Fort McKenzie and soon after your arrival here as possible. A later Start than 1st May so that the person who may go up in charge thereof can return here by the end of June.

With regard to the arrangements to be made before you come down, first, I presume you will have no Difficulty in fixing matters with J. Berger to trade with the Cootamahas, second, as it seems desirable that someone should go out with the Peigans, I know no persons are available as Isidore and I presume it cannot be necessary to send out any thing but ammunition & Tobacco, but this I leave to you. I suppose it should not be practicable for him to catch a few Beaver for the company while out with the Indians it would help pay his Salary. Third, as Mr. Culbertson send some person who can talk Blackfoot it might be well to engage L. Marcevan[200] for another year, not as an interpreter expressly, but to be employed as heretofore. I expect you have no other person more competent or useful; with this exception I do not wish you to make any new engagements with hands, such as are disposed to re-engage, on their arrival here, will have the opportunity of so doing.

You will bring down with you an accurate Inventory of all the property you leave behind, and the books of Accts, Mr Culbertson agreeing the balance of them to remain & transferring them to a new Book. With respect to the grievances of your men in consequence of some inattention on the part of Mr Mitchell on filling their appointments there does not appear to be any insurmountable difficulty the proper adjustment, had you received Mr. Hamilton's letter entrusted to Mr Harvey I presumed you would have set the matter to right at once it appears Mr Mitchell made no entry in Isidore's Acct. which he brought here last spring the charges objected nor do I find he alluded thereto in any way.

Mr Tulloch has been pretty well alarmed by various war parties from our quarter and I think needs no warning from me to be on his guard. At the commencement of the season there was excellent prospect of a great trade in Robes at this post but I am sorry to say they come in very slowly. As I propose writing you one more letter by the present express I will close this by assuring you that I am

Truly Yours

(Signed) [J. A. Hamilton]

Fort Union January 15th 1835

Mr Lewis Crawford [Fort Assiniboine]

Dear Sir

I duly received your letters of the 9th & 12th date accept my thanks for the same. L'ours paid his credit. If the Moose Dung visits you again let him know that if he will come here in the Spring with his band and a rare heap of robes a very respectable present of ammunition & Tobacco will be made him.

Mr Kipp writes in much better spirit with respect to trade than when Harvey came down, he expects to bring down at least 20 packs Beaver 10 packs rats & six hundred packs of robes. I forgot that you were without a tariff, So ~~one~~ send one; on accepting thereof you will start Joe Howard in company with Marchande, and Marchal for Fort McKenzie, give him 30 balls & powder & ½ lb tobacco & charge this post and add to the enclosed acct. what little advances you may have made him and enclose it in the letter you will write to Mr Kipp he is in debt but is so fond of spending, he would never cry "had enough." You have forgotten Mr Kennedy's acct. You need not expect Mr Lamont for some time to come, he is comfortably housed here & I hope he has no wish to move camp.

Believe me to be Dear Sir

Very Truly Yours

(Signed) J Archdale Hamilton

P.S. If you have need [of] any of the Newspapers send some of them on to Mr Kipp if you please. Mr [Demaray? [201]] will fill Joe Howard place.

January 16 1835

Mr J Kipp [Fort McKenzie]

Dr Sir

You will perceive I have suggested your bringing down the Carpenter as there is much work to do here but it would be well to have an extra boat built if you have the means in case it should be wanted in he Summer to bring down the person & extra men who will go up in the Keel boat

Yours &c.

[Signed] D.L. [Daniel Lamont]

Fort Union 3rd February 1835

Mr. Saml Tulloch [Fort Cass]

Dear Sir

Your several letters of he 26th Aug. 3rd Sepr. 11th Nov. and 4th February are before me; the first four I found here on my arrival here from St Louis on the 20th Decr the last on my return from Fort Assiniboin where I have been for a few days. Mr McKenzie started from St Louis last Septr for New York where he proposed taking the first packet for England. I expect he will make his arrangements to be here about the end of June next I observe with concern that your prospects of trade are so unfavourable your expenditure of the most costly articles appear to me unusually large for so very small a return, and although it appears you have been driven thereto by an unexpected opposition, yet there is an old adage, that Gold may be bought too dear, and view your present opponents in a very different light to the parties we had to contend with last year. I have made you up the articles you ask for, a small assortment that you not be wholly destitute of these articles, when Borgne's band comes in to trade.

It is quite out of my power to send the men you requested to rebuild your Fort & therefore my desire that you will make your arrangements to come down here in the Spring with your whole establishment as early as you think desirable to leave, of course bringing away every thing valuable. You will not trade any more horses for I have already more than I have use for. I send you two good hands in the place of the two lads who came down with La Bombarde. As you have the wherewith to come without your boats I hope you will not find it necessary to risk any of the Cos. property in Canoes. I would recommend you to take an Inventory, previous to your starting that you may know exactly what you put on board. Though you say it will be your last year in the country; I have known others say so as positively and yet change their minds. None of the Assiniboins who took your horses last summer have been in here since: I have however recovered two of the horses. The Crows stole every horse they had at Fort McKenzie, but only three. I suppose they did not tell you any thing about it. You neglected to state the weight of the Beaver Skins A. Gravelle delivered to you; for how long a time did the man you furnished remain with him? I sincerely hope by the time this reaches you that your health will be fully re-established. I think it should be well when you leave, to rail up your Doors & Fort Gates.[202] Accept of my best wishes & believe me to be, Dear Sir,

Yours Truly
(Signed) [Daniel Lamont]

Fort Union March 3d 1835
Mr. Halsey [Fort Pierre Chouteau]
Dear Sir

You will please credit Ft Union $4.92 being 2 cts per lb on [word?] Tallow sent to Fort Pierre Sept 20th it was part of Sublett &Cos. stock and is that [word?] this post six cents pr lb. Postage of single Letter from St Louis to New York is only 25 cts not 50 cts. You give the post credit for Mdze &c 7th July $98.80 cts. The account sent by Mr McKenzie a copy of the "Books here" was $119.40 cts will you explain how the difference arises. A fresh Invoice is enclosed, with the addition of silk hats & Table covers.[203] You place nothing to credit of this post for Sunds. as pr a/c taken by Mr McKenzie 20th Sept. and yet the amount was to be regulated on his arrival at Fort Pierre

I therefore now charge the whole subject to such deductions as may be correct. Mr McKenzie also took some packages of Mdze to St Louis which if not returned this post should be credited for there. You will find a copy of Inv. Mdze &c from Fort Clark Outfit received here ex S. Bt. Assiniboin Amt $325.15. also Sundry Mdze brought here in error part of Fort Pierre Outfit. The other articles regarding which you make inquiry, certainly did not come here. This post should have credit for errors in St Louis Invoice as pr Statement. Mr Sanford received 350 lbs Powder as p[er] entry in packing a/c 100 Kegs of 50 lb ea arrived here and tho whole is charged in St Louis Invoice, he was also to have 1050 lbs Lead but he said he should take it at Fort Clark if he had occasion for it but no more arrived here than is charged in St Louis Invoice. You charge P. Lefleur's[204] wages $140 for 12 mos. he is engaged for two years at $90 p[er] ann[um]. L. Crawford's engagement says $450 you charged $500. You charge wages A. Maxan[205] $230. No such person came here, in the St Louis Book you marked against his name "Not to be found." Modest Pressey's[206] wages you mark $210, should it not be $250? In the St Louis Book there is a blot on the figure but it may be read for $250 or 210, if the man were here the fact could be ascertained, but I have considered it $250. James Andrews[207] was left at Fort Clark. You charge Sundries for Mr Lamont $23.14 as no part thereof was delivered here Mr Lamont will instruct you what post to make Cr for it. Gardin[208] sends $10.50 passes to a/c. A list of men who left Fort Union 30th July with J. Mogan is sent herewith, also abstracts of Ludlow's[209] & L Crawfords engagements. As Mr Chardon did not give up pan, cup, plate &c in Ap[ri]l I presume his a/c should be charged therewith. Believe me Dr Sir

Yours truly
[Signed] D. L. [Daniel Lamont]

Fort Union 11 Mar 1835
A. Culbertson [Fort McKenzie]
Dr Sir

I give this to Pierre Legris an old servant of the Comp & a good beaver hunter who has contrived to have some money in the country, he has also paid Dupuis debt to the Coy. If they offer you beaver for sale $4 pr lb for well handled Spring beaver dry & well best, is the highest price that can be given: should they wish to sell out their horses & traps I by no means wish you to trade for them. When Dupuis arrived here last fall he had 6 traps which he says he bought from you were they included in the amts.

of a/c handed by himself On Aug 7 $166: all well. Accept my best wishes

Yours truly

D. L. [Daniel Lamont]

Fort Union March 26th 1835

Messrs Pratte Chouteau & Co. [Saint Louis]

Gentlemen

In July last Mr McKenzie took with him on leaving this post a scetch [schedule] of order for Mdze &c requisite for the trade of the coming season, the quantities of several articles were to be regulated by circumstances, upon an estimate of the expenditure of the season. I have ventured to fill up the blanks as per annexed list, and it will at least be some criterion for your guidance. In my letter to Mr McKenzie of 17th Sept last I suggested some necessary additions to the order a list whereof I now hand you with some addenda. Chiefs Coats could easily have been made here had Mr McKenzie sent the Lace as promised. I beg to notice that drafts drawn as advised in favour of P. Legris July 3rd 1834 on P Chouteau Jr. Agt. A.F.C. for $395.87 cts. P Legris July 23rd on Pratte Chouteau & Co for $160.25 are both cancelled, having been paid here. March 25th 1835 D. Lamont for U.MO 1834 drew on Pratte Chouteau & Co in favour of P Legris for $162.87 not transferable. In F.U. Invoice 1834 I observed Cusingle Bakles [surcingle buckles[210]] charged 6 doz ea 250 & 275 which is the price (and a high one) pr gross and 6 doz. ea came only the deduction should be

error in buckles 25.87

5p Cr on ditto 2.44

8 March Int on ditto 1.35

$31.66

The post should also have credit for 7 Kegs (350 lbs) Gun powder delivered by order to Mr Sandford, say 350 lbs powder 95.67

5 pr [?] ditto 4.78 31.66

100.65

132.11

Thomas Stensfeit[211] engaged for the mountains came here pr Steam Boat last year; what are the terms of his engagement, and what advances were made to him? What are the terms of Labusiere's[212] engagement, there is no entry thereof in the Name Book. Antoine Luteman came here spring 1832. I have not been able to ascertain what advances were made to him in St Louis. I presume Mr Lamont will furnish you ample particulars of the trade of this post and the prospects by last arrives from the black feet & Crow posts. I have the honor to be

Gentlemen

Yours Very Obediently

(Signed) J Archdale Hamilton

P.S. The acts of Manger du lard 1833 are much wanted.

Fort Union March 29th 1835

Kenneth McKenzie Esqr

Dear Sir

I presume that my letter of the 17th Sept. pr Francis & Oct 9th pr Miller have reached you, they are accompanied by copies of letters from Mr Tulloch & Mr Kipp and addressed to you in St Louis or en route dispatches being also sent to Fort Pierre in case the former did not reach you. On the 15th Nov. I sent further letters pr express to Fort Clark to await your arrival there, but as the fates had destined you to other shores, Mr Lamont early in Decr. ordered the dispatches to be forwarded to St Louis by the first mail, trusting they have found safe conveyance I have now to apprize you those affairs have progressed since Nov; on the 17th of that month La Lance & L'ours and about 80 warriors started to give battle to the Gros Ventres on the 1st Decr. the parties met near the village of the latter. La Lance & about 20 of his men were killed, 16 others severely wounded found their way here in miserable plight, the remainder got to their several camps as they best could: the unfortunate coup has very much interfered with the robe-making of the Gens de filles, Gens de roches & Gens de Canot bands, for war, war, war is their constant cry. Nor do they hesitate to declare that having lost the inducements to make robes, as they will no longer procure grog, they hunt barely for subsistence.

The old Gauché & his son were here 29th Novr. Very little to trade but a great deal to talk. La Bras Cassé & La Corne have been in this quarter all winter but very idle. Le Sonant & La Roche with the Crees who got credit here last season have not visited. The river closed here on the 5 Decr. Mr Lamont & Mr Laferrin[213] arrived here 20th Decr, they started for Fort Assiniboine 29th Decr. & Mr Lamont returned here Janry. 8th visited the Upper Fort again Febry. 15. returned here Febry. 22 and started again for the same place March 20th. Jackson & about 20 Lodges with him wintered on the Yellow Stone, this Camp has given us a good number of robes. Le Brechu came in here with bout 20 Lodges Janry. 9. & has been encamped here ever since. Le Enfant du fer entered at Les Montagnis des Bois [Wood Mountain], he came in with a respectable band and traded 500 robes: several smaller parties of Crees also from that quarter came in well laden with robes: at Fort Assiniboine the Crees have traded largely but not profitably, they have pressed hard on Cloth & blankets. The upper Indians have expressed themselves well pleased with having a Fort so near them, about 400 packs of Robes have been traded there without the aid of much wine (say 100 Gallons) & no alcohol. Three hundred & fifty packs of robes have been traded here and we are yet in expectation of the young Gauché, the Moose Dung &c with their several bands. On the 18 July the Gros Ventres visited Pellot's hunting camp on the Yellow Stone & took 20 horses but they were closely pursued and eventually got off with 6 only. I send you copies of letters from Mr Kipp & Mr Tulloch and the replies thereto. The Fort Cass ~~a/c is~~ account is a melancholy one, 80 Guns 56 Chiefs Coats 200 Blankets & 200 yds cloth expended, and only 4 packs Beaver & 80 packs of robes in store.

There has been no meat traded ~~traded~~ here this season but Pellot has kept the Fort well supplied. Sales in retail store fall very far short of former years. The bastions are completed with the exception of laying down the floors but the planks are all tongued & grooved. Saucier was employed until Christmas in finishing the attics. Timber & plank for the new stores are hauled and so soon as the boats are finished opperations will commence thereon. Halcrow declines a re-enggement. Fr. Deschamp Jr has been of no use, the old man wintered with Mr Crawford and did his duty. Mr Lamont proposes to send Moncrevié to the Blackfeet & to engage Mr Laferriere for the post. Mr Larpenteur has made himself very useful.[214] The stock of Tin & sheet Iron was all worked up long before Christmas last and the Lace you were to have sent for Chiefs Coats did not arrive. ~~La Gr~~ Legris & Dupuis wintered here and have started on a spring hunt with Compton, Vallé & Le petit Francais.[215]

The ice started in the Yellow Stone on the 20th Inst. & on the Mo below the mouth of the Y. Stone on the 22nd and is gradually disappearing opposite the Fort, the River about as high as last year, no snow on the ground. Expenditure of Mdze at Ft Assiniboine as follows Viz Red strouds 3 pict. Blue strouds, 3 pr. Blue LL 3 pr. Scarlet 3 pr Blankets of all kinds 76 pr. Guns 13. Powder 950 lbs. Balls 1700 lbs. Tobacco 2000 lbs. Wine 102 Gallons. The expenditure at this post of cloth & Blankets will not vary much from the above. As Mr Lamont considered it impracticable for any letters to be sent forward from the Lower posts this winter, no mail has left this place since his arrival which will sufficiently account for your not getting any letter from me on your arrival in New York, this will I trust will be in time to greet you in St Louis, & though much information may yet be lacking Mr Lamont will be able to supply the deficiency & I know he will make every effort to reach St Louis before you leave it, I shall be looking anxiously for you about the middle of July if you are not there by the end of that month my patience will be getting very thread bare.

of last year's credits there remain unpaid by

Gens de Filles	62 robes
Gens des Roches	13 "
Gens de Canot	30 "
Gens du Gauché	8 "

I have done all in my power to please the Indians who have visited the fort this season, have listened to them patiently, treated them with kindness & liberality & acting on your suggestions with regard to the presents, have sent every one away this spring apparently content. Old Deschamp and his five sons have started on a Beaver hunt. Mr. Gravelle is idling about the Fort. Not a breath of news from below since Mr Lamont arrived in December last, but I am daily expecting the return of two men who were sent down to winter with Mr Chardon. I am hourly expecting the steam boat having heard that she left her moorings to day she will not be long detained here, as all the packs are ready to be put on board. Mr Lamont will I presume will leave this on or about the 1st May when I shall have again the pleasure to assure you

My Dear Sir
Your Truly I am
Your Friend & Servant
(Signed) J Archdale Hamilton

Fort Union March 24th 1835
J. F. A. Sanford Esqr
Dear Sir

I had the pleasure on the 15th Nov. last, since then I have had no means of sending letters to the lower posts, I have none of your forms to acknowledge. The enclosed certificate is agreeable to the form you left me, the Indians were well contented with your liberal presents. The Young Gauché & the son of the old Gauché received the U S medals from Mr Lamont who made speeches suited to the occasion. La Lance was killed by Gros Ventres after a battle in which he was taken prisoner while endeavouring to save his sons life on the 30th Nov. or 1st Decr. last. The Gros Ventres stole 20 horses from us this winter (say 18th Janry) Pellot and other men very prompt in pursuit & recovered fourteen but the six best & fleetest carried their riders to their Village.

Some young men with the Chef qui parle stole five horses from Mr Tulloch; Some young men Gens des Canot stole three from Pellot but they were subsequently recovered by Dr Jackson. Le garçon de Sonnant & his comrade last week stole 2 fine horses from our band one belonging to old Deschamp the other to Halcrow but I have reason to believe this arose from a private quarrel & that the Indians will know whose horses they took. As I cannot leave this place until Mr McKenzies return I shall expect a letter from you before it will be possible for me to assure you viva voce[216] how truly I am

Dear Sir
Your Friend & Servt.
(Signed) J. Archdale Hamilton

Abstract of Merchandize (Indian Presents) delivered to Sundry Indians at Fort Union as per direction of JFA Sanford U.S. Agt.

[Annuities distribution to the Assiniboines at Fort Union, 1835][217]

[product]	Gens de files	Gens de roches	Le Gauche's band	Les Crees (L'enfant du fer)	[total]
Tobacco [lbs]	150	82	400	100	732
Lead [lbs]	175	100	400	150	825
Powder [lbs]	100	50	250	100	500
Blue Beads [lbs]	1	1	2	1	5
Vermillion [lbs]	1	1	2	1	5
Scarlet Cloth [yds]	7½	6	14	8	35½
Blue Cloth [yds]	8	6	14	7	35
Calico [yds]	40	21	50	40	151
Blankets	2	2	2	1	7
Knives [doz]	15	8	25½	12	60½
Firesteels [doz]	4	3	6	3½	16½
Look'g Glasses [doz]	2	2	3	2	9
Rings [doz]	9	6	12	9	36

I certify that the above presents were made to the Indians in my presence by request of J. F. A. Sanford U S Ind. Agt.

Fort Union March 24th 1835
Mr F A Chardon [Fort Clark]
Dear Sir

Agreeable to your request by Mr Lamont I have sent on board the Steam Boat Sundry articles as per Invoice which will I hope reach you in safety. The trade of the post is not yet over. I am yet expecting a considerable number of Robes from the Young Gauché, the Moose Dung & Labreume que marche with sundry whips [word?]. Mr Crawford has traded 400 packs and the General above 350 packs & Mr Kipp promises 600 packs & Mr Tulloch 200. On the 18th January your neighbors the Gros Ventres visited Pellots camp on the Yellow Stone and took away 20 horses but on being hotly pursued they left en route 14 and eventually got off with six. Le garçon & Sonnant lately stole Halcrow's horse & one of old Deschamp's. Dr Jackson & his band have worked well this winter, Le Brechu has been encamped at the Fort since Janry. 9th. Scarcely a peace of meat has been traded here this summer but Pellot has left our Larder in good order. Your old friend Lanford de fer came in last week at the head of a small band &

traded near 600 Robes. I shall have the pleasure of addressing you again next month by Mr Lamont in the mean time believe me to be

Dear Sir
Very Truly Yours
(Signed) J. Archdale Hamilton

Fort Union April 6th 1835
Mr Saml. Tulloch [Fort Cass]
Dear Sir

Many thanks for your letter pr Girard which I received the 3rd Inst. The Steam Boat left this post the day previous for St Louis with 800 packs.[218] Your men abandoned their canoe and travelled for several days by land, they remain here and Etienne Labursier[219] with Nobert Guilliotte[220] go up in their place to whom you may make any reasonable advances. I suspect Mr Lamont will start for St. Louis about the end of this month with the Blackfeet returns as ~~and~~ early in June I shall be looking out anxiously for your arrival, when you reach the mouth of the Yellow Stone if you send some one ahead all my disposable force shall be dispatched to your assistance: I should hope if Le Borgne's[221] band as rich in robes as you speak of, they will trade for such things as you have, if you are without such things as they want and place some faith in your promises for the future, you have never yet deceived them though I believe they have often deceived you.

I fancy your secret for remedying pains feet though so effecacious in your case would not meet the recommendation of physicians in the civilized world or be readily adopted by their patients.[222] I hear with much pleasure of your restoration to health. I believe that under you, Beckwith as also some others would render good services to the Company and yet perhaps under other authority their exertions might be less zealously directed. Our beaver return will be very small this season but the price in New York is lower than it has been for seven years or upwards, and this year I hope the supply will be greater & also find a better market. Mr McKenzie apprized me that he placed your money with the company at 6 p[er] Cent Int. p[er] annum which will increase your income about above a hundred Dollars. Mr Lamont joins his thanks to mine for two fine bows & arrows, he would like to get should fall in your way the skin of a male Big Horn with the head, horns, lower legs & feet left on. I trust the Crows have too much sense to allow Bonneville's people to trap in their country, it can never answer the purposes of this company to keep up an establishment there, unless they keep strangers from trapping. I hope there will be no Indians near you when you are preparing to start, in fact you should keep secret the period of your proposed departure, but I have no doubt you will make your arrangements so judiciously as not to suffer any annoyance. My best wishes attend you & be assured of a cordial greeting on your arrival, from yours truly

[Signed] JAH

Fort Union 6th April 1835
Mr Saml Tulloch [Fort Cass]
Dear Sir

The declaration in your letter of the 11th Nov. & 4th Febry with respect for your own plans for the summer now approaching were so positive and it being moreover out of my power to furnish the men you called for to render Fort Cass tenantable, I had no alternative but to instruct you as by my letter of Febry 23rd to make your arrangements to come down here in the spring with your whole establishment as early as you think desirable to leave, of course bringing away every thing valuable. Nothing has since occurred to induce or even enable me to vary from my instructions then communicated. I have even fewer men than at that time & though you have lowered your demand to five it is out of my power to furnish that number nor can I look for any increase until the arrival of Steam Boat or Keel Boat from St Louis which must be later this year than usual.

I am not conscious of having said one word in my last letter which could have led you to infer that the Crow trade would be abandoned and I now authorize you to say to the Chiefs that they shall certainly have a trader next season upon the principle originally avowed by Mr McKenzie that he would give them a fair trial and they will therefore have still an opportunity of redeeming their promises, but as we came into this country to make money it would be sheer madness to continue to trade with the Crows at this year's prices the prices of this season or last season.

Mr McKenzie will no doubt be here in good time to make such arrangements as will be satisfactory to you and your friends the chiefs but that this may be done effectually you must be hard and as cases are governed by circumstances I cannot do otherwise than request you to conform to my first instructions since my last I have sold or lost thirty horses, but when I arrive at Fort Pierre I will endeavour to obtain horses from the Sioux to come hither with Mr McKenzie to sell to the Crow next season, it would be better for you I think for you to sell what horses you have remaining than bring them down here. It strikes me as desirable that you should make some fixed arrangement with the Crows to the time they will be at the fort upon their hunt, and if necessary on your arrival here you can make arrangements with Mr Hamilton to send up a small equipment on horses to supply their immediate wants and relieve them of their peltries before a boat with complete equipment for the season could start but this I will leave to your management, satisfied that you will do what appears to you for the best. I have neither fear nor cares for any continued opposition by Capt. Bonneville, he has no funds of his own, his backers are bankrupted, and he could not get credit in St Louis for a Cent. he has lost his commission in the army which may make him wreckless & bluster a little for a season, and if he proposes to give what few Goods he has remaining to the Indians for little or nothing I shall not follow his example: I should think him much more likely to endeavour to sell out everything to you.

I am dear Sir
truly Yours
[Signed] D.L. [Daniel Lamont]

Fort Union 8 miles West of the Mouth of the Yellow Stone River
6th Aprl 1835
Capt Bonneville
Wind River Mountains
Sir

Having been informed that you have a Considerable parcel of Robes and Furs the produce of this Country which you propose to send to market this Spring, I take the liberty of making [word?] and tender of my Services, and should you feel disposed to make sale thereof at this post, I will pay you liberal prices in Cash or otherwise, as best may suit your convenience; but setting aside all matters of business, it should afford me much pleasure to have you at my [word?] a few days or weeks, and I will promise the best cheer the Country will afford with the [word?]

[Word?] of Your [word?] &c.
[Signed D. L. [Daniel Lamont]

Fort Union May 4. 1835
Mr Louis Turick[223] [Fort McKenzie]
Sir

Your letter dated 1st April in which you note ~~you state~~ your wish to work until Aug. 20 1836 ~~is before me~~ and then to pass down, is before me; in reply I have only to say that if Mr Culbertson does not require your services in the spring to come down with the Boats, I shall be satisfied by your working to the 20 Augt 1836 at Fort McKenzie and being free there on that day provided that you are not in debt to the company when your time of service is finished.

Yours Obediently
for Kenneth McKenzie
[Signed] J. Archdale Hamilton

Fort Union May 5th 1835
Mr A. Culbertson [Fort McKenzie]
Dear Sir

On the 24th Ulto. our friend Mr Kipp arrived here in safety with the Fort McKenzie boats and their respective cargoes, had he made the voyage the accustomed number of days, I think the new equipment would at this time have been half way to the Marias river. I have made every exertion to dispatch the Keel Boat with the least possible delay; she has a good crew, is well fixed, and under the command of J.B. Lafontaine[224] in whose prudence and judgement I have the utmost confidence, nothing doubting that should an unforeseen circumstance interfere, he will make a successful trip: I do not wish him to make any longer sojourn with you than will enable the Carpenter who accompanies him for that purpose, to build a boat capable of bringing down the balance of this season's robes and the men as pr List whose term of service will expire the Fall. I observe two names on the List are in debt, and as they will probably wish to make a new engagement I consent thereto on the terms heretofore given i.e. from the expiration of their present engagement until the summer of 1836 free in St Louis $100 & an equipment, or free summer 1837. $350 & two equipments.

Mr Brazeau will accompany his friend J.B. Lafontaine down. I have engaged Mr Harvey for another year having a high opinion of his integrity and bravery, the latter a very desirable quality in this country, he professes his willingness to render himself useful in any and every way that you may direct I hope you will find him a good aid. Mr J.B. Moncravie has been five years in the employ of the company and for the last 18 months and has had charge of the Store here, he has moreover considerable medical & surgical skill, he is conversant with the routine of business here & I trust you will find his assistance valuable, he has perhaps somewhat too much confidence in his own powers, there is scarcely any thing he will not undertake, and it would be a miracl [miracle] if you he universally succeeded, he has many good qualities, has rendered himself very useful here & his faults are very menial. J. Berger I have engaged for another year on the usual terms in full confidence that he will do his duty. The only instructions I conceive necessary to give with respect to Isidore Sandoval is to obtain possession of all the company's property entrusted to his care then forbid him the Fort and direct him to seek redress here. With regard to the policy to be pursued in conducting the trade of your post, your own judgement and experience will best direct you. The seasons in which Mr Kipp has conducted the Blackfoot trade the results have been favourable for exceeding other years, you have the opportunity to profit by his long experience in the Indian trade & I feel assured have not failed to improve it. A Very valuable Outfit is selected for you amounting at St Louis prices to $11200 & upwards without any charge for commission or transportation and though you justly observe it is a very heavy trade to part with so large an amount in Cloth and Blankets for Buffaloe robes yet to the extent that the company is desirous to push the robe trade in order to attach the various nations in your District, to the Missouri. They are aware a undesirable portion of cloth and Blankets must be supplied although the only profitable part of the trade is made in Beads Ammunition & Tobacco for Liquor cannot be obtained on any terms without open war with the President & his army and risking forcible expulsion from the country. I send you two Barrels of allcohol and six of wine make the most of it and do not sell a single drop of it to the men, we have long since ceased to do it here; explain to the Indians that our supply of liquor would have been larger had not the Steam Boat been kept here all winter for lack of water, and consequently unable to return here as time sufficient for the Outfit which is necessarily sent away at the early date to avoid a recontre with the Crows. Should the Crow Indians come near you again this summer do not spare them tooth or Nail. Should your expectations be realized of keeping the same Indians to trade with you as last winter and Buffaloe be found in plenty I have little fear but you will show a more favourable return than any of your predecessors in command, as in the Item of salaries this year, there is a reduction of several thousand Dollars. In the article of white Beads we are sadly deficient and as you may find a supply thereof absolutely necessary, I would suggest your sending down here in the fall all your spare horses under charge of some trust worthy person, (no one better than Mr Harvey if you can spare him when your first trade is over) and whatever is now wanting shall be furnished so far as your requests can be complied with. I would not advize your keeping more horses than are requisite for the use of the Fort. Horses are of but little value here, 12 or 15 Robes is the most we can get for them but I know in your Peigan trade you will be compelled to take a few horses & I believe you would have more difficulty in keeping then we have here.

You will receive full instructions by the return of your fall express with respect to your future arrangements and as I rely on Mr McKenzie's being here at that period let your communication be very ample respecting your trade & prospects. For several past seasons a very ill judged & unreasonable privilege has been given to the men at Fort McKenzie to spend more than their wages, under your management a new era must commence. I have made very liberal advances to the hands re-engaged & have prepared a schedule of the proportion which may be advanced monthly to the several parties, & justice to my colleagues compells me to say that if at the close of the season any one of their accounts exceeds the privilege conceded you will be made accountable for the amount thereof. Those men free in 1836 who passed the summer with you who have not exhausted their means you will apportion in the same manner & to those who have nothing left you will make only such advances as you deem absolutely necessary, carry forward the advances made during the spring on those a/cts who remain with you to the new Ledger and in making out the accounts of men who descend state in one line advances to Fort McKenzie to 31 March 1835 and in another, advances from that date to the day of their departure. The men who accompany J.B. Lafontaine from hence to return, have privilege to spend as pr [word?]. Nearly all the men have copies of their engagements corresponding with entries in the Ledgers. The two year men are entitled to the ordinary [two words?] on building the Boat & from Mr Kipp's is report of them I am inclined to think they will be able to build your boats next spring. Sell traps cheap to [name?] say two Robes each rather than loan them. Beaver packs should not go under the press. Articles in great demand by the Indians should not be sold to the men. I propose starting for St Louis in a few days and will take charge of your letters. The expenses of your post being necessarily very large the utmost care and economy must be exercised, for the expenses good or bad the expenses do not diminish.

As the Beaver trade for the last three years has been regularly declining notwithstanding every facility and encouragement we have given the Peigans, it appears to me that our best anchor will be, the Robe trade and by encouraging the Blood Blackfeet rather to make Robes, articles which they now obtain as luxuries will become necessities and they will be compelled to remain on the Missouri in order to procure them. Rats are a poor trade,[225] those you have sent down this year will scarcely sell for 10 cts each. As the present fort will scarcely last over the present year select a place suitable for renewing it. Mr Kipp strongly recommends the mouth of Marais River, examine the spot and report thereon. there are some hundred logs of fine timber I understand lying there, and an abundant supply can be obtained a few miles up the river and floated down if a boom were thrown across the mouth of the Marias, if possible employ your spare hands when Indians have left you, preparatory to this object. I presume it ~~must be~~ has been subject of conversation between you and Mr Kipp and that you are in support of his views & the advantages attending the site he recommends.

I send you a copy of a letter addressed to Louis Turlick in answer to his request to be set free at Fort McKenzie 20. Augt. 1836. You will do as you think proper next spring if he has means to equip himself for hunting but I would not give him equipment on credit. It is probable Dupuis & Legris may come out at your fort this summer; any beaver they may wish to sell & be paid in goods, you will buy of them, but I cannot authorize you to make contract for payment in money, certainly not at a higher price than three Dollars pr lb. Please add $4. to Mr Moncarvie's a/c furnished since the boat started. I send you a medicine pipe which appertained to Genl. Jackson, he is Chief of Gens des Roches. I know nothing of its virtues, and on no account make a present of it in Indian style, but if you can, sell it bona fide for a good horse do so, there are many more at this post can be furnished on the same terms. I have had no intelligence from the civilized world since my departure in September last: I will take care some newspapers will be forwarded you in the Fall. ~~Mr Kipp~~ Mr Hamilton and Mr Kipp have this instant have joined me in drinking your health with best wishes that every success may attend you. I know that you deserve it and I hope you may attain it and believe me to be

Dear Sir
Very Truly Yours &c &c
(Signed) [Daniel Lamont]

Fort Union 5 May 1835
J. B. Lafontaine [Pattron of the keelboat *Maria*]
Dear Sir

On leaving this place in charge of the keel boat Maria with a valuable outfit for Ft. McKenzie I ~~am~~ know you should have some written instructions to refer to in case of and, not that I deem it necessary to lay down any plan for your guidance, for the confidence I repose in you is founded on my opinion of your integrity, your prudence your caution your watchfulness and the [word?] care you have invariably evinced to promote the interest of your employers while tendering therefore my best wishes for your successful voyage I will merely state, that in assuming the command of the Boat & crew you will proceed to Ft. McKenzie 10 miles above Marias Rr, & deliver your cargoe to Mr Culbertson who is in charge & remaining there until a batteaux is constructed you will make your arrangements to descend taking charge of all the peltries Mr C may have to forward to this post. I ~~full~~ feel assured M. Moncrevoir & Mr Harvey will render you every assistance in their powers & may wind & water also be favorable to you as the sincere wish of

yours truly
(Signed) Danl Lamont

Fort Union 5 May 1835
Mr J B Moncrevois [Fort McKenzie]
Dr Sir

As in this life there are so many casualties that truly we know not what a day may bring forth, I hereby authorize you should any unfortunate accident have befallen Mr Culbertson to assume command of Ft. McKenzie & report without delay to headquarters conducting the establishment in a way best calculated to promote the interests of the Company. I pray that you may find all's well on arrival at Ft McK. & I confidently rely on your giving your best services in aid to MC.[226]

My best wishes attend you,
Yours truly
(Signed) Danl Lamont

Fort Union 5 May 1835
Mr A. Harvey [Fort McKenzie]
Sir

Should any unfortunate event deprive the Company of the services of Mr Culbertson & Mr Moncrevoir I hereby authorize you to assume command of Ft. McKenzie, well knowing that the property will be protected to the utmost of your power & every possible exertion be made by you to promote the interest for the Company. If such an event should occur you will report to this place all particulars without delay.

I wish you well and am
Yours truly
(Signed) Danl Lamont

Fort Union 4th July 1835
Kenneth McKenzie Esqr
Dear Sir

Having no instructions or a word of intelligence from below since last Decr. I am somewhat uneasy & undecided how to act, there are 850 packs Robes here, Pellot will bring 150 packs more, there is also 1700 lbs of Beaver and some other things and I have only two men whose terms of service has expired but n'importe.[227] When Pellot arrives there will I suppose be nearly men enough to man the Boats and if no steam boat arrives which from the extraordinary high water I have sanguinely expected to see here, I will dispatch them under charge of Mr Brazeau, with as much cargo as they can take.

Mr Tulloch is here and at my request awaits your arrival, the Crow trade this year has turned out much better than was feared leaving a better profit than last year and yielding good Robes say 350 packs (with 100 packs yet in the Village) & 1200 lbs Beaver, the Crows are very much humbled having lost two thousand Horses this season and are much distressed at Mr Tulloch's abandoning the fort. It is my opinion that you will continue the Crow trade, and you will not find it difficult to make an arrangement with Mr Tulloch if you think it desirable, although he is very much bent on going down; if you determine to renew the trade with the Crows and wish to be independent of Mr T. this will perhaps give you time to get some person here in his place before the season is too far advanced. The new stores are in part shingled and have a very imposing appearance. We are short of 10 py &12 py cut nails. All things going forward much as usual. We have been deluged with rain and are now grievously tormented with mosquitoes. Cattle far off, all the Half Breeds and women are out at camp near the old spot across the River. Anxiously awaiting your arrival

I am Dear Sir
Very Sincerely Yours
(Signed) J. Archdale Hamilton

Fort Union July 16th 1835
William Laidlaw Esqr [Fort Pierre Chouteau]
Dear Sir

On inspection of the accompanying papers you will observe Duplicate of Inventories, one set for your post the other for St Louis. The duplicate ledger I have made in accordance with agreed balances of last year leaving allowance for this years advances. The men who started for Fort McKenzie in May last were all allowed by Mr Lamont to spend freely; their Acct. appear heavy from the amount than in ordinary cases would have gone into next years a/c. being charged in this, the advances having been made long before the Inventory was taken, but each man knows what he is to spend pr month during the term of his engagement and Mr Culbertson is apprized that if the amount is exceeded he will have to make it good. In the statement of mens a/c who leave this post pr Boat with Mr Brazeau, I copy from duplicate Ledger balance that would be due them if they serve their full time, in stating their accounts for St Louis I presume it would be more correct simply to set forth their advances, and as they spend something while with you and as you have all the data, I merely make up the Accts. as between this post and Fort Pierre, having the remainder to be sent by you. I send two or three engagements of men who go down. Henry Charrin[228] who started the Keel Boat up to Fort McKenzie came down with Pellot, no man, no man on board having skill to steer a mackinac Boat down this far; and there being no one here of whose steering capabilities I have any knowledge I have deemed it most prudent to send Henry Morrin with the Boats as far as Fort Pierre, he goes with much reluctance having been promised by Mr Culbertson that he should return to Fort McKenzie immediately on his arrival here, his services will be relied on to steer the Keel Boat down next spring. You will of course arrange for his return here this fall. My stock of sugar is so nearly exhausted I can only furnish Mr Brazeau with sufficient to serve them to Fort Pierre. Fort Cass returns have proved much better than were expected, 320 packs Robes 1300 lbs Beaver &c. Mr Tulloch remains here at my personal request under the expectation that Mr McKenzie will continue the trade or supply here with Mdze to do it on his own acct. A fortnight since I sent two men to Fort Clark for news they have not returned, nor have I received a breath of intelligence of any thing that has been passing below since Mr Lamont arrived here last Christmas. I presume Mr Halsey has taken his departure or I should write to him, if still with you present my respects to him and received Dear Sir the assurance of esteem and friendship of

Yours truly
(Signed) J Archdale Hamilton

Fort Union July 17th 1835
Danl Lamont Esquire [Saint Louis][229]
Dear Sir

No messenger or friendly gale has bought me a line or breath of news since your departure a fortnight since I sent two men to Fort Clark for intelligence they have not retuned. Mr Tulloch arrived safe June 15th with 320 packs good Robes 1250 lbs Beaver &c he is very anxious to take up the Crow trade on his own account if the company will support him. Pellot was 25 days in getting to Fort McKenzie, he arrived here all safe the 9th Sept. he brought Morrin down as steersman for security, for the same reason I send him as far as Fort Pierre. The Deschamps brought in very little Beaver & the bunch Horses terribly injured. they have behaved very idle since their return, the old man is going to Red River I strongly suspect he has great portion of his hunt in cache. Jackson was treacherously killed lately by the brother of the young man who was killed by La Vachés son in the spring: it is said Jackson had taken the part of La Vache Blanche in some recent dispute, the body was brought here 10 days ago to receive funeral ~~rights~~ rites as a chief constituted by the Whites:[230] Ought not the U.S. Government to reimburse the company this expense? Mr Brazeau will fully detail to you the conduct of Fort McKenzies horse Guards, as the men are able, they surely ought to be made to pay. The new Stores have progressed equal to my expectation. The quantity of rain which has fallen here this season I should think is almost without precedent, the fort was quite a Lake for a month, the points of wood are deluged, grass is abundant every where, and Mosquitoes bad beyond all former example, the men cry out terribly and not without cause.

I send all accts. Inventories &c to Fort Pierre but the originals or duplicates will in due course find their way to you at St Louis. I forward one bill of Lading to Messrs Pratte Chouteau & Co with a statement of furs Robes &c on hand, all of which I hope safely to deliver in St Louis in September next or early in October. Three days march to get to cattle and when the meat arrives one half is spoiled. Twelve Lodges of Indians at the fort none others I believe very near. Mr Culbertsons letter was sent open I have taken a copy of it. "Time flies with leaden pinions"[231] Yet I hope ere long to assure you viva voce[232] that I am

Dear Sir

Very Truly Yours

(Signed) J. Archdale Hamilton

The Garden is very productive.[233]

Garden seeds wanted for Fort Union Fall 1835.

½ lb Turnip Beet ¼ lb long Carrot ½ # Kale ¼ lb Scarlet long Radish

4 lb Yellow summer turnip Radish ¼ # Red Summer Turnip Radish

¼ " White " " " ¼ lb Early Garden turnip

¼ " Turnip ½ lb Red onion 2 oz Cabbage lettuce

½ Gallon Early peas & ½ Gal. Early dwarf French beans

½ " Windsor Broad Beans 2 Oz Horse Radish

2 oz. Parsley 2 oz. Broad leaf Sage ¼ lb Mustard

2 " Savoy Cabbage. A Garden pot of thyme to come up by boat in the spring.

Fort Union July 18th 1835

Messrs Pratte Chouteau &Co [Saint Louis]

Gent.

I enclose Bill of Lading of packs of Buffaloe Robes for boats Julia, Jane, Margaret & Isabella under charge of J. B. Brazeau bound for St Louis to touch at Fort Pierre &c. You will also find an abstract of Furs &c remaining on hand, to be sent forward in September

Inventories, men's Accts and so forth are addressed to Fort Pierre to be looked over. B Bourdalne[234] No 21. on the List, who works his passage down, came on here half dead, from a Division of Capt. Bonnevilles party under Montero, who has been for the last year with 50 men trapping & trading in the Crow country he tells a wofull tale the leading features whereof Mr Tulloch had previously heard the from other quarters. The River has been higher during the whole month of June and to this day than at any period during my long residence here, full to the banks on many parts, this I attribute to the incessant and constant rains, no rise generally called the Mountain rise has been discernable. I beg you to refer to Mr Lamont for Fort Cass & Fort McKenzie news, and am

Gentlemen

Yours Very Obediently

(Signed) J Archdale Hamilton

List of men[235]

R Bouché	good
C. Guinnard	"
A. Guinnard	not worth his meat
F. Desmay	"
H Labadiere	willing but slow & sleepy
E Labusico	" "
J Bolingston	willing & active but ignorant
M Helvish	" " "
J Harris	good but slow
A Smith	" " not very industrious
L Bacarapa	Strong lazy often sick
J. Rouelle	not very good
J Praal	good to look after cows
J Blechere	Old
H Robert	Good
L V Wayotte	"
M Pressy	"
A. Lacroix	"
A Bledsoy	"
A Solomon	"
R Harper	"

Fort Union Sept 10 1835

Messrs. Pratte Chouteau Co [Saint Louis]

Gent

I this day send under charge of H Picotte & boats Enterprize & Fairmought balance of robes & beaver for last season see particulars annexed.

The part of this years outfits most required remains at Fort Pierre. On the 4th Inst. an express arrived from Crow Camp saying they have robes & beaver which they want to trade. Mr Tulloch has been waiting here three months daily expecting to see Mr McKenzie but his non arrival & the last years Crow trade leaving a much better balance than was expected I have deemed it advisable to send out a new equipment for that trade & consequently dispatched Mr T. & twenty men yesterday with suitable outfit & to build near the Rose bud.[236] On the 5th A. Harvey arrived with 33 horses from Ft McKenzie, all well, they had traded only 12 packs of beaver. I annex statement of small d[ra]fts drawn since my last. I am Gent &c

[Signed] JAH

List of Men.[237]

J Bare	is good but slow & often sick
M Dero	is lazy not worth half wages
A Freseau	of as now for this post
B Grendhouse	very so so
T Holmes	good
B Guislte	"
A Lureman	"
J Sevaillen	"
H Mallioux	"
J Roy	"
A Touchette	"
P. Kilneuf	"
A Coté	ruptured, descends at his own request.

❖ ❖ ❖

Ft Union Sep 9 1835

A Culbertson [Fort McKenzie]

Dear Sir

Your letter by Mr Harvey was delivered on the 5 Inst. horses & mules all safe. I refer you to Mr H for particulars of the Cos S. Boat & cargo. You will renew Lacomptes[238] engagement if you can see fit next spring on same terms as last year, he will deliver you an Iron grey horse or pay for it. I send two women purchased from the Crows by Mr Tulloch to be sent home to their friends the Gros Ventres & hope it will have a good effect. Ft Cass is abandoned but another fort will be built to suit the Crow Nation as regard to location.[239] I think you did well to remain in your present Fort. I can send no liquor but arrangements are made for a small supply next year. Morrin is gone to Ft. Pierre to return. I send you some newspapers & letters.

When Pinnand[240] has been as long in the Country as Deargen[241] & others he will have as good wages if he merits them & if he conducts himself well, as double in Spring an allowance equal to Equipment may be made him.

You have done as well or better with Indians than I expected. I have every confidence in your exertion to make a better trade this season than any of your predecessors My best wishes attend you. No news from below or of Mr McKenzie

Yours obediently

[Signed] JAH.

Scarlet sells at $12 pr yd.

❖ ❖ ❖

Ft Union Nov 24 1835

John Campbell[242] [Apple River Post]

Dr Sir

I arrived here safe 17 Nov. all well.[243] I start men tomorrow for Mandan's with 4 bales of Tob. & tea & liquor for you. I shall expect letters from you pr first opp[ortunit]y. I left Mdze for you at Ft. Clark & hope you have rec'd all in good order. I shall write again pr St Louis express.

Yours truly K. McK.

Fort Union 24 Nov 1835

M. Bellehumeur [Fort Clark]

Dr Sir

I arrived 17th Cur. I send you Mdze & [value of] horses as pr a/c

Amr. Bay [name?] not less than 30 Beaver skins

" dk Bay Lamont "25 or 30

Chestnut mare Eclipse "20 or 25

Brown Horse Blackfoot excellent runner

5 good Buffalo horses all bought for runners have supported their characters well.[244]

1 Sorrel horse white face & feet for Boullé[245] if he declines him sell him for beaver.

Mr Kennedy will remain with you rendering all assistance he can I send your statement of his a/c his wants will be few. I should not send him down but it being uncertain Mr May's[246] wintering with you I subject myself to inconvenience rather than you should want the means of communicating with me.

Let Vallé come back & the Dutchman[247] with him, send the bundle I described to you, furnish a train

& 4 good dogs. Adams is a friend of Newman's,[248] he is a stranger to me but you may advance him 50 or 60 dollars if he has need for so much. Advance to Vallé any little thing he may require. I charge Ft Clark with advances to Newman Adams & Le brua & horse for Brullé place the several sums to their accts. I send 4 bales Tobo. Marked [symbol "Y"], forward it & a bdle [bundle] marked C Campbell to Yanctona post. Newman cannot afford to spend much more. If you can ascertain that old Bigeau[249] or any of his party have made a start for this quarter send me news pr express & I will take care that wherever they may fix themselves they shall not trade to profit but go home lighter than they came out. I have encountered various opposition traders in my time & it has always been to their cost, if I can make nothing myself I will at least spoil the market for others. I have ever confidence in your attention & exertions for my interest. Yours &c

[Signed] K. McK.

My compliments to Mr May.

Fort Union 10th Decr 1835

Major Fulkerson[250]

Indn Agt

Dear Sir

For several years past on my return to this post from my visits to St Louis or Fort Pierre, I have been always been accompanied by Mr Sandford, and the Indians ~~have taken~~ of this District have then regularly received their presents from the U.S. Government, but this season after after an unusually protracted absence returning alone, and without any thing to give away my situation for the past three weeks has been any thing but agreeable, and not without great sacrifices have I been able to keep the Indians in any approach to good temper; they cannot or will not discriminate between their traders and the Government, and those Chiefs especially who have been peculiarly noticed or have been to Washington City say their great Father assured them they should never want for ammunition & Tobacco, so long as they traded on this side the lines, and behaved well to the Whites, nor can they believe their great father would tell a lie. I have therefore the odium of keeping back their presents. I never was an advocate for large and indiscriminate distribution of presents; a good and industrious Indian may be encouraged to greater exertions by a well timed gratuity, but when all receive alike, every good effect is destroyed and the nation claims as a right what was intended as a boon. I annex you a statement of Sundry articles left by Mr Sanford to be distributed after my departure last year, and during his month residence here he must have dispersed nearly an equal amt. to the Gens de Canot and some bands of Crees; you will at once perceive how utterly impossible it is for me to be equally profuse, and may hence imagine what I have to endure from the disappointed and of course discontented red Skins.

This place is barren of news. I arrived here on the 17th Novr. having walked all the way from the Mandans, because it was impracticable to ride, the winter has set in exceedingly early (20th Oct) and with unusual rigor.[251] I shall look forward with pleasure to meeting you & Mrs. Fulkerson at Fort Pierre next Spring, and remain

Dear Sir

Yours Very Obediently

(Signed) Kenneth McKenzie

Abstract of Merchandize (Indian Country) delivered to Sundry Indians at Fort Union as per direction of J.F.A. Sanford U. S. S. I. A.

As signed by D. Lamont

Fort Union 10th Decr 1835

J. B. Cabanné Esqr [Cabanné's Post[252]]

Dear Sir

This will be accompanied by my usual express for St Louis and with your friendly aid I trust it will reach its destination in good season. Your kind attentions to me have been so constant and of so decided a character, that although I cannot sufficiently thank you I shall never cease to think of them. My trip from your place to Fort Pierre was very pleasant but from thence forward, I had a great deal of trouble. The boat with Outfits for the Upper trade had left Fort Pierre before my arrival. I had therefore to take charge of some very essential articles for the Yanctona trade,[253] and what with carts breaking down and horses giving out, I made but very slow progress, and on my getting a little above heart river I found the boat ice-Locked, the Landing and securing the cargo detained me some time: I was obliged to remain many days at the Mandans to make arrangements as far as practicable to baffle our opponents: I did not reach this place untill the 17th Novr. (having walked the whole distance from the Mandans) and find my Indians in such bad humour from being disappointed of their customary Government presents & the uncertainty of obtaining liquor for their Robes, that nothing short of almost profuse liberallity on my part will induce them to make peltries, "No liquor no trade" is the prevailing sentiment with the Assiniboines, and I am now more than ever convinced that no trading can be done without it here. I know I may rely only on a continuance of your kind exertion to assist me herein, and with such a friend in need, I feel perfectly at my ease. I have written Mr. Chouteau to engage Martin Dorion,[254] but if you will take the trouble you are much more likely to effect it for me.

I leave the entire arrangement to you. I cannot at present say whether he will be wanted at this post or with the Sioux, but I presume it would be immaterial to him. I should wish him to come up in the Steam boat in the Spring. Accept my assurances of respect & esteem and believe me ever to remain

Dear Sir
Very Truly Yours
(Signed) Kenneth McKenzie

Fort Union Decr 10th 1835
Messrs Pratte Chouteau & Co. [Saint Louis]
Dear Sirs

I did not arrive here untill the 17th Novr. having been upwards of six weeks making the trip from Fort Pierre. You are aware that a portion only of the Outfit for this post was forwarded from Fort Pierre in July, arriving here in Sepember, the remainder with the exception of such articles as were retained for the trade of the lower posts were forwarded in September with the Outfit for the Yanktona: the Boat was taken by the ice near heart river where the Cargo was landed and proper measures taken for its protection. It is a mortifying reflection after spending so much money in Steam boats the whole Summer should be too short to transport goods from St Louis to this place, and that this Company should be subject to the derision of our pitiful opponents, inasmuch as with all our appliances and means to boot we could advance no further than heart River with the Outfit for our winter's trade; it is true the winter has set in with great force unprecedently early this year, but there is no excuse for our being thus taken by surprise. I send herewith order for Fort Union & Fort Clark Outfits for next year, and rely on your exertions to fulfill it to the ~~utmost~~ letter; in addition thereto the Tobacco & Liquor at C. Bluffs must come to this post, there is also a box of beads some Iron & perhaps some other things remaining at the Bluffs but having left the packing acct. at Fort Pierre my memory will not serve me to particularize them, but be they what they may, with the exception of Liquor & Tobacco they should be deducted from the present order. The order from this place may appear large, but by no means unnecessarily so when I inform you that but little more than half the equipment of this year came hither; Beads, Guns, Lead, Powder &c were required at Fort Pierre: Cloth, Blankets &c at Fort Clark and moreover I have been compelled to send Tobacco from hence for the Mandan & Sioux trade. I fear the Steam Boat cannot bring the Cargo for this place, Fort Clark, Fort Pierre, & the Agents goods in addition, I therefore suggest your starting a Keel Boat as early as possible with the Outfit for Fort Pierre, it can easily make the trip in good season for their trade. You are aware I have no Keel boat for the Blackfoot Outfit of next year and must therefore have one towed up by the steam boat. The number of men on this establishment is considerably reduced this year at the four posts there are all in all but 84 and of these I cannot depend on more than 20 remaining with me, since the sale of Liquor has been stopped they save their money and no doubt will go down and spend it.

I shall require fifty men to be engaged for next season for this upper trade; they must be good, likely men, not ignorant useless boys, who are mere cumberers of the ground, should such come I will send them back instanter; nor can high wages be afforded now it is almost a cash charge to the Outfit. I must again caution you about such unreasonable advances to the hands, it is a direct temptation or premium to be indifferent, independent & faithless. I shall require a Carpenter, old Luteman would answer well on moderate [wages], he is slow but sure. I shall also want a Blacksmith, please send my boy Prince.[255] I am anxious you should engage Martin Dorion. I cannot say at present whether he will be wanted for this post or the Sioux, of course it will be immaterial to him which post he winters at. If Mr Halsey does not return to the Country (of which he will apprize you) I shall require a Clerk for Fort Pierre and one for this place, they must be good accountants, fully competent to the charge of a set of Books, if Mr. Halsey returns one will suffice. With respect to traders I can give you no instruction, I believe Mr Culbertson will go down, Mr Tulloch & Mr Laferriere will probably remain, but verily I will not tempt them by the offer of high salaries. On no consideration engage S. P. Winter or J. B. Brazeau, recent information from the Blackfeet confirms what I had long suspected, that the latter is a chip of the old block, and the former is like unto him.

I have never been able to ascertain what advances were made to the Manger du Lards of 1833, please furnish me therewith, C Marion, D. Jabotte & Fr. Landry[256] are all that are at this post. Also state the wages of P Kamming[257] who came up this year In the Invoice of the year, charge is made of Kettle ears, rivets &c as packed in box marked P.C.&C/103 and which could not be found on board the Steam Boat on her arrival at Fort Pierre, a further charge is made independent of the contents of the missing box of 18 doz. packs both black ears ea $\frac{21\frac{7}{8}}{0}$ $\frac{28[?]}{1}$ = $9 N.Y. and again towards the end of the Invoice the same entry is repeated, none of these articles can be found nor do they appear in the packing Account. I have no later news from Blackfeet post than was communicated by Mr Hamiltons letter of Sepr. 10th by H. Pecotte. Mr Tulloch was putting up his new fort near the mouth of the Rosebud on the 30th Octr, no subsequent intelligence. I found on my arrival that the post established last year called Fort Assiniboine was kept up Mr Laferriere in charge. I cannot safely hazard an opinion on what quantity of peltries my District may yield this season; last year these upper Indians received from the Government 1000 lbs Tobacco 40,000 Balls & powder 75 doz Knives besides Cloth Blankets &c &c and getting nothing this year they are careless and indifferent and say they are without Tobacco and ammunition and consequently cannot go out to hunt; I verily believe if I were destitute of Liquor I should not trade a hundred packs of robes. Pray be careful in sending good Tobacco, that which came up in 1834 I cannot even give away, & trading it is out of the question. I find I shall want a man for the Blackfeet post who is able to build boats, a professed carpenter is not required, you will please attend to this. I have ordered a few things of Mr Orthy[258] and will thank you to pay his bill. If you have an Iron Screw with fixings not in use that could be made serviceable here for pressing Robes, please to send it.

Two hundred or more lodges of Crees who traded here last year are gone to the North, they did not like the wine of last season but if we give them whiskey, they will come and see us again. Le Gens de Gauché have been at the North all fall, about 150 Lodges are just returned but they have not a Robe dressed or a skin in camp, nothing but liquor will keep these Indians to us, in fact without it is a mere waste of time and money to keep up this post. There must be some mistake in 3 ps Wt. Blkts of this year at such an advance on former prices the quality ought to be maintained but these are the meanest I ever saw in 1833 we had better blankets at 9/. [word?] Blankets we well know are much advanced but not a hundred pct.

[Unsigned] [Kenneth McKenzie]

Ft. Union 10 Dec [1835]

Wm Laidlaw Esqr [Fort Pierre Chouteau]

D Sir

I enclose a/c B. Depuis[259] as requested. Please send statement of Bapt Dauphins[260] a/c he wintered at Mandans. Pray inform me of acct. of wages to P Kemming & send a/c of advances at Montreal &c to C Morrin D Jabotte & J Laudry. Mr McKenzie arrived here 17 Nov I had given up all thoughts of seeing him having been assured by Mr C.[261] that nothing but his death or some unforeseen catastrophe should prevent my being relieved from my irksome duty early in the Summer I consented to remain here for the Sumr. purely for Mr L's[262] accomd. & would never have contemplated that I should have been thus made a tool of. As I dare not to attempt to make the trip to St Louis at this inclement season I strive to reconcile myself to my unfortunate lot. I trust I shall find you in the spring enjoying your accustomed health & remain D Sir Yours respectfully

[Signed] JAH.

As our tin smith[263] will now be able to furnish the river with tin kettles please inform me the quantity of each size required for your post & its dependencies, we have a super abundance of hawk bells & should be glad to supply your demand.

Fort Union Decr 10th 1835
Ramsey Crooks Esqr [New York]
Dear Sir

Could I but fancy myself seated opposite to you by your own comfortable fireside with a bottle of your excellent port on a small table between us, we should see the bottom of it before I had recounted to you half my adventures "by flood & field" since we parted last summer but abandoning the flights of fancy and coming down to sober reality, I am alone in a smoky room, the thermometer 15 below zero, and although my ink is not frozen, my pen will neither move so nimbly, nor my ideas flow so freely as I could desire, when writing to my good friend Ramsey. I think I told you of my mortification when I [was] appealed to in the old country respecting the falls of Niagara, to be obliged to confess I had not viewed them. I congratulate myself on having lived to see this most sublime of natures works. I am not going to weary you with a description of what many may attempt but no one can adequately perform, words may convey ideas but they often fail to pourtray feelings; you have been there and I doubt not felt as I did, how utterly impossible it is for language to do justice to the scene. At Cincinnati the news of our disasters recorded in the Columns of a newspaper, of the loss of our un-insured Steam Boat first reached me on this subject, especially the total disregard of our interests by our Agents, I shall have more to say to you on another opportunity to say "it was forgotten" is poor satisfaction for the loss of thousands! Misfortune never comes alone, and news of loss upon loss met me on my arrival at St. Louis the 17th July, but a truce to gloomy reflections.

What will you say at my neglecting to write to you during a whole month that I remained in St. Louis? You will know it was not from want of inclination: how shall I excuse myself; first Mr Lamont was occupied in making his arrangements for entering into a new business,[264] and transferring his interest in this, to our friend Mitchell; second, Mr. Laidlaw was on a sick bed and really very ill, I had consequently a good deal on my hands; and further, knowing of your absence from home, I delayed from day to day until the hurry of my departure fairly prevented my writing to you at all: well, say you, enough of apology and let us proceed. On the 17t Aug. I left St Louis by Steam boat for Council Bluffs, where I procured horses and came on to Fort Pierre, M. Laidlaw unwilling to leave his bones in St Louis gave his Physician the slip, took the stage to Independence, furnished himself with horses, and riding fast came up with me at the Vermillion trading house whence we proceeded to Fort Pierre, while there I made arrangements for Mr Mitchell to take out an equipment to Laramie's Fork on the river Platte, to trade with the Sioux and Chayennes, a fine Buffaloe Country, and where Sublett & Co established a post last winter.[265] The Steam Boat from St Louis this summer came no higher than Fort Pierre, although there never was a finer stage of water than at the time she arrived there, but there was no person on board to direct the self-willed Captain & no one at Fort Pierre to enforce his proceeding to this place, the consequence has been, that after all the money we have expended on Steam Boats,[266] our boat with outfit for the upper posts was taken by the ice a little above Heart River where I found her ice-locked on the 20 Oct. I was detained a considerable while in seeing her cargo landed and property secured, but at length reached the Mandans, where we have opposition again this year, and but for the circumstance of our opponents boat being taken by the ice far below ours, it would have extended to this place and I still expect that during the winter I shall have to contend with them at one or two of the Indian camps. I arrived here the 17th Novr. having walked and lead my horse the whole distance from Fort Clark. They told me in St Louis that the Crow post was abandoned, I was well pleased to find a new equipment was sent thither and another to the post established last year near the spot where the steam boat Assiniboine wintered. [word struck out] It is impossible at this time to form any idea of this seasons returns cattle are tolerably abundant and the prospects fair at the several posts. I shall be satisfied if this post equals last year from whence there were shipped 4100 lbs. Beaver skins, 1970 packs Robes 4000 fox Skins 9000 Rats &c &c though unfortunately so small a portion thereof got to market. Eleven of our oldest Clerks and Interpreters have left the service this summer and no new ones have been engaged to fill their places. I have had some difficulty in supplying the different posts efficiently, I have not much fear of our doing quite as well without them, and we are certainly relieved of some very heavy salaries.

And now my good friend, being fixed in my wintering ground I must take my leave of you untill the next express for St Louis, in the mean time you have my ardent wishes for your health happiness, & prosperity. Please to present my respects to Mr Whetten[267] and if he will do me the favour to consider himself a letter in my debt, I shall feel very much obliged to him. I have room only to assure you My Dear Sir, that I am ever most faithfully & cordially

Yours &c &c
(Signed) (Kenneth McKenzie)

Fort Union 10th Decr 1835
Mr M Bellhumeur [Fort Clark]
Sir

I send down Papiche & Laramie[268] with express for St Louis, these men will return after a day or so and I wish you to send J Beaugard with them, furnish the latter with a train & 3 dogs & my men with an extra dog and send up by them, two Kegs of large cut nails, one Keg to each train. When your Inventory was taken you had 4 Kegs & I have none. Send also a soldering iron which you have, my tinsmith is in great want of it. You will I hope be able to get on with your fine acct untill I can furnish you a permanent clerk. I am axious that the express should be sent forward without the least delay, every hour is of consequence, I should wish. Delorme to go on with it to Fort Pierre should man being sent with him by you as far as Campbell's,[269] and I have written to him to furnish a man to accompany Delorme to Fort Pierre. I know I may rely on your exertions and that you will do the best in your power.

My compliments to Mr May
I am Sir
Yours &c &c
(Signed) Kenneth McKenzie

Fort Union Decr. 10th 1835
Mr Colin Campbell [Ogallalla Post]
Dear Sir

I have this day made up my usual winter express for St Louis and sent two of my men with it to Fort Clark being very short of hands I have instructed Belhumeur to send Delorme forward with the packet to Fort Pierre; further his progress in any way that lies in your power for I am very anxious that no time should be lost. I sent you from hence on the 24th Novr. 214 lbs Tobacco with some Tea & Sugar and hope all this you have received all safe. The Robe trade is very slack here I hope it is much brisker with you. Accept my best wishes.

I am
Yours Obediently [Kenneth McKenzie]

P.S. I have instructed Belhumeur to send a man with Delorme as far as your place, but must request you to furnish a man in his room to go with Delorme to Fort Pierre, a good leg and one who knows the road, & will soon find his way back to you.

Fort Union 10th Decr. 1835
To his Highness Prince
Maximilian de Neuwied
Sir

Flattering myself that sometimes when your thoughts wander to the Banks of the Missouri they may linger for a moment at Fort Union. I embrace the opportunity of the usual winter express to St Louis to apprize you that I found the Fort in status quo on my arrival here the 17th Ulto. Mr. Kipp has left Fort Clark for Canada, Mr. Hamilton who was my locum tenens[270] during my long absence is wintering with me, and the beauties of the Rhine & especially the hospitalities of Chateau de Neuwied are frequent subjects of our conversation; I shall ever retain the most agreeable reminiscences of your polite attentions, and regret that I can only return you my poor thanks. Mr Lamont apprized you of the loss of our Steam boat last spring with your several cases of animals & birds on board, collected with so much toil and trouble! your loss is irreparable,

I sincerely regret it and should feel happy could I in any way supply the defficincies thus created in your valuable collection of Natural History. Our Cargo of furs &c destroyed was of very considerable pecuniary value, from sixty to eighty thousand Dollars, a total loss, no part being insured.[271] My voyage across the Atlantic was as agreeable as a good ship with experienced Captain, sumptuous fare, and pleasant Company could possibly render it. On my way out to St Louis I visited that most sublime of natures works, The falls of Niagara, but what pen can describe so magnificent a scene, and still less the feelings excited by a contemplation thereof. I reached St Louis July 17th and after a month's sojourn commenced my voyage to this place, which occupied three months, the winter set in with great force unusually early the Missouri was closed on the 23rd Octr. Since my arrival I have been pretty constantly occupied in "talks" with the red Skins, a great contrast to the very agreeable manner in which my time was passed at this period of last year, in fact my rambles in Germany, France and England yielded me so much delight, I am anxious for a repetition of the like enjoyment. You will please command my services in this country or in the U. States in any way they can be available. I make tender of my best wishes for the continuance of your health & vigor to enjoy the many good things of this life which surround you, and have the honor to be,[272]

Sir
Your Highness's
Most Obedt & Very humble Servant
(Signed) Kenneth McKenzie

Fort Union 10th Decr 1835
Henry K. Ortley Esqr [Saint Louis][273]
Dear Sir

Various untoward circumstances occurred to protract my voyage so that I did not arrive here until the 17th Ulto fully a month later than I contemplated. I am however in good health & vigor and ready for a hard winter's campaign if my Indians will but crowd in their peltries upon me until I cry "hold, enough." None of the luxuries of life having found their way into my cellars or stores during my absence, and the Stock I left there being almost wholly diminished. I must request you to put up for me sundry articles as pr annexed order, have them carefully packed in boxes marked with my name, and sent on board the Steam Boat when she starts for this place, Pierre Chouteau & Co will pay your Bill on your presenting it to them. Some people find pleasure in contrast but you can readily immagine how dull this place must appear, after my gay and busy life with its ever varying & always interesting scenes of the last twelve months. I know not when we shall meet again, the sooner the better say I, and until the day arrives, may you be as happy and prosperous as you can desire, is the sincere and ardent wish of

Your friend &c &c
(Signed) Kenneth McKenzie

Order for Sundry Articles to be shipped by H. K. Ortley Spring 1836 pr Steam boat addressed to K. McKenzie Fort Union.

10 Gallons best french Brandy
10 " " Hollands Gin
1 Doz ½ pint bottles Capers
½ " Qrt " best Catsup
10 lbs Almonds in shell
=1 Box Fr. [French] Plums
½ Bushl Pearl Barley
1 Box Herrings
A Budget of newspapers
1 Box Segars

Notes

1. For a biography of this trader, *see* W. Raymond Wood, "James Kipp: Upper Missouri River Fur Trader and Missouri Farmer," *North Dakota History* 77, nos. 1–2 (2011): 2–35.
2. The German explorer and naturalist Alexander Philipp Maximilian, Prince of Wied-Neuwied (1782–1867) traveled under the name Baron de Braunsberg in the United States. Robert Campbell referred to him in his journal as "the Dutch Prince of Leyden" after a dinner at Fort William. During his studies with private tutors and at German universities, Maximilian showed an aptitude for the "natural sciences," eventually coming under the tutelage of Alexander von Humboldt. From 1800 to 1815, Maximilian served with the Prussian Army, rising to the rank of Major General, and was awarded the Iron Cross.

   Karl Bodmer (1809–1893) was one of the most

talented artists to travel the upper Missouri. Born into a family of artists in Zurich, Switzerland, Bodmer trained in Zurich and Paris before moving to Germany. There, his skills caught the interest of Prince Maximilian, who asked Bodmer to document his travels through the Great Plains. Bodmer's contract for the trip stipulated that upon their return to Germany all sketches and watercolors would become the property of Maximilian in return for a stipend, round-trip passage, and payment of all expenses in America.

David Dreidoppel worked as a servant for Maximilian's family and was also a skilled taxidermist and hunter. He had accompanied Maximilian on a Brazilian expedition from 1815 to 1817. Mildred Goosman, "Karl Bodmer: Earliest Painter on the Upper Missouri," *Montana: The Magazine of Western History* 20 (Summer 1970): 36–38; Orin A. Stevens, "Maximilian in North Dakota, 1833–1834," *North Dakota History* 28 (Oct. 1961): 163–64. The Prince's stay at Forts Union and Clark is described in Maximilian, Prince of Wied, *The North American Journals of Prince Maximilian of Wied*, 3 vols., ed. Stephen S. Witte and Marsha V. Gallagher (Norman: University of Oklahoma Press, 2012).

3. The Mandan people lived in villages along the Missouri River in present-day North Dakota and practiced both horticulture and bison hunting. By the 1830s, they mostly resided near the mouth of the Knife River, near Fort Clark. Raymond Wood and Lee Irwin, "Mandan," in *Handbook of North American Indians*, Vol. 13: *Plains*, pt. 1, ed. Raymond J. DeMallie (Washington, D.C.: Smithsonian Press, 2001), pp. 349–64.

4. The Mandan village of Mih-Tutta-Hang-Kusch was located next to Fort Clark in central North Dakota. The Gros Ventres referred to here are likely the Hidatsa people, who lived a few miles upstream near the Knife River. While many at the time knew the Hidatsas as the Gros Ventre of the Missouri, they had no relation to the Gros Ventre people who lived in present-day northern Montana and southern Alberta and Saskatchewan. Instead, the Hidatsas shared a close linguistic and historic relationship with the Crows. Like other Missouri River tribes, the Hidatsa practiced settled agriculture and had become deeply involved in the fur trade by the early nineteenth century. Frank Henderson Stuart, "Hidatsa," in *Handbook of North American Indians*, 13: *Plains*, pt. 1, pp. 329–48; Loretta Fowler and Regina Flannery, "Gros Ventre," ibid., pt. 2, pp. 677–94. For a history of interactions between American fur traders and American Indians at Fort Clark, *see* W. Raymond Wood, William J. Hunt, Jr., and Randy H. Williams, *Fort Clark and its Indian Neighbors: A Trading Post on the Upper Missouri River* (Norman: University of Oklahoma Press, 2011).

5. Kenneth McKenzie (1797–1861) was the chief agent of the Upper Missouri Outfit and bourgeois (manager) of Fort Union until 1835. At nineteen, he had immigrated to Canada, where he found employment as a clerk with the North West Company on a standard six-year apprenticeship contract. In November 1821, he, along with William Laidlaw, Daniel Lamont, James Kipp, Honoré Picotte, and others left the Selkirk colony via the Red River trail to Prairie du Chien on the Mississippi River and then on to Saint Louis. In the spring of 1822, the group, along with two American citizens, organized Tilton, Dudley and Company, better known as the Columbia Fur Company. Ray H. Mattison, "Kenneth McKenzie," in *The Mountain Men and the Fur Trade of the Far West*, 10 vols., ed. Leroy H. Hafen (Glendale, Calif.: Arthur H. Clark, 1965), 2:217–24. *See also* Michael M. Casler and W. Raymond Wood, "The Rise and Fall of the Columbia Fur Company: Rethinking the Fur Trade on the Northern Great Plains," paper delivered at the 2018 National Fur Trade Symposium, 26–29 Sept. 2018, Bismarck, N.Dak.

6. Hugron Beaugard, hired from Saint Jean Baptiste Parish in Montréal in 1832, is number seventy-two in the AFC Voyageur Contracts Database. Joseph Beauchamp, hired from Faubourge St. Laurent Parish Montréal the same year, is number sixty-one in the AFC Voyageur Contracts Database. Beaugard and Beauchamp were both assigned as winterers in Fort Clark at 1833. AFC Voyageur Contracts Database, Centre du Patrimoine, Saint Boniface, Manitoba, used with permission by Nicole St-Onge and Robert Englebert (hereafter cited as AFC Voyageur Contracts). UMO Employee Database created and used with permission by William J. Hunt, Jr. (hereafter cited as UMO Employee Database). *See also* William R. Swagerty, "A View from the Bottom Up: The Workforce of the American Fur Company on the Upper Missouri in the 1830s," *Montana: The Magazine of Western History* 43 (Winter 1993): 29–30.

7. The 1832 UMO roster lists Henry (Hyacinthe) Morrin as a boatman. The 1832 roster also lists a "Batelier" and an 1827 entry for him at "Fort Clark I" lists a debt of

$77.69. He was the "Patroon" (steersman) for Prince Maximilian's mackinaw in 1833–1834. The 1830 roster lists Louis Vachard (Vacha, various spellings) as a voyager assigned to Fort Tecumseh. He is first mentioned in trader Jacob Halsey's Fort Tecumseh journal on 28 November 1830. Maximilian mentions him as part of his boat crew for the downriver trip to Fort Clark. "Equipment Intended for the Upper Missouri for the Winter of 1827–28," reverse side: unnamed ledger of men's accounts with the Columbia Fur Company (1824–1825), Fur Trade Collection, Missouri Historical Society Archives; UMO Employee Database; Charles Larpenteur, *The Original Journal of Charles Larpenteur: My Travels to the Rocky Mountains Between 1833 and 1872*, ed. Michael M. Casler (Chadron, Nebr.: Museum Association of the American Frontier, 2007), p. 48n3; Michael M. Casler and W. Raymond Wood, eds., *Fort Tecumseh and Fort Pierre Chouteau: Journal and Letter Books, 1830-1850* (Pierre: South Dakota Historical Society Press, 2017), p. 27; Maximilian, *North American Journals*, 3:28n34.

8. Francis Auguste Chardon (1795–1848) was born in Philadelphia. He worked for the prominent fur trader Bartholomew Berthold in Saint Louis in 1817, and while it is unknown when he went west, he later lived among the Osage Indians. He was working for the UMO by 1827. New evidence suggests that Kenneth McKenzie ordered Chardon to take a group of men and the keelboat *Otter* from the Mandan post to build a new post on the Yellowstone River in August 1828, which early documents refer to as the "Yellowstone Post." It becomes Fort Union within two years. In 1829, Chardon became manager at Fort Floyd on the White Earth River and at Fort Tecumseh the next year. Chardon became known as a fort builder and would be associated with every major post on the Missouri. On 21 April 1848, he died at Fort Pierre Chouteau and was buried in a now unmarked grave. Ray H. Mattison, "Francis A. Chardon," in *Mountain Men and the Fur Trade*, 1:225–27, and "Kenneth McKenzie," ibid., 2:217–24; Annie H. Abel, ed., *Chardon's Journal at Fort Clark*, by F. A. Chardon (Pierre: South Dakota Department of History, 1932), pp. xx–xxv.

9. James Archdale Hamilton Palmer (?–1840) remains one of the more mysterious figures of the upper Missouri fur trade. The circumstances leading to his departure from his native England are unclear. "Mr. Hamilton" is first mentioned in the Fort Tecumseh journal on 2 September 1830 as "an English gentleman traveling for curiosity" two years before he becomes the bookkeeper at Fort Union (Casler and Wood, *Fort Tecumseh and For Pierre Chouteau*, pp. 23, 240n52). Several times during his tenure at Fort Union he was left in charge of the post. Hamilton left for Saint Louis in 1836 and served as the cashier for Pierre Chouteau and Company. He died in February 1840 and was buried in the city's Episcopal cemetery. Erwin N. Thompson, *Fort Union Trading Post: Fur Trade Empire on the Upper Missouri* (Medora, N.Dak.: Theodore Roosevelt Nature and History Association, 1986), pp. 20–21; Mattison, "James A. Hamilton (Palmer)," in *Mountain Men and the Fur Trade*, 3:163–66.

10. Kipp removed the Mackinaw boat from the river for winter on 15 November 1833. Maximilian, *North American Journals*, 3:60.

11. The 1830 UMO roster lists Michel Dubreuille (Dubruille, Dubreueille, various spellings) as a voyager. UMO Employee Database.

12. David Dawson Mitchell (1806–1861), was born in Virginia and joined the American Fur Company in 1828. He came to the UMO as a clerk in 1830 was a partner by 1835, and replaced Jacob Hawley as bourgeois at Fort Union after a disastrous smallpox epidemic in 1837. Four years later, he was appointed the United States Superintendent of Indian Affairs, Central Division, at Saint Louis. He took part in the United States–Mexican War, leading the detachment that captured the city of Chihuahua. Mitchell married Martha E. Berry in Kentucky in 1840. He died in Saint Louis in 1861. Samuel Tulloch (1801–1880), a trapper and trader, signed on with William Henry Ashley and Andrew Henry in 1822, and was one of the original "Ashley Hundred." He then joined the UMO. In 1827, Kenneth McKenzie sent Tulloch and a brigade of men to trap in the mountains. He helped build a post for the Crow Indians on the Yellowstone River five years later which was named for Secretary of War Lewis Cass. After Fort Cass was abandoned in 1835, Tulloch built Fort Van Buren, also on the Yellowstone River. In 1839, he left the fur trade and moved back to Missouri. Abel, *Chardon's Journal*, pp. 233–34n99; Hiram M. Chittenden, *A History of the American Fur Trade in the Far West*, 2 vols. (Lincoln: University of Nebraska Press, 1986), 1:386–87 and 2:938; Ray H. Mattison, "David Dawson Mitchell," in *Mountain Men and Fur Trade*, 2:241–46; Larpenteur, *Original Journal*, p. 11n15.

13. The 1830 UMO roster lists Michel Gravelle (Gravil, various spellings) as a clerk/interpreter assigned

to Fort Union. His name first appears in an 1825 Columbia Fur Company account book at "Fort Clark 1" and then on 10 April 1827 as having a debt of $101.50 at Fort Clark. In 1831–1832, he had gone to Washington to serve as an interpreter for an Indian delegation from the upper Missouri. He was assigned to Fort Cass before trapping for Fort Union, where he became Jack Rem ("Jack Ram") Kipling's son-in-law. Larpenteur notes the departure of Gravelle and "Little Frenchman," his brother-in-law, from Fort Union for more beaver trapping in a 12 September 1835 entry. The Blackfeet killed both men that fall near the headwaters of the Milk River. The Deschamps mentioned here could be any of the grown sons—Francois, Jr., Charles, or Joseph—of an infamous Métis family that migrated to the upper Missouri around 1827. One of the Deschamps murdered Jack Rem Kipling in 1836, prompting a large group of the fort's employees to kill six members of the family in retaliation. UMO Employee Database; "Equipment Intended for the Upper Missouri," reverse side, Fur Trade Collection; Jim Hardee, "An 1824–1825 Columbia Fur Company Ledger," *Rocky Mountain Fur Trade Journal* 5 (2011): 138; Larpenteur, *Original Journal*, pp. 49n18, 50n23 and n40; Robert W. Thomson, "'This Wicked Family': A Biography of the Deschamps Family of Fort Union: Their Feuds, Fights, and Violent Demise," *Montana: The Magazine of Western History* 54 (Winter 2004): 2–15.

14. For biographical information on Robert Campbell, *see* George R. Brooks's introduction to "The Private Journal of Robert Campbell," herein. *See also* William R. Nester, *From Mountain Man to Millionaire: The Bold and Dashing Life of Robert Campbell* (Columbia: University of Missouri Press, 2011).
15. For more on the Gens de Gauche, *see* note 68 of "The Private Journal of Robert Campbell," herein.
16. The 1833 UMO roster lists Duchaine (no first name found) as a voyager assigned to Fort Union. The 1831 UMO roster lists Charles Durocher as a winterer assigned to Fort Union. UMO Employee Database; Abel, *Chardon's Journal*, pp. 358, 425.
17. Peter Miller, occupation not listed on the 1831 UMO roster, was assigned to Fort Clark. He may have been a boatman, as Jacob Halsey mentions a Peter Miller in a 15 February 1832 letter to Hamilton: "you mention Peter Miller, as one of the men who remained at Fort Clark, or returned here for 'Louis Vallé' [keelboat] consequently, the term of his engagement ($90 for services ending fall of 1832) was forwarded to Fort Clark" (Casler and Wood, eds., *Fort Tecumseh and Fort Pierre Chouteau*, p. 86). A seemingly different Peter Miller was a skilled carpenter who built the bastions at Fort Union. Swagerty, "View from the Bottom Up," p. 21; UMO Employee Database.
18. The 1833 UMO roster lists common laborer J. Maloney and Thomas Holmes as assigned to Fort Union. In 1835, Larpenteur claimed that Holmes had performed most of the masonry work at the fort. UMO Employee Database; Thompson, *Fort Union*, p. 41; Harold H. Schuler, *Fort Pierre Chouteau* (Vermillion: University of South Dakota Press, 1990), pp. 144–45; Larpenteur, *Original Journal*, p. 49n6.
19. Jean Baptiste Moncrevie (1797–1885) served as a clerk at most of the upper Missouri posts over the course of many years. A gifted artist, he has been credited with the painting above the front gates at Fort Union and creating friendship certificates for Indian chiefs. Moncrevie carried letters back and forth between Fort Union and Fort William in 1833–1834. Robert Campbell referred to him "Doctor McCrevee." He had left the Missouri by 1849 and worked at Fort John in Nebraska before retiring to a nearby ranch. Charles E. Hanson, Jr., "J. B. Moncravie," in *Mountain Men and the Fur Trade*, 9:289–98; John C. Ewers, "Jean Baptiste Moncravie: Fort Union's First White Artist," in *Fort Union Fur Trade Symposium Proceedings* (Williston, N.Dak.: Friends of Fort Union Trading Post, 1994). pp. 53–58; Campbell, "Private Journal," note 18.
20. The winter express linked the fur trading forts on the upper Missouri during the winter with news and orders for trade goods, which were then passed on to the company offices in Saint Louis. Generally, a trusted individual would travel from fort to fort on snowshoes or a dog sled carrying packets of letters, trade orders, and other information critical for doing business, and would be replaced with a new person once they reached their destination. The men chosen for this task were not allowed to carry any messages except those relating to business. Ben Innis, *How t' Talk Trapper: 252 Words and Phrases* (Williston, N.Dak.: Sitting Bull Trading Post, 1983), p. 11; Casler and Wood, *Fort Tecumseh and Fort Pierre Chouteau*, p. 243n91.
21. Kenneth McKenzie left Fort Pierre Chouteau on 22 October 1833, returning to Fort Union. Casler and Wood, *Fort Tecumseh and Fort Pierre Chouteau*, p. 118.

22. The Poplar River flows into the Missouri from the north near present-day Poplar, Montana.

23. The Assiniboine people once ranged from the upper Missouri to as far north as the Saskatchewan River and as far east as the Red River. Most of the tribe had migrated south by the late-eighteenth century due to trade opportunities and the abundant bison population. An Assiniboine chief chose the location of Fort Union, which became the tribe's primary trading post. Raymond J. DeMallie and David Reed Miller, "Assiniboine," in *Handbook of North American Indians*, 13: *Plains*, pt. 1, pp. 572–95.

24. Each Assiniboine family generally had between six to twelve dogs, but they did not appear to have as many horses as other Plains tribes. Robert H. Lowie, *The Assiniboine*, Anthropological Papers of the American Museum of Natural History (New York: American Museum of Natural History, 1909), p. 15.

25. Fort Jackson also was called the Poplar River Post.

26. Thomas Glenday, a former American Fur Company employee, worked for Sublette and Campbell, who assigned him to move up the Yellowstone River with Pierre Vasquez and trade with the Crow Indians. Pierre Louis Vasquez was an experienced mountain man who had accompanied Campbell from Saint Louis. Campbell, "Private Journal," note 12; LeRoy R. Hafen, "Mountain Men–Louis Vasquez," *Colorado Magazine* 10 (Jan. 1933): 14–21.

27. By early 1800s, the Crow people had become skilled mounted bison hunters and traders. The tribe had two divisions, the Mountain Crows, who lived in the vicinity of the Bighorn, Wind River, and Absaroka ranges, and the River Crows, who lived on the upper Missouri and the surrounding northern plains. Due to their substantial range, the Crows played a key role in linking upper Missouri tribes with Great Basin and Plateau tribes to the west. The opening of Fort Union provided new opportunities for the Crows, who were more active in the beaver trade than any other plains tribe. Fred W. Voget, "Crow," in *Handbook of North American Indians*, 13: *Plains*, pt. 2, pp. 695–717.

28. Pierre Urtubise (Ortubise, various spellings) worked as a Dakota language interpreter at the time Maximilian was at Fort Clark. The 1830 UMO roster lists him as an interpreter assigned to Fort Clark. He is later assigned to the White River post. Pierre Urtubise was described as "a half-breed Sioux interpreter and trader" and "a good young man; but he has one failing, he is fond of liquor" (Janet Lecompte, "Charles Autobees," in *Trappers of the Far West*, ed. LeRoy R. Hafen [Lincoln, Nebr.: Bison Books, 1983], p. 22). Maximilian, *North American Journals*, 3:53n3; UMO Employee Database; Abel, *Chardon's Journal*, p. 228n81; Swagerty, "View from the Bottom Up," p. 43.

29. Michel Bellehumeur (various spellings) worked as a Mandan language interpreter while Maximilian was at Fort Clark, though Kipp, the bourgeois, knew the language better. The 1824–1825 account book lists Bellehumeur at "Fort Clark 1" in debt $250.17. The 1833 UMO roster lists him as a trader assigned to Fort Clark. Jim Hardee, "1824–1825 Columbia Fur Company Ledger," p. 139; Maximilian, *North American Journals*, 3:53n2; UMO Employee Database.

30. The 1833 UMO roster lists Alexis Durant as a hunter assigned to Fort Clark. UMO Employee Database.

31. Apple River, today's Apple Creek, enters the Missouri River from the east near Bismarck, North Dakota.

32. The 1829 UMO roster lists Baptiste Deguire as a voyager assigned to the Kansas Outfit. In 1830, he was assigned to the Arikaras. In 1833, he worked at Fort Pierre and then Fort Cass. The 1832 UMO roster lists him as a boatman. UMO Employee Database; Donald Jackson, *Voyages of the Steamboat Yellow Stone* (New York: Ticknor & Fields, 1985), p. 168.

33. Samuel Tulloch built Fort Cass in 1832 on the right bank of the Yellowstone River, a few miles below the mouth of the Bighorn River in present-day Treasure County, Montana.

34. For a short biography of Andrew Sublette, *see* Leroy R. Hafen, "Mountain Men: Andrew Sublette," *Colorado Magazine* 10 (Sept. 1933): 179–84.

35. Fort William was built on the north side of the Missouri River. Today, the site sits about two hundred yards due west of the Missouri-Yellowstone Confluence Interpretive Center at Fort Buford State Historic Site, North Dakota.

36. "L'Anje Guerir" is French for "The Healing Angel." This could be Francois L'Ange, who the 1833 UMO roster lists as an engagé assigned to Fort Union. UMO Employee Database.

37. The 1830 UMO roster lists Pierre Narcisse LeClerc as a clerk/trader at Fort Union. He operated as an independent trader the following year. By 1833 he headed the Sioux Outfit for Sublette and Campbell. UMO Employee Database; Abel, *Chardon's Journal*, p. 440n21; Campbell, "Private Journal," note 28.

38. The 1832 UMO roster lists Francois Croteau as a voyager assigned to Fort Clark. UMO Employee Data Base; Jackson, *Voyages of the Steamboat Yellow Stone*, p. 168.

39. The North West Company let Honoré Picotte go following its merger with the Hudson's Bay Company in 1821. With his brother, Antoine Picotte, and nephew, Joseph (Henry) Picotte—who became a well-known fur trader on the Missouri and is often confused with his uncle, who was also nicknamed Henry—he joined the party traveling to Saint Louis from the Selkirk colony in 1821 and was among the original partners and traders of the Columbia Fur Company. Honoré Picotte was sent to the Bad River, where he built Fort Tecumseh in 1822. He remained there until William Laidlaw replaced him as manager in 1827. After being reassigned to Fort Floyd, Picotte left the upper Missouri in 1828. He soon rejoined the UMO and served as manager at various posts. In 1835, he became head of the new Sioux Outfit headquartered out of Fort Pierre Chouteau, and by 1846 he was the chief agent on the upper Missouri. In 1848, Alexander Culbertson succeeded him as chief agent but Picotte continued with the company in Saint Louis. John S. Gray, "Honoré Picotte, Fur Trader," *South Dakota History* 6 (Spring 1976): 186–87, 202; Chittenden, *History*, 1:387; Abel, *Chardon's Journal*, pp. liii, 163, 202–3n20, 263n247.
40. *See* Campbell's "Private Journal" for 5 October 1833.
41. Pierre Didier Papin (1798–1853) was a member of one of the original French families that settled in Saint Louis. He joined the fur trade with B. Pratte and Co. in 1825. The next year a letter mentions him trading at the Mandan villages opposite William P. Tilton. In the 1827 merger between B. Pratte and Co., the AFC, and the Columbia Fur Company that created the UMO, Ramsay Crooks chose Papin to represent the company's interests on the Missouri River by conducting inventories and transferring property and men to the UMO. In 1829, he started P. D. Papin and Co., but by 1830 he had sold out and joined the UMO. Over the next twenty years he worked as a clerk or manager at various posts for the company. Papin died suddenly in 1853 and is buried near Scottsbluff, Nebraska. [B Berthold] to Jean P. Cabanné, 9 December 1826, Chouteau Family Papers, Missouri Historical Society Archives; Chittenden, *History*, 1:328; William A. Goff, "Pierre Didier Papin," in *French Fur Traders and Voyagers in the American West*, ed. LeRoy R. Hafen (Lincoln, Nebr.: Bison Books, 1997), pp. 239–52.
42. This post was located at the White River below Fort Pierre Chouteau. Abel, *Chardon's Journal*, p. xxvi.
43. Joshua Pilcher (1790–1843) came to Saint Louis during the War of 1812 and worked as a hatmaker and merchant. After joining the fur trade, he accompanied the Long Expedition in 1819 and became a leading partner of the Missouri Fur Company the next year. He organized Joshua Pilcher and Company in 1824. Pilcher then served as acting Indian Agent at Rock Island until he replaced J. P. Cabanné as resident trader at Council Bluffs in 1833. In March 1835, he accepted an appointment as subagent for the Sioux of the Missouri, whose agency was below Fort Pierre Chouteau. Ray H. Mattison, "Joshua Pilcher," in *Mountain Men and the Fur Trade*, 4:251–60.
44. Council Bluffs is located on the west bank of the Missouri River some twenty-nine miles north of the mouth of the Platte River. Lewis and Clark counseled with the Otoe and Missouri Indians at this locality on 2 August 1804, hence the name. Today, a replica of the military post Fort Atkinson, one of the many posts built on the site, sits near its midpoint. Clark, 2 Aug. 1804, *The Journals of the Lewis and Clark Expedition*, Vol. 2: *August 30, 1803–August 24, 1804*, ed. Gary E. Moulton (Lincoln: University of Nebraska Press, 1987), pp. 435–38.
45. Daniel Lamont (1798?–1837) was a Scotsman who came to Saint Louis from Canada in 1821. An original member of the Columbia Fur Company, he managed the Lands' End post across the river from Fort Snelling at the confluence of the Mississippi and Saint Peters (now Minnesota) rivers. He came to the Missouri River in 1827 as one of the three partners of the UMO. There, he oversaw logistics for the company and served as manager at various posts. He was acting bourgeois of Fort Union during the winter of 1834–1835 while his good friend, McKenzie, was touring Europe. Lamont left the fur trade in 1835 and went into business with Peter and Joseph Powell in dry goods wholesaling firm of Powell, Lamont and Company. William Laidlaw soon joined him, and the company enlarged their market and began dealing buffalo and beaver from the upper Arkansas River and Santa Fe until Lamont died in 1837 at age 39. Chittenden, *History*, 1:326, 388; Abel, *Chardon's Journal*, pp. 16–17, 293n335; Casler and Wood, "Rise and Fall."
46. Pierre Chouteau, Jr., was part of a family that dominated the western fur trade for the better part of a century. Janet Lecompte, "Pierre Chouteau, Jr.," in *Mountain Men and the Fur Trade*, 9:92–123, and "The Chouteaus and the St. Louis Fur Trade," in William R. Swagerty, *Papers of the St. Louis Fur Trade* (Bethesda, M.d.: University Publication of

America for the Missouri Historical Society, 1991), pp. xiii–xxii.

47. This comment is the first reference to McKenzie's still at Fort Union.

48. The Blackfoot people ranged throughout the plains east of the continental divide, chiefly in present-day northern Montana and Alberta. The tribe has three primary divisions: the Blackfoot, Blood, and Piegan. The southern branch of the Piegan are known as the Blackfeet. Relationships between the Blackfoot nation and American traders had been turbulent until the American Fur Company built Fort Piegan (1831) and Fort McKenzie (1832). The tribe subsequently became active in the fur trade. Hugh A. Dempsey, "Blackfoot," in *Handbook of North American Indians*, 13: *Plains*, pt. 1, pp. 604–28.

49. Much like the winter express, the "upwards express" moved from post to post up the Missouri River.

50. William Laidlaw came to the Selkirk Colony on the Red River sometime before 1816 and served as agricultural superintendent, teaching farming and animal husbandry to the settlers. In 1819, he introduced the first use of the steel-tipped plow to the Red River valley. After the death of Lord Selkirk, Laidlaw left the Red River with McKenzie, Lamont, Kipp, and others in 1821, and traveled to Saint Louis, where he became one of the partners of Tilton, Dudley and Company. He built and managed Fort Union at Traverse des Sioux on the Saint Peters (Minnesota) River, which eventually became a depot for the transfer of goods west and furs east. In December 1823, he brought six wagonloads of trade goods overland from Fort Washington on Lake Traverse to the Mandan villages for James Kipp. Laidlaw, among other Columbia Fur Company traders, escorted several Yankton, Wahpeton, and Sisseton representatives to the Grand Peace Conference at Prairie du Chien in August 1825. With the merger of the companies on 9 July 1827, William Laidlaw and Daniel Lamont became partners in the UMO and received salaries and stock. Laidlaw then moved to the Missouri River, where he took charge of Fort Tecumseh and later Fort Pierre Chouteau. Laidlaw remained in the upper Missouri fur trade until 1844, when he retired to Liberty, Missouri, where he lived with his Sioux Indian wife Mary Ann, until his death on 9 October 1852. He is buried in Mount Zion Cemetery, in Mosby, Missouri. Alexander Ross, *The Red River Settlement: Its Rise, Progress and Present State* (London: Smith, Elder and Co., 1856), pp. 77–78; Ray H. Mattison, "William Laidlaw," in *Mountain Men and the Fur Trade*, 3:167–72; Rhoda Gilman, Carolyn Gilman, and Deborah M. Stultz, *The Red River Trails, 1820–1870: Oxcart Routes Between St. Paul and the Selkirk Settlement* (Saint Paul: Minnesota Historical Society, 1979), pp. 4–5; Lavender, *Fist in the Wilderness*, p. 361; Lawrence Taliaferro to Oliver Bostwick, 2 April 1826, Chouteau Family Papers, Missouri Historical Society Archives; Wood, "James Kipp," p. 5; Dale L. Morgan, *Jedidiah Smith and the Opening of the West* (Lincoln: University of Nebraska Press, 1964), p. 60; Casler and Wood, "Rise and Fall."

51. *Manager du Lards* (pork eaters) is a reference to those employees hired in Montréal by AFC recruiter Gabriel Franchère. For a discussion on their journey to the upper Missouri, *see* Casler and Wood, *Fort Tecumseh and Fort Pierre Chouteau*, p. xii; Swagerty, "View from the Bottom Up," p. 25.

52. Charles Trudelle was hired as a voyager in Montréal in 1832 and assigned to the "Rivière Missouri." He is number 1067 in the AFC Voyageur Contracts.

53. Jacqués Berger, also referred to as Jacob Berger, was a former Hudson's Bay Company employee who had come down to the United States from Canada. Fluent in the Blackfoot languages, Berger persuaded the traditionally hostile tribe to trade with the Upper Missouri Outfit. He worked out of both Forts McKenzie and Union as an interpreter. Larpenteur, *Original Journal*, p. 67n2; David Smyth, "Jacques Berger, Fur Trader," *The Beaver* 69 (June/July 1987): 44–45; Casler and Wood, *Fort Tecumseh and Fort Pierre Chouteau*, p. 244n6.

54. Alexander Harvey was clerk/trader with a reputation for violence against Indians and his fellow fur trade personnel. In 1840, he murdered Isadore (Isodoro) Sandoval in the company store at Fort Union. Two years later, he conspired with Francis Chardon to kill several Blackfoot chiefs at Fort McKenzie. Ray H. Mattison, "Alexander Harvey," in *Mountain Men and the Fur Trade*, 4:119–23; Thompson, *Fort Union*, p. 47.

55. The steamboat *Assiniboine*, built in Cincinnati, Ohio, in 1833, was a side-wheel measuring 130 x 20 x 6 feet and weighting 149 tons. On its maiden voyage in 1833, it brought Prince Maximilian's party to Fort Union. The boat became stranded on an 1834 trip to Fort Union and wintered near the Poplar River. In the spring of 1835, it headed downriver but caught fire and burned near Sibley Island near present day Bismarck, North Dakota. Casler, *Steamboats*, pp. 18–19; Larpenteur, *Original Journal*, p. 13n29;

Enrollment Papers, *Assiniboine*, Enrollments 1832–1834, Vol. 7939-B, pp. 375–76, Custom House Records—Port of New Orleans, Bureau of Marine Inspection and Navigation, Record Group 41, National Archives, Washington, D.C.

56. For Duchaine, *see* note 16.
57. The 1830 UMO roster lists Louis Leger as a voyager assigned to Fort Clark. UMO Employee Database.
58. Stapin; no information.
59. Edwin L. Patton was a clerk for the UMO assigned to Fort McKenzie. Prince Maximilian met him there in August 1833 and noted that he been acting director prior to David D. Mitchell. On 14 August, Patton and eleven engagés left for Fort Union in a pirogue heavily loaded with fur returns. Patton, who had plans to leave the fur trade and return home to Alabama, commanded the boat all the way to Saint Louis. In 1834, he was first William Sublette's clerk and then manager at Fort William (Laramie). After the sale of the fort in the spring of 1835 to Fontenelle, Fitzpatrick and Company, Patton brought the post returns to Saint Louis. Maximilian, *North American Journals*, 2: 353, 368–69; Dale L. Morgan and Eleanor Towles Harris, "A Galaxy of Mountain Men: Biographical Sketches," in *The Rocky Mountain Journals of William Marshall Anderson*, ed. Morgan and Harris (San Marino, Calif.: Huntington Library, 1967), pp. 341–43.
60. The Milk River, which Lewis and Clark named for its milky appearance, joins the Missouri River from the north in central Montana. At the time, many referred to it by its French name, *River au Lait*.
61. The Poplar River.
62. Antoine Janis (various spellings) accompanied Robert Campbell to the 1833 Rocky Mountain rendezvous and traveled with him down the Yellowstone River to build Fort William. He then managed the Poplar River Post alongside William B. Almond. Larpenteur, *Original Journal*, p. 11n20.
63. The Yankton and Yanktonai Sioux lived between the Missouri River to the west and the Big Sioux and Red rivers to the east. They formed part of the Seven Council Fires, or *Oceti Šakowiŋ*, known by Americans as the Sioux. By the 1800s, the Yankton and Yanktonai considered themselves a single people and spoke the same language, though they had several distinct bands due to their large geographic range. Raymond J. DeMallie, "Yankton and Yanktonai," in *Handbook of North American Indians*, 13: *Plains*, pt. 2, pp. 777–93.
64. The Hidatsa Indians. *See* note 4; Frank Anderson Stewart, "Hidatsa," ibid., pt. 1, pp. 329–48.
65. Thomas Fitzpatrick was a member of the Rocky Mountain Fur Company. On 24 June 1833, he and his men departed the rendezvous with Robert Campbell, Milton Sublette, Nathaniel Wyeth, and Captain William Drummond Stewart. Fitzpatrick left them at the Bighorn River to trap in Crow country. Chittenden, *History*, 1:257, 302.
66. For a detailed analysis of the Cabanné/Leclerc liquor affair, *see* Barton H. Barbour, *Fort Union and the Upper Missouri Fur Trade* (Norman: University of Oklahoma Press, 2001), pp. 159–65; Mark William Kelly, *Lost Voices on the Missouri: John Dougherty and the Indian Frontier* (Leavenworth, Kans.: Sam Clark, 2013), pp. 444–68.
67. Lucien Fontenelle (1800–1840) entered the fur trade in 1819 as a trader for the Missouri Fur Company assigned to Council Bluffs. He remained with the company until its charter expired in 1824. In 1827, he went to the mountains with Joshua Pilcher and led a hunting brigade. He had returned to Bellevue, a trading post south of present-day Omaha, by September 1828. Fontenelle made an agreement with the UMO in 1830 to return to the mountains with Andrew Drips. For the next several years, Fontenelle led supply trains and hunting brigades for the AFC. In 1835, he and Thomas Fitzpatrick formed Fontenelle, Fitzpatrick and Company, then merged with the former partners of the Rocky Mountain Fur Company and purchased Fort William. At the 1836 rendezvous, Joshua Pilcher, representing Pratte, Chouteau and Company, purchased Fort William and the remaining assets of Fontenelle, Fitzpatrick and Company. Lucien Fontenelle died at Bellevue in early 1840. Morgan and Harris, "Galaxy of Mountain Men," pp. 307–12; Alan C. Trottman, "Lucien Fontenelle," in *Trappers of the Far West*, pp. 123–41; Chittenden, *History*, 1:389.
68. The Rocky Mountain Fur Company.
69. Milton Green Sublette (1801–1837) and his older brother William would sign on with Ashley and Henry in 1822. The younger Sublette worked as a trapper in the southwest until 1829, when he joined his brother to bring supplies to the rendezvous on the Popo Agie River. In 1830, he became a partner in the newly created Rocky Mountain Fur Company (RMF). By 1834, the scarcity of beaver fur, rising costs of supplies, and increased competition from AFC trapping brigades led to the RMF's collapse and reorganization. Sublette, Thomas Fitzpatrick, and Jim Bridger merged with Lucien Fontenelle and Andrew Drips. Soon after, Sublette aggravated an old arrow wound in his left leg that he had received

on the Gila River in 1826, forcing him to leave for Saint Louis, where Dr. Barnard Farrar performed two amputations on the leg. Determined to return to the mountains, Sublette rode in a cart with the supply caravan as far as Fort William, where he remained until dying in April 1837 from what is thought to have been malignant bone cancer. Doyce B. Nunis, Jr. "Milton G. Sublette," in *Mountain Men and the Fur Trade*, 4:331–49; Morgan and Harris, "Galaxy of Mountain Men," pp. 363–69; Dr. R. W. Gaul, "Death of the Thunderbolt: Some Notes on the Final Illness of Milton Sublette," *Bulletin of the Missouri Historical Society* 18 (Oct. 1961): 33–36.

70. The Northwest gun was one of the most important trade items at any fort on the upper Missouri. American Indians reportedly preferred them to any other gun. For more information on Northwest guns *see* Charles E. Hanson, Jr., *The Northwest Gun* (Lincoln: Nebraska State Historical Society Publications in Anthropology, 1956); James A. Hanson and Dick Harmon, *The Encyclopedia of Trade Goods*, Vol. 1: *Firearms of the Fur Trade* (Chadron, Nebr.: Museum of the Fur Trade, 2011), pp. 143–200; note 84, herein.

71. Brass faucets for kegs.

72. Francis T. Chardon was Chardon's Osage son. His other son was Francis Bolivar Chardon. Abel, *Chardon's Journal*, pp. 208n36, 209n39, 209n44, 210n48, 304–5n404.

73. Sir William Drummond Stewart (1795–1871), a half-pay captain of the British Army, accompanied Robert Campbell to the 1833 rendezvous. Stewart traveled throughout the west for the next seven years. He was the second son of Sir George Stewart, Seventeenth Lord of Grandtully, Fifth Baronet of Murty, and of Catherine, eldest daughter of Sir John Drummond of Logiealmond, a cadet of the Earls of Perth. He became Sir William Drummond Stewart by right of succession and inherited the estates of Grandtully and Murthly castles when his brother John died on 20 May 1838. Mae R. Porter and Odessa Davenport, *Scotsman in Buckskin: Sir William Drummond Stewart and the Rocky Mountain Fur Trade* (New York: Hastings House, 1963), pp. ix, 4, 172–74, 271. *See also* John I. Merritt, *Baronets and Buffalo: British Sportsman in the American West, 1833–1881* (Missoula, Mont.: Mountain Press Publishing Company, 1985).

74. Fitzpatrick's party was moving up the Tongue River valley to obtain permission to trap on Crow lands when this incident occurred. He blamed the American Fur Company for instigating the Crows to rob him. Later, the Crows traded forty-three beaver skins at Fort Cass. Chittenden, *History*, 1:302.

75. William Backhouse Astor (1792–1875), John Jacob Astor's son, was the president of the American Fur Company, a position he held until its sale in 1834. Maximilian, *North American Journals*, 3:346–47n60.

76. Dr. George W. McKenney, son of Thomas L. McKenney, United States superintendent of Indian affairs from 1824 to 1830, had hoped to become a clerk in the fur trade. Kenneth McKenzie had taken him under his wing to teach him the trade but claimed the good doctor did not have the temperament for dealing with Indians. Abel, *Chardon's Journal*, p. 221n73; Campbell, "Private Journal," note 74.

77. William Clark (1770–1838) of Lewis and Clark Expedition fame served as superintendent of Indian affairs in Saint Louis from 1822 until his death in 1838.

78. Pierre Gaboleau may have been an engagé at Fort Union; no information. Abel, *Chardon's Journal*, p. 356.

79. This packet of letters would not reach Fort Clark until Christmas day 1833. Kipp had prepared to travel to Fort Union by dog sled but did not depart Fort Clark until December 29. Afterward, a large snowstorm forced him to take refuge at the "Maitari village" because of the extreme cold. Kipp would not return to Fort Clark until 23 January 1834 (Reuben Gold Thwaites, ed., "Part III of Maximilian, Prince of Wied's Travels in the Interior of North America, 1832–1834," in *Early Western Travels, 1748–1846*, 32 vols. [Cleveland: Arthur P. Clark, 1906], 24:49–63). Maximilian, *North American Journals*, 3:108, 112, 246–47.

80. The 1831 UMO roster lists Baptiste Lebrun as an engagé assigned to Fort Clark and Francois Delorme as a winterer assigned to Fort Union. Cyprien Denoyer (Desnoyer) had been with the Columbia Fur Company and came over with the merger. The 1830 UMO roster lists him as a voyager assigned to Fort Tecumseh. The same roster lists Joseph Papin as a boatman assigned to Fort Clark. UMO Employee Database; Charles E. DeLand, ed., "Fort Tecumseh and Fort Pierre Journal and Letter Books," *South Dakota Historical Collection*, Vol. 9, notes by Doane Robinson (Pierre: State Publishing Company, 1918), p. 144n127.

81. Jacob Halsey arrived on the upper Missouri in 1826 as a clerk for the Columbia Fur Company at Fort

Tecumseh and later at Fort Pierre Chouteau. He would serve at various posts for the UMO and was a partner by 1837. He and his family boarded the steamboat *St. Peters* at Fort Pierre Chouteau for the 1837 trip up to Fort Union, as he had been appointed the new bourgeois. Smallpox broke out on the boat around Fort Leavenworth, and shortly after leaving Fort Clark the Halsey family became ill with the disease. His wife died in childbirth aboard the boat. Halsey arrived at Fort Union very ill along with his newborn daughter and three-year-old son. He lost his entire family to smallpox during his time at Fort Union. Perhaps as a result, his performance was unsatisfactory. David D. Mitchell replaced him as bourgeois that fall. Halsey died in 1842 after riding his horse into a tree while intoxicated near Liberty, Missouri. Abel, *Chardon's Journal*, pp. 211–12n50; Chittenden, *History*, 1:391; Thompson, *Fort Union*, p. 46. *See also* Michael M. Casler, "'This Outrageous Desease': Charles Larpenteur's Observations of the 1837 Smallpox Epidemic," *Rocky Mountain Fur Trade Journal* 10 (2016): 18–35.

82. In 1833, the upriver journey of the steamboat *Assiniboine* carried a liquor still destined for Fort Union. Kenneth McKenzie sought a way around the prohibition of liquor in Indian Territory and set up a distillery at the fort producing "as fine liquor as need be drunk" (Thompson, *Fort Union*, pp. 29–32). The government's discovery of the illicit still had serious repercussions for the American Fur Company and damaged McKenzie's career as a fur trader. Rebuked by the company and ordered out of Indian country for a year by the Indian Department, McKenzie left Fort Union in late summer 1834. Chittenden, *History*, 1:358–62; Mattison, "Kenneth McKenzie," pp. 217–24. *See also* Casler and Wood, "Rise and Fall."

83. Better known as peace medals, colonial powers vying for control of the Interior of North America issued these symbols of sovereignty. Fur traders used the Silver Astor medals to grant authority to Plains Indian tribes, but their distribution only disrupted relations between the United States government and the Indians. Francis Paul Prucha, *Indian Peace Medals in American History* (Bluffton, S.C.: Rivilo Books, 1994), pp. 52–53.

84. To save the expense of paying for "Barnett" Northwest guns from London, the American Fur Company placed an order with Belgium gun makers and had each lock stamped "Barnett." The result, as an agent explained in 1833, was shabby workmanship: "The Stocks are a little too heavy, and not crooked enough, — but the worst of it is that every stock is made of two pieces joined at the breech and this the Indians cannot endure. When the stock is new and varnished, you hardly discover this imperfection, but when they have been used, or exposed to the wet, it has an ugly effect, and very often the Indians bring them back to be exchanged for better, or those who have them on credit will not pay for them" (John E. Parsons, "Gunmakers for the American Fur Company," *New York Historical Society Quarterly* 6 [Apr. 1952]: 183). *See also* Hanson and Harmon, *Encyclopedia of Trade Goods*, 1:309–19.

85. John B. Whetton, merchant. Abel, *Chardon's Journal*, p. 274n268.

86. The 1833 UMO roster lists Lewis Crawford as a clerk assigned to Fort Clark. Crawford, who had probably been a clerk/trader for the Columbia Fur Company, came to the UMO after the 1827 merger. In 1836, he was with Joshua Pilcher at Fort William. He is mentioned numerous times in the letter books of Fort Tecumseh, Fort Pierre Chouteau, and Fort Union. UMO Employee Database; Abel, *Chardon's Journal*, p. 229n36; Morgan and Harris, "Galaxy of Mountain Men," pp. 257, 304; Casler and Wood, *Fort Tecumseh and Fort Pierre Chouteau*, p. 259.

87. Mr. "C" is Francis Chardon. For Pierre Urtubise (Ortubise), *see* note 28.

88. Alexander Culbertson joined the AFC as a bookkeeper/clerk in 1829 at the age of twenty. In the summer of 1833, Culbertson was sent to Fort McKenzie. There, he helped entertain Prince Maximilian, who was witness to Culbertson's wedding to a Piegan woman for whom he paid one-hundred dollars. The UMO rosters list Culbertson as an agent/bourgeois from the 1830s through the 1860s. In 1843, he transferred to Fort Laramie on the Platte River to reorganize the trade in that area. The next year, he was suddenly recalled to Fort McKenzie after Chardon and Harvey fired a cannon at a group of Blackfeet Indians coming to trade. He and Kenneth McKenzie, who had been called out of retirement, spent the next year regaining the Blackfeet's trust. Culbertson built Forts Lewis and Benton among the tribe. In 1879, he left the Fort Peck Agency, where he had been trading, and went to Nebraska to live with his daughter, Julia. He died four months later at age seventy. UMO Employee Database; Henry A. Boller, *Among the Indians, Four Years on the Upper Missouri, 1858–1862* (Norman: University of Oklahoma Press, 1965), p. 62; W. Raymond Wood, ed., *Twilight of the Upper*

Missouri Fur Trade: The Journals of Henry A. Boller (Bismarck: State Historical Society of North Dakota, 2008), p. 43n12; Maximilian, *North American Journals*, 2:253n42; Ray H. Mattison, "Alexander Culbertson," in *Fur Traders and Mountain Men of the Upper Missouri*, ed Leroy R. Hafen (Lincoln, Nebr.: University of Nebraska Press, 1995), pp. 253–56; Casler and Wood, *Fort Tecumseh and Fort Pierre Chouteau*, p. 260. For an in-depth biography of Alexander Culbertson, *see* Lesley Wischmann, *Frontier Diplomats: The Life and Times of Alexander Culbertson and Natoyist-Siksina* (Spokane, Wash.: Arthur H. Clark Company, 2000).

89. At this time, the Bad River at Fort Pierre, South Dakota, was called the Little Missouri.

90. Alexander's uncle, John Craighead Culbertson had been the resident trader at the AFC post across from Fort Snelling (the former Columbia Fur Company Lands' End post) at the confluence of the Mississippi and Saint Peters (Minnesota) Rivers. Alexander had begun his career as a fur trader there under the guidance of his uncle. Maximilian, *North American Journals*, 2:253n42, 349n70.

91. In 1833, Asiatic cholera, a bacterial disease caused by contaminated water, was spreading up the Missouri River. Barbour, *Fort Union*, pp. 138–39; Kelly, *Lost Voices on the Missouri*, p. 430.

92. Almanza was probably an engagé; no information.

93. Michael Sylvester Cerré (1803–1860) nicknamed "Lami," was brother-in-law to P. D. Papin and cousin to the Chouteau family. At this time he was serving Capt. Benjamin Bonneville in 1825 as one of his two field "Captains," the other being Joseph Reddeford Walker. His brother, Gabriel Pascal Cerré, also worked for the UMO as a clerk assigned to Fort Clark. Casler and Wood, *Fort Tecumseh and Fort Pierre Chouteau*, p. 237n10; Abel, *Chardon's Journal*, p. 209n45; Robinson, notes, in "Fort Tecumseh and Fort Pierre Journal and Letter Books," ed. DeLand, pp. 97–98n23.

94. A factotum, or handy man, performs all kinds of work.

95. By the early nineteenth century, the Kootenai people largely lived west of the continental divide, in present-day northwestern Montana, northern Idaho, Washington, and British Columbia. The tribe had two bands, the lower and upper Kootenai, the latter of whom frequently crossed the divide to hunt bison. The tribe had lived on the plains before moving west, perhaps due to pressure from the Blackfeet. Bill B. Brunton, "Kootenai," in *Handbook of North American Indians*, Vol. 12: *Plateau*, ed. Deward E. Walker, Jr.(Washington, D.C.: Smithsonian Press, 1998), pp. 223–37.

96. David Mitchell sent out a group of traders and men from Fort McKenzie to find and establish trade with the Kootenai Indians. Prince Maximilian records in his field journal that they left on 30 August 1833. Maximilian, *North American Journals*, 2:400.

97. Nathaniel J. Wyeth (1802–1856) was born to a wealthy family in Cambridge, Massachusetts. Influenced by Hall J. Kelly's Oregon Colonization Society, he put together a small party of twenty men to travel to Oregon in March of 1832. During his western travels, Wyeth interacted with many in the fur trade, even entering into a contract to deliver goods to the Rocky Mountain Fur Company. He established Fort Hall on the Snake River. Despite Wyeth's best efforts, his schemes did not pan out and he returned east by 1836. McKenzie famously blamed Wyeth for reporting the still at Fort Union to authorities at Fort Leavenworth. Chittenden, *History*, 1:435–57. *See also* Nathaniel J. Wyeth, *The Journals of Captain Nathaniel J. Wyeth's Expeditions to the Oregon Country 1831–1836*, ed. Don Johnson (Fairfield, Wash.: Ye Galleon Press, 1984).

98. John Dougherty Jr.; no relation to Indian Agent John Dougherty. The 1830 UMO roster lists Dougherty as a clerk assigned to Fort Clark. An 1830 AFC document lists Dougherty as a clerk/interpreter at Fort Union. The 1832 UMO roster lists him as a clerk. He was sent to Fort McKenzie, where he died of cholera, in 1833. The 1830 UMO roster lists Thomas Dickson as an interpreter assigned to Fort Clark. The next year he is listed as a clerk/interpreter at the Yanctonnais post. Abel describes him as the son of Robert Dickson, formerly of the North West Company, who worked for the Columbia Fur Company at Fort Washington on Lake Traverse. Colin Rose, a free trapper, was killed along with Hugh Glass and Hilain Menard after leaving Fort Cass in the spring of 1833. UMO Employee Database; Abel, *Chardon's Journal*, pp. 227n81, 229n88; Barbour, *Fort Union*, p. 139; Jackson, *Voyages of the Steamboat Yellow Stone*, p. 168; Clay J. Landry, "Hugh Glass: The Rest of the Story," *Rocky Mountain Fur Trade Journal* 10 (2016): 1–17.

99. There were three men with the last name "Martin" on the upper Missouri at the time: Jacque, Lamant, and Michel, all of them boatmen. This is possibly Michel Martin, who was assigned to Fort Clark. William Laidlaw mentions in a letter dated 10 January 1834 that "two of our men were killed

near Fort Cass" (Casler and Wood, *Fort Tecumseh and Fort Pierre Chouteau*, p. 124). UMO Employee Database; Jackson, *Voyages of the Steamboat Yellow Stone*, p. 169.

100. The Hudson's Bay Company.
101. Francois, Jr., Charles, and Joseph Deschamps. Thomson, "'This Wicked Family,'" p. 10; Larpenteur, *Original Journal*, p. 49n18.
102. The 1830 UMO roster lists Thomas Kipland as a winterer assigned to Fort Union. UMO Employee Database.
103. An 1832 license for men employed on the upper Missouri lists Samuel P. Winter as a clerk/trader at Fort Union. James P. Beckwourth was born into slavery in Virginia in roughly 1800 to a black slave and her white owner. In 1824, after being manumitted by his father, he went west in William Ashley's supply expedition to the Rocky Mountains. For the next several years he worked for the Rocky Mountain Fur Company. In 1828, he began living among the Crows. Soon thereafter, Kenneth McKenzie employed him to encourage the Crows to trade with the Upper Missouri Outfit, a relationship that lasted until 1836. UMO Employee Database; Abel, *Chardon's Journal*, pp. 227–28n81, 273n266; Chittenden, *History*, 2:679–81; Elinor Wilson, *Jim Beckwourth, Black Mountain Man and Chief of the Crows* (Norman, University of Oklahoma Press, 1980), pp. 73–78; T. D. Bonner, *Life and Adventures of James P. Beckwourth, Mountaineer, Scout, Pioneer, a Chief of the Crow Tribe* (Minneapolis: Ross & Haines, 1965), pp. 207–8, 212–14.
104. The 1834 UMO roster lists Joseph E. Pellot (various spellings) as a clerk/trader assigned to Fort Union. He and Joseph Brazeau had been sent up the Yellowstone River about twenty-five miles to establish a temporary post to trade with local American Indian tribes, which was later referred to as "Brazeau House." Larpenteur described Pellot as an excellent buffalo hunter. In 1835, he was assigned to Fort McKenzie. The 1829 UMO roster lists Joseph E. Braseau (Brazeau) as a clerk assigned to Fort Union. He is mentioned in the Fort Tecumseh Journal on 23 October 1830 boarding the keelboat *Fox* bound for Fort Clark. Kenneth McKenzie sent Brazeau and Pellot to establish a post on the Yellowstone as part of his "divide and conquer" strategy in dealing with Robert Campbell. In 1835, McKenzie refused to rehire Brazeau as a clerk, and sent him to Saint Louis. UMO Employee Data Base; Larpenteur, *Original Journal*, pp. 48n3, 50n23; Jackson, *Voyages of the Steamboat Yellow Stone*, p. 168; Casler and Wood, *Fort Tecumseh and Fort Pierre Chouteau*, p. 26.
105. Jacqués (Jacob) Berger, *see* note 53.
106. Mistakenly written as ".800 cents" rather than eight hundred dollars.
107. The 1830 UMO roster lists Joseph Papin as a boatman assigned to Fort Clark. UMO Employee Database.
108. Louis Saucier was a carpenter who, along with Antoine Luteman, took part in a construction project at Fort Union in 1835. Saucier specialized in finish work, such as doors and windows. Saucier built the mackinaw that Prince Maximilian used to descend from Fort McKenzie in the fall of 1833. Abel, *Chardon's Journal*, p. 377; Maximilian, *North American Journals*, 2:418; Larpenteur, *Original Journal*, p. 48n1.
109. For more on Charles Durocher, *see* note 16.
110. For more on this practice *see* Michael M. Casler, "Fur Traders as Undertakers on the Upper Missouri," *Museum of the Fur Trade Quarterly* 43 (Fall/Winter 2007): 107–14.
111. Johnson Gardner joined Ashley and Henry as a trapper in 1823. He was present when the company was attacked at an Arikara village that same year. He departed for the mountains with John H. Weber after leaving the Missouri River, and for the next several years he led groups of trappers in the Rocky Mountains under brigade leaders Weber and Jedediah S. Smith. In 1830, when he accepted a note of $1,321.48 from Smith, Jackson and Sublette for his beaver furs and moved back to the Missouri River to work as a free trapper. This note served as his working credit at UMO posts for the next few years. He opened his account at Fort Union on 12 July 1831. The next year, Gardner signed a contract to trap and sell his furs at the fort. In the spring of 1833, some of the Arikaras who had recently killed Hugh Glass came into a camp that Gardner shared with a group of trappers near the confluence of the Yellowstone and Powder rivers. When the trappers noticed some of the visitors carrying items belonging to Glass and his companions, they allegedly scalped and burned alive several Arikaras. Johnson Gardner would be killed by the Arikara sometime after January 1835. Harrison Clifford Dale, *The Ashley-Smith Explorations and Discovery of a Central Route to the Pacific, 1822–1829* (Cleveland: Arthur H. Clark, 1918), p. 107n210; James D. McLaird, *Hugh Glass, Grizzly Survivor* (Pierre: South Dakota Historical Society Press, 2016), pp. 87, 103–5; Robert M. Utley, *A Life Wild and Perilous: Mountain Men and the Paths to*

the Pacific (New York: Henry Holt, 1997), pp. 76, 142; Maximilian, *North American Journals,* 2:115, 127–28; Aubrey L. Haines, "Johnson Gardner," in *Mountain Men and the Fur Trade,* 2:157–59; Casler and Wood, *Fort Tecumseh and Fort Pierre Chouteau,* pp. 128–29, 139, 147.

112. The 1834 UMO roster lists Pierre Villandré (Valandre, various spellings) as a hunter assigned to Fort Clark. The 1830 UMO roster lists Pierre Legris as voyager number 217, assigned to Fort Union. In 1831, he is listed as voyager number forty-seven. This passage indicates that he was a beaver hunter by this point. Chardon mentions that Legris and Villandré sold their beaver catch at Fort Clark on 7 November 1834. The next day, Chardon noted that Legris, Joseph Dupuis, and a "Black foot wife" had left for Fort Union (Abel, *Chardon's Journal,* pp. 13–14). Ibid., pp. 290n321, 291n323, 291n324; UMO Employee Database; Larpenteur, *Original Journal,* p. 55n65; Casler and Wood, *Fort Tecumseh and Fort Pierre Chouteau,* p. 144.

113. Vortefeuille; no information.

114. The company kept a close accounting of firearms issued to employees and required that they be returned. Maximilian included Alexis Tibeau, Pierre Beauchamp, and Urban Boldue, a boatman, on a list of the men who accompanied him to Fort McKenzie in 1833. The 1828 UMO roster lists Tibeau (Thibeau, various spellings) as a patron assigned to Fort Clark. The 1833 UMO roster lists Beauchamp as a voyager assigned to Fort Clark. UMO Employee Database; Maximilian, *North American Journals,* 2:257; Swagerty, "View from the Bottom Up," p. 30; Jackson, *Voyages of the Steamboat Yellow Stone,* p. 168; Robinson, notes, in "Fort Tecumseh and Fort Pierre Journal and Letter Books," ed. DeLand, pp. 97–98n23, 239.

115. The 1831 UMO roster lists Antoine Guion as a voyager assigned to Fort Clark. He also accompanied Maximilian to Fort McKenzie in 1833. UMO Employee Database. Maximilian, *North American Journals,* 2:257.

116. For an eyewitness account of the battle, *see* Maximilian, *North American Journals,* 2:393–98.

117. Isadore (Isodoro) Sandoval was a clerk for the Upper Missouri Outfit, assigned first to Fort Union and later to Fort McKenzie. Tension between Sandoval and the notoriously ill-tempered Alexander Harvey erupted during a trip to bring the spring returns downriver. In 1840, a year after he was fired, Harvey journeyed back to Fort Union, where he shot and killed Sandoval in the store. Thompson, *Fort Union,* p. 47; Barbour, *Fort Union,* p. 257n7; Casler and Wood, *Fort Tecumseh and Fort Pierre Chouteau,* p. 244n11; Wischmann, *Frontier Diplomats,* p. 321; Charles Larpenteur, *Forty Years a Fur Trader* (Lincoln: University of Nebraska Press, 1989), pp. 142–46. On Harvey, *see* note 54.

118. The 1830 UMO roster lists Joseph Howard as a winterer assigned to Fort Union and later to Fort McKenzie. UMO Employee Database. For a transfer of property in Saint Louis from Howard to Chardon while at Fort McKenzie, *see* Abel, *Chardon's Journal,* p. 246n185.

119. The 1830 UMO roster lists Auguste Hamille as a winterer assigned to Fort Union. The 1832 UMO roster lists Jean B. Marchand as a voyager assigned to Fort Union. In 1836 he was part of the group of employees who killed six members of the notorious Deschamps family. UMO Employee Database; Jackson, *Voyages of the Steamboat Yellow Stone,* p. 169; Larpenteur, *Original Journal,* p. 49n11.

120. The Plains Ojibwa people moved west from the woodlands of the northern Great Lakes beginning in the eighteenth century, in part seeking opportunities in the growing fur trade. Unlike their eastern relatives, the Plains Ojibwas combined woodland hunting and gathering practices with mounted bison hunting, which allowed them to spread from present-day western Manitoba and Saskatchewan to as far south as North Dakota. Patricia C. Albers, "Plains Ojibwa," in *Handbook of North American Indians,* 13: *Plains,* pt. 1, pp. 652–60.

121. The 1829 UMO roster lists Charles Doucette (Douartte, Dousset, Doucet, various spellings) as a voyager assigned to the Yanctonnais and later Fort Clark. The manner of his death is unknown. UMO Employee Database.

122. Milton G. Sublette, *see* note 57.

123. William Sublette, *see* Brooks's introduction to Campbell, "Private Journal."

124. Michel Dubreuille, *see* note 11.

125. A. (Antoine?) Martin was shot to death in one of the rooms at Fort McKenzie by a member of the Blood, or Kainai, band of the Blackfoot people on 12 August 1833. Maximilian, *North American Journals,* 2:368–69.

126. The 1830 UMO roster lists Louis Ladéroute (Laderente, Laderoute, Laderonte, various spellings) as a voyager assigned to Fort Tecumseh. Maximilian included him on the roster of men who accompanied him to Fort McKenzie in 1833 and later listed him as number fifteen among the men assigned there. UMO

Employee Database; Maximilian, *North American Journals*, 2: 257, 411.

127. Jacob Halsey wrote on 21 October 1834 that Gardner "is still at the mouth of the Running Water River, waiting for the Poncaws, he has passed the summer there, and done nothing in whatever in the way of trade, there Being no Indians there" (Casler and Wood, *Fort Tecumseh and Fort Pierre Chouteau*, p. 139).
128. No information on these three men.
129. President Andrew Jackson appointed Colonel Henry Dodge (1782–1867), who had recently played a key role in the Black Hawk War of 1832, as the commander of a regiment of mounted rangers that traveled to the Red River in 1834. They continued on to the Rocky Mountains the following year. After abandoning plans to journey to the Pacific, Dodge became the first governor of Wisconsin Territory in 1836, and would later represent the state of Wisconsin in the United States Senate. Morgan and Harris, "Galaxy of Mountain Men," pp. 291–92.
130. The steamboat *Assiniboine*. *See* note 55.
131. "Pitch" referred either to a natural product such as pine tar or a petroleum based, tar-like substance. Traders combined pitch with tow or hemp rope to make oakum, which they used for caulking timber joints in mackinaws and keelboats.
132. Hunter; No information.
133. Labonnharde; No information.
134. Legrie Carriera is probably Michel Carrière (Carrier, Cassier, various spellings), a free beaver trapper. In one of the Fort Pierre Letterbooks, William Laidlaw described him as working with another trapped named Janus Parker. Abel, *Chardon's Journal*, p. 313n445 and n449; Casler and Wood, *Fort Tecumseh and Fort Pierre Chouteau*, pp. 107–8. For Valandré, *see* note 104.
135. The one-year contract suggests that T. Louette was an engagé; no information.
136. David D. Mitchell, *see* note 12.
137. Losett; No information.
138. The 1830 UMO roster lists John Latrace (Latress, Latross, various spellings) as a voyager assigned to the Yanctonnais. He is at Fort Clark by 1834. Hainelle; no information. The 1830 UMO roster lists Narcisse Daignaux (Diagneau, Daigneau, various spellings) as a voyager assigned to Fort Union. Maximilian lists him as number thirty-five among the employees at Fort McKenzie in 1833. The 1832 UMO roster lists Frederick Girard (Gerrard) as a voyager assigned to Fort Union. UMO Employee Database. Maximilian, *North American Journals*, 2: 411; Jackson, *Voyages of the Steamboat Yellow Stone*, p. 168.
139. Augustine Sibeau; no information. Alexis LaBombarde spent many years at Fort Union as a hunter, providing meat for the fort's personnel. In 1843, he supplied the Audubon party with meat. Audubon wrote, "He is a first-rate hunter, and powerfully built; he wears his hair long about his head and shoulders, as I was wont to do; but being a half-breed, his does not curl as mine did" (John Francis McDermott, ed., *Up the Missouri with Audubon: The Journal of Edward Harris* [Norman: University of Oklahoma Press, 1951], p. 84n84). LaBombarde married a daughter of the Assiniboine leader Iron Arrow Point, thus becoming a brother-in-law to both the fur trader and ethnographer Edwin Denig and The Light, a well-known member of the tribe. Rudolf Friederich Kurz, *Journal of Rudolf Friederich Kurz*, ed. J.N.B. Hewitt, trans. Myrtis Jarrell (Washington, D.C.: Smithsonian Institution, 1937), pp. 238, 250, 274, 324; Larpenteur, *Original Journal*, p. 51n30. On The Light, *see* note 183.
140. Luiss; no information.
141. The 1830 UMO roster lists Justin Grosclaude as a voyager assigned to Fort Union. He was on the upper Missouri for many years. UMO Employee Database; Abel, *Chardon's Journal*, p. 301n377; Jackson, *Voyages of the Steamboat Yellow Stone*, p. 168.
142. Fort de Prairie likely refers to one of the posts in the Fort de Prairie Department in southern Saskatchewan, which Fort Edmonton administered. Smyth, "Jacques Berger," p. 40.
143. The 1829 UMO roster lists John McKnight as a clerk/trader assigned to the Mandan post (Fort Clark). UMO Employee Database; Abel, *Chardon's Journal*, p. 227n81.
144. Winter and Beckwourth, *see* note 103.
145. Joseph Brazeau, *see* note 104.
146. *Grosse-corne* is the French term for the bighorn sheep (*Ovis canadensis*). At Fort McKenzie, Maximilian paid Pierre D. Papin one hundred dollars to obtain a bighorn skin for his collection. Papin and Dreidoppel returned on 23 August 1833 with the skin of a small bighorn. At Fort Union, McKenzie had promised a horse to any hunter who could bring in a live bighorn, but none could be obtained. Maximilian, *North American Journals*, 2:138, 240; John G. Lepley, "The Prince and the Artist on the Upper Missouri," *Montana: The Magazine of Western History* 20 (Summer 1970): 47; George R. Stewart, Jr., "Popular

Names for the Mountain Sheep," *American Speech* 10 (Dec. 1935): 283–88.

147. Maximilian fell ill on 11 March 1834, eventually coming close to death. Baptiste LeClair, the cook at Fort Clark, thought the prince had scurvy, and began giving him a broth of wild onions (*Allium mutabile*) mixed with small white flowers (*Allium reticulatum*). Within four days, the prince began to recover. The prince was well enough to depart Fort Clark for the downriver post of Fort Pierre on 18 April. Maximilian, *North American Journals*, 3:272–82; Stevens, "Maximilian in North Dakota," p. 167; Abel, *Chardon's Journal*, p. 312n443; Kenneth W. Porter, "Negroes and the Fur Trade," *Minnesota History* 15 (Dec. 1934): 429.

148. James Filteau was the steersman for the mackinaw taking Prince Maximilan's party back to Saint Louis. Maximilian refers to him as "Fecteau" in his journals. He reported having problems with Filteau and J. Maloney (*see* note 18) after they obtained liquor from the steamboat *Assiniboine* as it was passing upriver. Swagerty, "View from the Bottom Up," p. 29; Maximilian, *North American Journals*, 3: 283, 291, 298.

149. The 1832 UMO roster lists Martin Fecteau (Fetceau, Facts, Facto, various spellings) as a voyager not assigned to any post. UMO Employee Database; Jackson, *Voyages of the Steamboat Yellow Stone*, p. 168.

150. Maximilian's party arrived at Fort Pierre on 26 April and in Saint Louis on 27 May 1834. Maximilian, *North American Journals*, 3:287, 328; Casler and Wood, *Fort Tecumseh and Fort Pierre Chouteau*, p. 135.

151. The party finally had fresh buffalo meat to eat on 24 February but ran out of sugar and had to sweeten their coffee with molasses. Maximilian, *North American Journals*, 3:263.

152. C. Morrin; no information.

153. The 1831 UMO roster lists Narcisse Manta as an engagé assigned to Fort Union. That year, he engaged to the company for eighteen months. Rather than re-engage, Manta offered to work off his debt if Hamilton would provide him transportation downriver. In a September 1834 letter to Chardon, Hamilton notes that Manta had gathered hay for the fort's animals. Manta left with Pierre Legris for Fort Clark around 1 October 1834. He would later be associated with the Sioux outfit until 1836. UMO Employee Database; Abel, *Chardon's Journal*, pp. 286–87n306, 290–91n321, 291n326.

154. Jean B. Marchand, *see* note 119.

155. The 1831 UMO roster lists Francois Montagne (Montaignis, Montaigne, various spellings) as a voyager with no post assignment. The 1832 UMO roster lists Daniel Wilson as a hunter with no post assignment. Sicanze is more than likely a misspelling of Sibeau (see note 139). UMO Employee Database; Jackson, *Voyages of the Steamboat Yellow Stone*, p. 169.

156. Frederic Kocland was a clerk assigned to Fort Cass and Fort Union. Larpenteur, *Original Journal*, p. 51n30.

157. After bragging about his "Fort Union Wine" in other letters, Kenneth McKenzie now begins his mea culpa after being reported for having a still in Indian country.

158. John P. Bourke was a storekeeper at the Selkirk colony in Canada. He was wounded at the Battle of Seven Oaks in 1816, when Francois Deschamps, Sr., murdered Governor Robert Semple and others, triggering the family's flight to the Missouri River. Kenneth McKenzie would have probably known Bourke from when he worked for the North West Company in the same area. His name came readily to mind when McKenzie needed to shift the blame for the still at Fort Union. Ross, *Red River Settlement*, pp. 35–40; Barbour, *Fort Union*, pp. 166–71; Thompson, *Fort Union*, pp. 4–7.

159. Michael "Lami" Cerré, *see* note 93.

160. Pascal Gabriel Cerré, *see* note 93.

161. For a reproduced copy of this bill, *see* Maximilian, *North American Journals*, 2:235.

162. The 1830 UMO roster lists Amable Hugron (Hunot, various spellings) as a winterer assigned to Fort Union. He was part of the boat crew who went with Maximilian and party to Fort Clark in October 1833. UMO Employee Data Base; Abel, *Chardon's Journal*, p. 241n148; Maximilian, *North American Journals*, 3:28–30.

163. Toussaint Charbonneau of the Lewis & Clark Expedition.

164. The 1829 UMO roster lists Jean Baptiste Brulé (Brulle, various spellings) as a voyager assigned to the Missouri. Brulé was hired from the Saint Cuthbert parish in Montréal, and is number 181 in the AFC Voyageur Contracts. UMO Employee Database.

165. The 1830 UMO roster lists Louison Frainier (Freniere, Funier, Frenier, Frainiere, various spellings) as a clerk/trader assigned to Fort Union. He was assigned to the Apple River post for the Yanctonnais. Here, he is being sent to escort one of the Vachard

brothers (Charles or Louis) and a skin canoe loaded with meat to Fort Pierre Chouteau. UMO Employee Database; Casler and Wood, *Fort Tecumseh and Fort Pierre Chouteau*, pp. 133–34.

166. Fort Jackson at the Poplar River.
167. John Morgan; no information. This passage describes him as the patroon of a small fleet of mackinaw boats loaded with furs and robes headed to Saint Louis.
168. The steamboat *Assiniboine*.
169. Pierre D. Papin, *see* note 41.
170. Kenneth McKenzie refused to hire either of these men and had them sent back to Saint Louis. Swagerty, "View from the Bottom Up," p. 29.
171. Jean Letup was an engagé whose contract had expired. He still owed the company money, which they hoped to collect in Saint Louis.
172. In 1834, due to unseasonably low water, the steamboat *Assiniboine* became stranded for the winter on the upper Missouri.
173. John Carlisle was captain of the steamboat *Assiniboine* on its 1834 voyage to Fort Union. McKenzie ordered Fort Assiniboine to be built to protect the boat where it had become stranded over the winter. Relations between the traders and boat crew soon became strained. Carlisle's conduct is discussed in letters to follow. Abel, *Chardon's Journal*, p. 298n363; Larpenteur, *Original Journal*, p. 13n29; William E. Lass, *Navigating the Missouri: Steamboating on Nature's Highway, 1819–1935* (Norman: Arthur H. Clark, 2008), pp. 82–84; James A. Hanson and Samantha Eickleberry, "Marginal Men: Lesser Lights of the Fur Trade in the American West, 1800–1865," *Museum of the Fur Trade Quarterly* 50 (Fall/Winter 2014): 13; Tracy Potter, *Steamboats in Dakota Territory: Transforming the Northern Plains*, (Charleston, S.C.: History Press, 2017), pp. 51–52.
174. The Crows had surrounded the fort and run off all the local game, forcing the starving men inside to cut up rawhide parfeches to boil for food.
175. Fort Assiniboine, at the mouth of the Poplar River.
176. Rotten Belly was a prominent River Crow leader. He led the Crows' siege of Fort McKenzie in 1834, which ended when a Blackfeet party came to the fort to trade. Rotten Belly died in a failed charge on a Blackfeet camp after the Crows fled the fort. His actions and subsequent demise led the Blackfeet to push the Crows south. The tribe rarely ventured north of the Musselshell River after 1840. Voget, "Crow," p. 697. For an in-depth biography of Rotten Belly, *see* Denig, *Five Indian Tribes*, pp. 161–84.
177. For detailed archaeological information on these structures *see* Erwin N. Thompson, *Fort Union Trading Post: Historic Structures Report, Part II, Historical Data Section* (Washington, D.C.: Department of the Interior, National Park Service, 1968), p. 195; Lynelle A. Peterson and William J. Hunt, Jr., *The 1987 Investigations at Fort Union Trading Post: Archeology and Architecture* (Lincoln, Nebr.: Midwest Archeological Center, National Park Service, 1990), pp. 115–17, 126–29.
178. La Bras Cassé, more commonly known as Broken Arm, was a Cree Indian chief who accompanied The Light (*see* note 183) to Washington, D.C., in 1831. George Catlin painted Broken Arm's portrait in Saint Louis and the Canadian artist Paul Kane met him near Fort Edmonton in 1848. Ewers, *Indian Life*, pp. 86–89; Paul Kane, *Paul Kane's Frontier: Including Wanderings of an Artist Among the Indians of North America*, ed. J. Russell Harper (Austin: University of Texas Press, 1971), p. 142.
179. The 1833 UMO roster lists Joseph Halcrow (Halcrow, Halcro, Alcrow, Acrow, various spellings) as a clerk/trader assigned to Fort Union. Maximilian claimed he was an interpreter for the Assiniboines. UMO Employee Database; Maximilian, *North American Journals*, 2:234n12; Larpenteur, *Original Journal*, p. 48n3.
180. Rocque; No information.
181. An Assiniboine Indian. Charles Larpenteur mentions him numerous times in his journals in the 1830s.
182. John Francis Alexander Sanford (1806–1857) began clerking for William Clark in the office of the superintendent of Indian affairs in 1825. That year, Sanford became Missouri subagent for the upper tribes, a position he held for the next seven years. Sanford married Pierre Chouteau, Jr.'s daughter Emilie in 1832. After regaining his former position two years later, he went to work for his father-in-law at Pratte, Chouteau and Company as a lobbyist in Washington, becoming immensely wealthy. Sanford is best remembered today as the defendant in *Dred Scott v. Sandford* [sic]. In 1846, Scott, a black slave, had sued Irene Emerson—Sanford's sister, and the widow of John Emerson, who had purchased Scott in 1830—for his freedom. A series of retrials and appeals followed, and in 1853, Emerson, who had moved from Missouri to Massachusetts, transferred ownership to Sanford, who then became the defendant. The case eventually went to the Supreme Court, which in 1857 ruled in favor of Sanford. The decision, particularly Chief Justice Roger B. Taney's incendiary majority opinion, stoked outrage and amplified antislavery

sentiment in the North. The suit allegedly caused Sanford to have a mental breakdown. He died in an asylum in New York in May 1857, two months after the ruling. Abel, *Chardon's Journal*, pp. xxxviii, 251n215, 252n217 and n219; Janet LeCompte, "John F. A. Sanford," in *Mountain Men and the Fur Trade*, 9:351–59.

183. General Jackson (Wah hé muzza, Lye-jan-jan, The Light, or the Shining Man), was the eldest of fifty or so children of Chief Iron Arrow Point of the Stone Band of Assiniboines. Iron Arrow Point (Iron Flint, and Le Gros Francais) had been the leader of the few Assiniboines living on the Missouri River when Lewis and Clark passed through the area. In 1828, Kenneth McKenzie established Fort Union on the advice of Iron Arrow Point and appointed The Light a "soldier" at the post. His primary responsibilities were maintaining order among the Assiniboines when they came to trade and retrieving any of the fort's horses that were stolen. In 1831, The Light was one of four American Indians from the upper Missouri to visit Washington, where he and President Andrew Jackson reportedly exchanged names. Subsequently, many referred to The Light as General Jackson. En route to the nation's capital, The Light met George Catlin in Saint Louis and the artist painted his likeness. The party returned to the upper Missouri on board the *Yellow Stone* on its pioneering voyage to Fort Union. John C. Ewers, *Indian Life on the Upper Missouri* (Norman: University of Oklahoma *Press*, 1968), pp. 76–90; Edwin T. Denig, *Five Indian Tribes of the Upper Missouri: Sioux, Arickaras, Assiniboines, Crees, Crows*, ed. John C. Ewers (Norman: University of Oklahoma Press, 1988), pp. xxxii, 86–88.

184. Andrew Bennett replaced Benjamin Young as captain of the *Yellow Stone* in the fall of 1831, working the lower Mississippi. He was captain when the *Yellow Stone* reached Fort Union the next year and in 1833, when it arrived at Fort Pierre Chouteau along with the *Assiniboine*. There, it loaded up with furs and robes before turning back to Saint Louis. Bernard Pratte, Jr., had taken the *Assiniboine*, along with Maximilian's party, to Fort Union. In the fall of 1833, he captained the *Assiniboine* on the lower Mississippi. John Carlisle replaced him the following spring and led the ill-fated 1834 trip to Fort Union. Jackson, *Voyages of the Steamboat Yellow Stone*, pp. 27, 84, 110; Lass, *Navigating the Missouri*, pp. 82–84.

185. The Mountain-du-Bois or Wood Mountains, are the hills on the Canadian side of the then-unsurveyed international boundary north of Fort Union in present-day Saskatchewan. The Assiniboine, Cree, and Plains Chippewa Indians often wintered here. Larpenteur, *Original Journal*, p. 55n66.

186. McKenzie ordered the building of Fort Assiniboine on the left bank of the Missouri at the mouth of Poplar River to protect the stranded steamboat *Assiniboine* and trade with the Assiniboines and Crees in the area.

187. The 1830 UMO roster lists Auguste Bourbonnais (Bourbonnet, Bouronet, Bourbinnais, various spellings) as assigned to the Yankton post. He had come down from Fort McKenzie to reengage. UMO Employee Database; Swagerty, "View from the Bottom Up," p. 32; Jackson, *Voyages of the Steamboat Yellow Stone*, p. 168.

188. The 1833 UMO roster lists Alexander Kennedy (Kiffer, Keefer, various spellings), "AK" in the text, as a clerk assigned to Fort Clark. In the fall of 1834, he was dispatched from Fort Union to winter at Fort Assiniboine with Lewis Crawford. Kennedy kept a brief journal at Fort Clark, published as an appendix in Abel, *Chardon's Journal*, pp. 206–7n33, 323–30. UMO Employee Database.

189. The Plains Cree people, part of the expansive Cree Nation, began migrating to the plains of western Canada beginning in the late-seventeenth century, becoming a distinct tribe by the 1790s. The development of the fur trade accelerated their move westward. The group had spread throughout the prairies, parklands, and river valleys of present-day Alberta and Saskatchewan by the early nineteenth century. The group blended woodland hunting practices with mounted bison hunting and served as a conduit between western tribes and Canadian fur traders. Regna Darnell, "Plains Cree," in *Handbook of North American Indians*, 13: *Plains*, pt. 1, pp. 638–51.

190. The 1831 UMO roster lists Peter (Pierre) Welsh as having no job title or post assignment. Ebert; no information. Both men may have been freemen trappers. UMO Employee Database.

191. Baria Prennard; no information. The 1831 UMO roster lists Louis Marechal (Marchall, Marchal, various spellings) as a boatman. He is number seventeen on the list of men at Fort McKenzie in 1833. The 1830 UMO roster lists Michel Cancellai (Carisalle, Carifell, various spellings), who would also accompany Maximilian to Fort McKenzie, as a winterer assigned to Rivière Bois Blanc (White River). UMO Employee Database; Maximilian, *North American Journals*, 2:257, 411.

192. The 1829 UMO roster lists Joseph Dupuis (Dupois, various spellings) as a voyager assigned to the Kansas

Outfit. He is assigned to Fort Union the next year. He is number 360 in the AFC Voyageur Contracts. UMO Employee Database.

193. Chouquette Pierrot (Pierot, various spellings) is number twenty-four on Maximilian's list of men working at Fort McKenzie in 1833. Maximilian, *North American Journals*, 2:411.
194. Alacompt and Carpentier; no information.
195. The 1830 UMO roster lists Charles Rondin (Rodin, Roundin, Roqui, various spellings) as a voyager in assigned to the Yanctonnais. He is number ten on Maximilian's list of men working at Fort McKenzie in 1833. UMO Employee Database; Maximilian, *North American Journals*, 2:411.
196. Thomas Dickson, *see* note 98.
197. An iron for clothes.
198. Francois Deschamps Jr., *see* note 101.
199. Joseph E. Brazeau, *see* note 104.
200. L. Marcevan may be Marcereau, who Maximilian listed as working at Fort McKenzie. No other information. Maximilian, *North American Journals*, 2:411.
201. Perhaps Louis Demaray (Demarais, Demary, various spellings) or Narcisse Daignaux, both listed as a voyagers on the 1830 and 1831 UMO rosters assigned to Fort Union. One of these men replaced Joe Howard, a winterer. UMO Employee Database.
202. Fort Cass was abandoned in the spring. Samuel Tullock built Fort Van Buren in the fall of 1835 on the right bank of the Yellowstone near the mouth of the Tongue River. Mark H. Brown, *The Plainsmen of the Yellowstone: A History of the Yellowstone Basin* (Lincoln, Nebr.: Bison Books, 1969), pp. 30–31, 77.
203. Inventories taken at Fort Union in 1834 list "36 red silk hats" and "green & scarlet table covers." Thompson, *Fort Union*, pp. 132–33.
204. Joseph Lafleur was hired from St. Joseph De Chambly parish in Montréal as a winterer, no destination recorded, and is number 603 in the AFC Voyageur Contracts. Swagerty, "View from the Bottom Up," p. 27.
205. The 1830 UMO roster lists Francois Maxan as a voyager assigned to the Yanctonnais. A "Maxans" is listed as a winterer at Fort Union in 1835. UMO Employee Database.
206. Modest Pressey was employed at Fort Union. His wages suggest he was an interpreter. Hanson and Eickleberry, "Marginal Men," p. 62; Casler and Wood, *Fort Tecumseh and Fort Pierre Chouteau*, pp. 150–51.
207. James Andrews, hired in Montréal in 1829, was a voyager assigned to Rivière Missouri and is number thirteen in the AFC Voyageur Contracts. The 1830 UMO roster lists him as assigned to Fort Tecumseh. The same year at Fort Union, McKenzie, worried that Andrews would desert, sent him to Fort Tecumseh for horses. There, Chardon made arrangements with Prince Paul of Württemberg for Andrews to accompany him to Saint Louis on the condition that the prince would pay his account of $187.72. UMO Employee Database; Abel, *Chardon's Journal*, pp. 221–222n73, 229–230n90, 295n337.
208. The 1831 UMO roster lists Jean B. Gaudin as an engagé with no post assignment. UMO Employee Database.
209. The 1830 UMO roster lists Michael Ludlow as a winterer assigned to Fort Union. UMO Employee Database.
210. These buckles were used to secure a saddle or pack saddle to a surcingle belt around a horse's girth.
211. Thomas Stensfeit (Stensfut); no information.
212. The 1830 UMO roster lists Louis Labusier (Labusier, Labussiere, various spellings) as a voyager assigned to the Sawans. He is also on the 1832 roster. UMO Employee Database; Jackson, *Voyages of the Steamboat Yellow Stone*, p. 169.
213. The 1830 UMO roster lists Marcelin P. Lafferrier (Lafiere, Laferriere, Laferiere, various spellings) as a clerk/trader assigned to Fort Union. In 1832, he is a storekeeper and trader at Fort Union. He assisted Lewis Crawford at Fort Assiniboine during the winter of 1834–1835. UMO Employee Database; Abel, *Chardon's Journal*, p. 378; Larpenteur, *Original Journal*, p. 49n14.
214. Sublette and Campbell originally hired Charles Larpenteur (1807–1872) as a common hand. He traveled to the 1833 Rocky Mountain rendezvous before accompanying Campbell down the Yellowstone to help build Fort William. He appears to be the only member of that concern to move over to Fort Union after the sale of that company to the American Fur Company, where Kenneth McKenzie hired him as a clerk, beginning his forty-year career on the upper Missouri. His autobiography, *Forty Years a Fur Trader on the Upper Missouri*, was first published in 1898 and his original journal in 2007. UMO Employee Database.
215. The 1834 UMO roster lists J. Vallee (Vallé, various spellings) as a hunter with no fort assignment. His name is mostly associated with Fort Union. Baptiste Contois (Compton in some accounts), and "le Pette Francais" (Little Frenchman) were Métis. Contois, from the Red River Settlements, died at Fort Union

in the 1837 smallpox epidemic. The Little Frenchman was Jack Rem Kipling's son-in-law. UMO Employee Database; Bernard DeVoto, *Across the Wide Missouri* (Boston: Houghton Mifflin, 1975), p. 418n5; Abel, *Chardon's Journal*, p. 61; Thomson, "'This Wicked Family,'" pp. 2–15; Casler, "'This Outrageous Desease,'" pp. 30–31.

216. Latin for "with the living voice."

217. The rows and columns in this table have been reversed for simplicity in formatting.

218. The steamboat *Assiniboine*.

219. The 1831 UMO roster lists Etienne (Eugene) Labursier as a boatman with no post assignment. UMO Employee Database.

220. Norbert Gulliotte was hired in 1832 from Bourg De William Henry parish in Montréal as a voyager assigned to Rivière Missouri and is number 501 in the AFC Voyageur Contracts.

221. Le Borgne was an Assiniboine chief otherwise known as Iron Arrow Point. *See also* note 183.

222. Hamilton suffered from gout that periodically rendered him "very crabbed" (Larpenteur, *Original Journal*, p. 50n20).

223. Louis Turlick, a clerk at Fort McKenzie. Here, he is discussing the expiation of his current engagement.

224. J. B. Lafontaine was the patron of the keelboat *Maria* en route to Fort McKenzie. Casler and Wood, *Fort Tecumseh and Fort Pierre Chouteau*, p. 129; Hanson and Eickelberry, "Marginal Men," p. 40.

225. Muskrats.

226. "MC" is Mr. Culbertson. This rare order of succession letter reflects the fact that Fort McKenzie was considered the most dangerous post on the upper Missouri. *See also* the following letter to Alexander Harvey.

227. French for "no matter."

228. Henry Charrin was a boatman; no other information.

229. Daniel Lamont, James Kipp, and Lewis Crawford departed Fort Clark on 19 May 1835. They left Fort Pierre Chouteau for Saint Louis around 1 July, on a flotilla of bateaux. Abel, *Chardon's Journal*, p. 32; Casler and Wood, *Fort Tecumseh and Fort Pierre Chouteau*, p. 149. *See also* note 45 on Daniel Lamont.

230. For an eyewitness account of the funeral and burial of The Light, *see* Larpenteur, *Original Journal*, pp. 26–28n33.

231. This quote comes from Friedrich Schiller's poem "The Immutable." The full poem reads: "Time flies on restless pinions—constant never. Be constant—and thou chainest time forever" (Schiller, *Schiller's Poems and Ballads*, trans. Lord Lytton Edward [London: George Routledge and Sons, 1887], p. 60).

232. *See* note 216.

233. John Dougherty described his plans for a garden at Bellevue in 1828: "I wish you to bring or send down all the asparagus and horseradish roots you can find, put them up in a box with earth over them" (Kelly, *Lost Voices on the Missouri*, p. 764n153). *See also* David J. Wishart, *The Fur Trade of the American West, 1807–1840* (Lincoln: University of Nebraska Press, 1979), pp. 101–4; Thompson, *Fort Union*, pp. 43–44; Barbour, *Fort Union*, p. 60.

234. B. Bourdalow's tragic account to Charles Larpenteur appears in Larpenteur, *Original Journal*, pp. 23–24, 50n28. *See also* Gary Peterson, "Antonio Montero and the Portuguese Houses: An Outpost on Powder River," *Rocky Mountain Fur Trade Journal* 2 (2008): 38–40.

235. The 1832 UMO roster lists C. (Louis) Guinard and Alexis Guinard as voyagers with no post assignment and Joseph Harris as an engagé assigned to Fort Union, where he worked as a carter and part-time hunter. The 1835 UMO roster lists Asa Smith as a winterer assigned to Fort Union, where he worked as a carter and common laborer. The same roster lists John Prill (Praal) as a common laborer and A. Bledsoe as winterer, both at Fort Union. Joseph Ruel was a hunter at Fort Union. Henry Robert (Robar) has no job or post assignment on the 1830 UMO roster. The 1834 UMO roster lists Alexis Lacroix as a trader with no post assignment, but he is assigned to Fort Union in 1835. For Modest Pressey, *see* note 206. R. Bouché, F. Desmay, H. Labadiere, E. Labusico, J. Bolingston, M. Helvish, L. Bacarapa, J. Blechere, L. V. Wayotte, A. Solomon, and R. Harper; no information. UMO Employee Database; Abel, *Chardon's Journal*, p. 282n283; Larpenteur, *Original Journal*, p. 49n6, n9, n15, n17; Robinson, notes, "Fort Tecumseh and Fort Pierre Journal and Letter Books," p. 214n267.

236. Fort Van Buren.

237. The 1830 UMO roster lists Maxan Derois (Deroy, various spellings) as a voyager assigned to the Yanctonnais. Henry Mailloux, hired in 1832 from Saint Constant parish in Montréal, was a hunter assigned to Rivière Missouri and is number 731 in the AFC Voyageur Contracts. The 1831 UMO roster lists Joseph Roy (Roi) as a boatman assigned to Fort Union. The 1829 UMO roster lists Alexis Touchette as a voyager assigned to Fort Union. The 1832 UMO roster lists Jean Baptiste Cotte (Coté, Cota, Cote,

various spellings) as a voyager assigned to Fort Union. For Thomas Holmes, *see* note 18. J. Bareis, A. Freseau, B. Grendhouse, B. Guislte, A. Lurman, J. Sevaillen, and P. Kilneuf; no information. UMO Employee Database; Larpenteur, *Original Journal*, p. 49n13.

238. The 1831 UMO roster lists Paul Lecompte as assigned to Fort Union. UMO Employee Database.

239. Fort Van Buren was built near the junction of the Yellowstone River and Rosebud Creek in present-day Rosebud County, Montana, a few miles east of the town of Forsyth.

240. The 1830 UMO roster lists Louis Pinian as a winterer assigned to the Cheyenne River Post. UMO Employee Database.

241. The 1830 UMO roster lists Charles Degrai (Deargen, Degray, Degre, various spellings) as a clerk/interpreter assigned to the Yanctonnais. UMO Employee Database.

242. John Campbell was a clerk/trader; no other information.

243. Kenneth McKenzie returned to Fort Union after a sixteen-month absence.

244. George Catlin noted the importance of good buffalo ponies when he accompanied Kenneth McKenzie on a buffalo hunt in 1832, writing, "He leads the party, mounted on his favorite buffalo horse (i.e. the horse amongst his whole group which is best trained to run buffalo)" (George Catlin, *Letters and Notes on the Manner, Customs, and Conditions of North American Indians.* [London: by the author, 1841], p. 24).

245. The 1835 UMO roster lists Boulié (no first name), who seems to be a hunter, as assigned to Fort Clark. UMO Employee Database.

246. The 1830 UMO roster lists William P. May as a clerk with no post assignment. He was assigned to Fort Clark in 1837. May became a beaver hunter after his first engagement expired and is mentioned in journals kept at Forts Tecumseh, Pierre Chouteau, Clark, and Union. UMO Employee Database; Chardon, *Journal*, p. 274n269.

247. The "Dutchman" referred to here is Peter Miller. *See* note 17 and note 38 in Campbell's "Private Journal."

248. David Adams first went west as a trapper with Capt. Benjamin Bonneville in 1832. After leaving Bonneville, he worked as a beaver trapper on the upper Missouri before becoming a small trader on the southern plains. Newman (no first name) was a beaver trapper who worked with Adams and William P. May. Charles E. Hanson, Jr., ed., "A Letter to David Adams," *Museum of the Fur Trade Quarterly* 33 (Fall 1997): 2–5; James A. Hanson, "The Amazing Journal of David Adams," *Museum of the Fur Trade Quarterly* 34 (Summer 1998): 1–2; Hanson and Eickleberry, "Marginal Men," p. 55. *See also* Charles E. Hanson, Jr., ed., *The David Adams Journals*, (Chadron, Nebr.: Museum Association of the American Frontier, 1994)

249. The 1830 UMO roster lists Louis Bissonette (Bigeau, Bazille, Basil, Bissonet, various spellings) as a clerk assigned to Fort Clark, where he was post manager. He had entered the fur trade with the Saint Louis Missouri Fur Company as a trader with the Mandans. By 1833, he was with the short-lived opposition company. UMO Employee Database; John C. Luttig, *Journal of a Fur-Trading Expedition on the Upper Missouri, 1812–1813*, ed. Stella M. Drumm (Saint Louis: Missouri Historical Society, 1920), pp. 148–49.

250. William Clark appointed William Neil Fulkerson to replace John F. A. Sanford as subagent for the upper Missouri Tribes. Abel, *Chardon's Journal*, p. 252n223.

251. Approximately 175 miles.

252. Cabanné's Post was on the Missouri about twenty-three miles above the Platte River. Gail DeBuse Potter, "Trading Posts of the Central Plains," *Museum of the Fur Trade Quarterly* 43 (Fall/Winter 2007): 77; Casler and Wood, *Fort Tecumseh and Fort Pierre Chouteau*, p. 240n45.

253. Apple River Post.

254. The 1830 UMO roster lists Martin Baptiste Dorion as an interpreter with no post assignment. He is mentioned as the Sioux interpreter in the Fort Tecumseh and Fort Pierre Chouteau journals and letter books. UMO Employee Database; Swagerty, "View from the Bottom Up," p. 20; Casler and Wood, *Fort Tecumseh and Fort Pierre Chouteau*, pp. 8, 17–20, 24, 31, 33, 43.

255. Prince may have been one of McKenzie's slaves.

256. C. Marion was hired in Montréal in 1833 as a tinsmith with no destination listed and is number 743 in the AFC Voyageur Contracts. He would later be assigned to Fort Union. Francois Landry was hired in 1833 from Laprairie parish in Montréal as a winterer with no destination listed and is number 632 in the AFC Voyageur Contracts. The 1835 UMO roster lists D. J. Jabotte as assigned to Fort Union. UMO Employee Database.

257. P. Kamming; no information.

258. H. K. Ortley, a merchant in Saint Louis. *See* "Order for Sundry Articles" in the final letter.

259. Baptiste Dupis, a trapper, was wounded in the foot during the battle at Fort McKenzie in 1833. Maximilian, *North American Journals*, 2:394, 411.

260. Baptiste Dauphin wintered at Fort Clark 1834–1835; no information. There were six other men on the UMO rosters between 1829–1832 with the last name of "Dauphin." Abel, *Chardon's Journal*, p. 295n345.

261. Pierre Chouteau, Jr.

262. Daniel Lamont, *see* notes 45 and 50.

263. C. Marion, *see* note 256.

264. *See* note 39.

265. Fort William (John).

266. The steamboat *Diana* only reached Fort Pierre Chouteau after Captain Halstead insisted on returning to Saint Louis. Casler, *Steamboats of the Fort Union Fur Trade*, p. 22; Casler and Wood, *Fort Tecumseh and Fort Pierre Chouteau*, pp. 148–49.

267. *See* note 77.

268. The 1830 UMO roster lists Vital Papiche as a voyager assigned to the Yanctonnais and later to Fort Union. Jean-Baptiste Laramé was hired in 1832 from L'Assomption parish Montréal as a voyager assigned to Rivière Missouri and is number 652 in the AFC Voyageur Contracts. UMO Employee Database.

269. Colin Campbell's post served the Ogallalas at the forks of the Cheyenne River. Abel, *Chardon's Journal*, pp. 206–7n33; Casler and Wood, *Fort Tecumseh and Fort Pierre Chouteau*, p. 240n44.

270. Latin for "one holding a place."

271. The *Assiniboine* caught fire and burned to the waterline on 3 April 1835 near present-day Bismarck, North Dakota. The loss included 1,185 packs of furs and Maximilian's natural history collection which had been stored at Fort Union to be shipped to Germany. Hiram M. Chittenden, "List of Steamboat Wrecks on the Missouri," in *Annual Report of the War Department: Report of the Chief of Engineers*, Pt. 6 (Washington, D.C.: Government Printing Office, 1897) pp. 3870–92; Casler, *Steamboats of the Fort Union Fur Trade*, p. 12.

272. Kenneth McKenzie departed Fort Union in late summer 1834 for an unplanned vacation to Europe. McKenzie had already intended to travel to Saint Louis to sign the articles that would renew the agreement between the Upper Missouri Outfit and the Western Department for another four years. Upon reaching Saint Louis, however, Pierre Chouteau, Jr., informed him that, like Jean Pierre Cabanné and Peter A. Sarpy, he was banned from entering Indian Country for one year due to the still incident. The articles of agreement were left unsigned, and by default the Upper Missouri Outfit ceased to operate as a semi-independent company, instead becoming an accounting entry on the books of Pratte, Chouteau and Company. In 1835, Chouteau created the Sioux Outfit and appointed Honoré Picotte as its head. The move angered Daniel Lamont and William Laidlaw, prompting the pair to quit and enter the robe trade on the southern plains until Lamont's death. McKenzie wrote this letter to Maximilian to thank him for his hospitality after his return to the fort in 1835. His time there was short, as he returned to Saint Louis soon thereafter. By 1840, McKenzie had become a wholesale grocer in Saint Louis. He expanded into wholesale liquor eight years later and had amassed a fortune by the time of his death on 26 April 1861. Thompson, *Fort Union*, pp. 29–32; Chittenden, *History* 1: 358–62; Mattison, "Kenneth McKenzie," pp. 217–24; Kelly, *Lost Voices on the Missouri*, p. 467; Casler and Wood, "Rise and Fall."

273. Saint Louis merchant Henry K. Ortley. Maximilian, *North American Journals*, 3:332n1.

James Kipp, 1873. *Brigham Young University*

This 1832 George Catlin painting shows Fort Union and its surroundings, including the mouth of the Yellowstone River.
Smithsonian American Art Museum

Kenneth McKenzie. *Missouri Historical Society*

Robert Campbell. *Missouri Historical Society*

The steamboat *Yellow Stone*, seen aground on a sandbar in this famous reproduction of Karl Bodmer's original watercolor, entered the Missouri en route to Fort Union in April 1833. *Missouri Historical Society*

This lithographic print of Karl Bodmer's *Fort Union on the Missouri*, published circa 1843, shows a group of Assiniboines arriving at the fort in 1833. *Yale University Art Gallery*

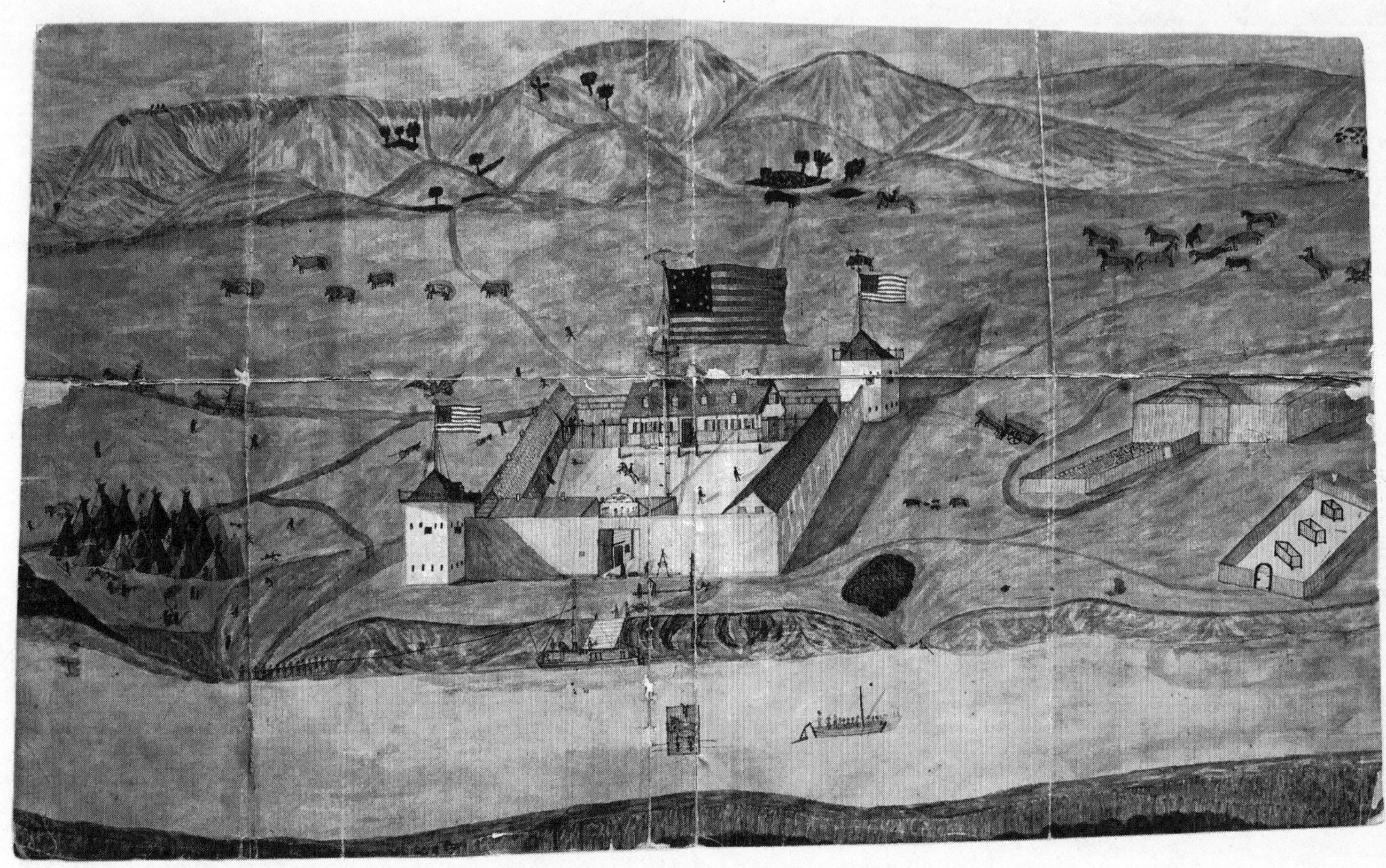

Jean Baptiste Moncravie depicted Fort Union (left) and Fort William (right) in this painting, c. 1843. *Midwest Jesuit Archives*

The Keelboat, by Paul Rockwood. Such vessels remained important even after steamboats were introduced. *National Park Service*

George Catlin painted the Blackfoot chief Stu-mick-o-sucks (Buffalo Bull's Back Fat) at Fort Union in 1832. *Smithsonian American Art Museum*

George Catlin painted this downriver view of Fort Clark and the neighboring Mandan village in 1832. *Catlin,* The North American Indians *(Philadelphia: Leary, Stuart & Co., 1913)*

John Mix Stanley completed this portrait of Alexander Culbertson in 1856, three years after accompanying him on a trip between Forts Union and Benton. *Fort Benton Montana Museums and Heritage Complex*

Bodmer portrayed himself and Maximilian, with David Dreidoppel in the background, being introduced to Hidatsa chiefs by Toussaint Charbonneau outside Fort Clark in this vignette from 1833. *North Dakota Parks & Recreation Department*

Karl Bodmer's *Skin Lodge of an Assiniboin Chief* depicts an Assiniboine camp near Fort Union in 1833. *North Dakota Parks & Recreation Department*

Fort William Feb 28th 1834.

Mr James Bridger

Dr Sir Last Season whilst in the mountains it was not in my power to meet you but I had some Conversation with Mr Fitzpatrick respecting you in which I told him in Case of any Change in your affairs it was my wish that you and him would Come in here and join us. and that I had no doubt we could make some arrangement for your advantage

As Mr Vasquez is now going to meet you I thought better to address a few lines to yourself and to offer any thing in our power to do for you

I hope your hunt has resulted favourably.

Respectfully Your
Obt Servant
Robert Campbell

Robert Campbell wrote this letter to the famed mountain man James Bridger on 28 February 1834. *Missouri Historical Society*

This photo of Robert Campbell's grave was taken in Bellefontaine Cemetery, Saint Louis, Missouri, in 2012. *W. Raymond Wood Collection*

2

THE PRIVATE JOURNAL OF ROBERT CAMPBELL

Transcribed and Annotated by George R. Brooks

Introduction

The Missouri Historical Society has had the good fortune recently to acquire a document of extreme significance, the private journal of Robert Campbell for the period of September 21 through December 31, 1833, covering a portion of his residence at Fort William on the Upper Missouri.* To any serious student of the fur trade, or even the casual reader of histories of Western expansion, the importance of Robert Campbell needs no further explanation, and this introduction will be but a repetition of well-known facts. For the great majority, however, and especially for St. Louisans, Campbell is remembered only as the owner of a handsome mansion on Lucas Place which now, with its original furnishings, is a museum of an elegant Victorian way of life, and the man himself has been all but forgotten.

Campbell arrived in St. Louis from a small town in his native Northern Ireland in 1824. A young man of twenty, he was suffering from a chronic respiratory ailment and soon sought the advice of the leading St. Louis physician, Dr. Bernard G. Farrar. Farrar suggested a rugged outdoor life to cure his symptoms, and so Campbell ultimately joined the trapping operations of General William Ashley in the Rocky Mountains; the prescription not only restored his health, but led him into a career that proved the basis of a large personal fortune. After several years as an expedition leader and an associate of the Rocky Mountain Fur Company, Campbell, with another Ashley veteran, William Sublette, formed a partnership in 1832. The firm of Sublette and Campbell continued in the trade for about a decade, although Campbell himself retired from active life in the West in 1835 to settle in St. Louis, using the capital gained from the fur trade to expand his wealth through a variety of commercial and mercantile operations. At his death in 1879 he was one of the city's leading citizens, and certainly one of the richest.

In the fall of 1833, when the journal commences, Sublette and Campbell had embarked on an ambitious project of opposition to the giant American Fur Company of the Astors and Chouteaus. The undertaking can be interpreted in two ways—and there are compelling arguments for both—either as bluntly straightforward or cunningly subtle. At any rate, the partners set about establishing a series of new posts hard by the existing American Fur Company "forts," with the idea, perhaps, of luring away the Indian trade as an end in itself, or as a means of creating harassments to force the larger firm to terms. The project enjoyed only limited success *per se*; after the Indians had satisfied their curiosity at the new posts they drifted back to trade with the older company. But the opposition must have been convincing enough, for in February of 1834 the American Fur Company officials met with Sublette in New York to divide the trade between the two along geographical lines, the former taking the Upper Missouri area, and the latter confining his company's activities to the mountains.

Fort William, named for Sublette, was situated just below the confluence of the Missouri and Yellowstone rivers. It was some three miles distant by land, and about six by water, from the American Fur Company's Upper Missouri Outfit headquarters, Fort Union, then under the command of Kenneth McKenzie. A shrewd, experienced trapper and the self-styled "King of the Missouri," McKenzie emerges in the journal as the personification of Campbell's opposition and troubles.

After separate journeys during the summer of 1833—Sublette up the Missouri with provisions, and Campbell on a trading expedition through the Rockies—the two partners met at the mouth of the Yellowstone in late August and set about erecting their post. Sublette stayed about three weeks, ill much of the time, and then started his return trip to St. Louis, taking the furs Campbell had obtained. The latter, left in charge of the fort, started his journal the day of Sublette's departure.

Up to now, the principal source for information about Fort William has been Charles Larpenteur's classic, *Forty Years a Fur Trader on the Upper Missouri*;[1] other documents such as the *Fort Union Letter Book*,[2] and scattered references in narratives and letters have been valuable for piecing together facts on activities outside the fort, but only Larpenteur offers anything approaching a feeling for the life within. It is with some regret, therefore, that we cannot find him mentioned by Campbell, despite

Larpenteur's implications that he was one for impressing his superiors as a promising young man. Without destroying the value of his contributions, the omission of Larpenteur from this journal seems rather to confirm a suspicion that his imagination about his personal importance "cherished," as Elliott Coues wrote, "aspirations beyond his powers of accomplishment."[3]

Campbell's journal,[4] a record of significant historical importance as a day-by-day account of a crucial period in the history of the Western fur trade, also reveals the human drama within Fort William among (and partly because of) the band of independent *engagés* it housed. The diary, in addition, captures the thoughts and moods of a rather lonely and certainly conscientious author who evinces sometimes the elation of victory, but more often the despair inherent in a seemingly hopeless struggle against McKenzie and Fort Union. The journal concludes on such a note of reflection, giving way to a final prayer for deliverance in the New Year; one month later Sublette and the American Fur Company came to terms in New York.

The Private Journal of Robert Campbell

Fort William. September 21 1833. Saturday.
Mr Wm L Sublette started by sun rise with the Keel Boat Gallant[5] dismantled of her Cargo Box, and the rigging which was taken [on] board. In the Keel Boat was the returns from the Mountain Outfit consisting of Beaver and Otter skins with some two or *three* Buffalo Robes. Mr Sublette took the greater number of our indifferent hands down and took a few good men amounting in all to Eighteen men—with these men we entered into a new engagement releasing them on their arrival below; after all were on board the amt. was nearly 30. After Mr Sublettes departure I started all hands to move up and we were all in the Fort that evening. Mr Tebo[6] came down with our first raft of Pickets, they were 18 feet long and hewed on one side averaging 10 to 12 inches in diameter. I sent to the Fort the Tub and Sirringe Mr Sublette had borrowed.[7]

Mr Chadron[8] and another man came down after night to see me Without any particular business apparently, but in all probability with some design. They remained until 11 o clock and talked quite sociably.

22 Sunday—I remained in the Warehouse today and after dinner took Mr Janis[9] and Mr Vasques[10] out to the Hills to look for Rock for Chimneys. I succeeded in finding some at about 3 miles distance. Mr Vasques and myself rode up to Fort Union to see the fort and see Mr Hamilton[11] who had sent word he had been sick the day previous. We sat an hour and returned. The old Gentleman shewed me the buildings even to the Ice House and Stables and every convenience of the fort. The Ice House serves for Lumber having a door in the floor and a descent by rope ladder to the Ice.

23—I had all the goods removed into the ware House intended for it and moved into my own House without floor or covering in order to fit out Vasques & Glenday[12] and the party with them to hunt.

24—The men brought down 50 Logs and we kept working at our Houses.

25—Vasques and Glenday were preparing to start today and I had Letters and instructions for them but something was wanting and they could not start.

26—I succeeded in starting them today with 8 men and eight animals having desired Mr Vasques to make out loading for 6 animals. I started Charboneau[13] along to go on express to Fitzpatrick.[14] After starting and crossing the river I directed Manchester[15] and another man to go on hunting and not to stop for Mr Vasques. When Vasques and Glenday went to pack up they had 7 Loads and some extra Baggage. Glenday mounted on a couple of Logs and came back for another animal. I had none and was about to go up and take back part of the equipment but on reflection I concluded to take one of the hunting mules although aware they could have gone on with the number they had. Mr Vasques would not have come back. A man who deserted from the Fort of Tullock[16] came to my Camp and reported that he had been 11 days on the way, that Buffalo were close at hand. The man reported that Winters and Jim Beckwith[17] with two men started to the Crows to Winter there.

27—Last night rained severely and the Houses that were covered with mud let through but those

[that] were covered with dirt kept it out. The weather was very unpleasant and I covered my other houses with dirt.

28th—The weather still unpleasant. I had 3 loads of Rock hauled and a chimney raised about 5 foot high. I received a note from Mr Hamilton stating that he heard a man of theirs had arrived at our fort and requesting that I should desire him to go up. I wrote him an answer stating that the man arrived and applied to me for employment but I declined not knowing his engagements to the Am fur Co and that the man would go up. I got 2 raft Logs. I had a window and door in my House and a floor laid.

Sunday 29th—The little doctor[18] came down to see me and dined with me. I commenced and transfered all the mens accounts from the Book in which they were kept as they did not suit me in their state. I placed them in their proper form. The Dutch Prince of Leyden and his companion arrived from the Blackfeet—he has 2 Bear a fox and other curiosities.[19]

30th—I commenced planting my pickets and got up 38. Had sawyers at work. Got the roof on the second House of the men and had a man cutting Hay. The Hunters arrived with 2 cows being a timely supply. Vasques & Glenday did not find him and consequently he brought back the mule I directed them to take.

Tuesday October 1st—I started off the Hunters again with directions to come loaded when they again returned. I continued raising my pickets and covering second House for the men. The weather continued disagreeable.

2nd—I received a note from Mr Hamilton inviting me to dine and to be made acquaint with the Baron Bransburgh or Prince of Newyd[20] in Germany. I went and passed a pleasant evening in this society. He is a man about fifty years of age who has devoted a great part of his time to travel in the prosecution of subjects for natural History. He has made the tour of South America in search of animals insects and plants heretofore un-described, and thinking our Indian country might afford materials to increase his stock of new discovery, the Prince arrived in St Louis last Spring with an artist (who sketches remarkably well) and a secretary, and embarked in a Steam Boat for this place. He then proceeded to the Blackfoot Fort where he intended to pass the Winter and visit the Rocky Mountains but the living on dried meat was so unpalatable that he concluded on returning. He found it would be unsafe to live amongst the Indians and that operated much on his return. He speaks of wintering at the Mandans. I found him fond of enquiry and anxious to possess all the information he could respecting the mountains in which I endeavoured to satisfy him. He was unfortunate in having his collection wet on descending the river but is now busily engaged in drying them.[21] I invited him to visit me which he promised. I returned about sun set. 2 chipeway and 1 assinaboine Indian came here from Broche[22] and Band De Canoe[23] who are on Knife river amongst Buffalo.

3rd—I set 3 men to make a Perogue today and sent after a raft of pickets to the other side. Five Indians of the Cree nation came to the Fort from their village which was some distance off. I gave them a little Tobacco but did not succeed in getting rid of them. They remained all night. They appear worthless scamps. One of my canoes had broke loose last night but I recovered it a short distance below. I sent after Rock to make a chimney in the mens House but from the distance to haul the Pickets with the few animals I proceed rather slowly. The weather too is disagreeable.

4th—I started Tom Kipland[24] and another man in a canoe up the Yellowstone to kill deer or Elk. I started off the Indians and sent the Canoe to the opposite side to keep it out of their way.

5th—Two men[25] came from the Fort of Tullock who had started on a hunting expedition with Harris[26] but the party broke up without doing any thing. These men met Mr Vasques on the way to whom they sold 2 Horses for 80$ and Vasques drew on us for the amount in Cash. Two of the men also gave orders for mer'd to the amount of six Dollars which I paid in the store. I was dissatisfied with Mr Vasques conduct for purchasing Horses or anything except Beaver Fur to pay in Cash. No doubt he required the Horses but he could have done without unless he could have paid in merch'd. I felt disposed however to honour his dft. Mr Chadron came to the Fort to see the man who did not await his arrival. One of the men owed the Am fur Co 205—(the man who had the order) and Chadron wished to stop him. A canoe was up in the fork of the Yellow stone and the man came down at night. I got the remainder of our Logs from the other side.

Sunday 6—Early this morning I received a note from Mr Hamilton requesting me to retain in our hands the amt. of the 80$ but observing if such were not the custom in company to not allow friendship to interfere. I wrote him in answer that our usage was not to stop any money in our hands but if they got the order I would willingly pay them. The men started off immediately having purchased of me a canoe for 10$ which reduced the draft to 70$ for which I drew on Mr Sublette in St Louis at 3 days and wrote him a letter of advise to that effect. I wrote Mr Dougherty[27] that I would send down a Perogue in two or three days and requesting him to have 60 Bushels corn on hand for Tebo. I directed him in case he sold any thing to these men to endorse it on the back of the order. I wrote Mr Leclerc[28] requesting him in case they bought of him to endorse it on the order, and in case he hired them to have the order if possible—and requested the man not to let the Am fur Co have the order. Yesterday Tom Kipland arrived with an Elk. Our hunters did not arrive here. Almond[29] and several of the men visited the other Fort.

7th—I continued raising the pickets and sent 3 men to work at the Perogue and two to make a canoe with Mr Janis. The Hunters came in having killed six cows but loaded lightly. I concluded as the Buffalo were so far off [30] I would have the mules brought here and send out on the opposite side the Missouri where if I find Buffalo it will be more convenient for me. I suppose it was too late as they have not crossed there tonight. The Cattle thrive well and furnish us with abundance of milk.[31]

8th—I started the hunter and Tom Kipland across the river directing them to go not more than two days if they found no cows but to return with the Bull meat. I got the Perogue and Canoe down here to finish them off.

9th—I started two men hunting in the canoe and directed them to go up the Yellowstone to kill Elk. I got the Perogue finished and started Joe Tebo and three men to the Gro Vont Village for corn. I wrote Mr Dougherty as per copy. A man came from the Crow Indians and told me Rotten Belly was on Gray Bull[32] and Burn on Little Horn.[33] Am fur Co with Burn.

10—The man who came from the Crows last night deserted from fort Union in company with another man. They stole a skiff which they calculated on leaving here and taking our canoe but fortunately it was not launched. Mr Chadron came to look about it and breakfasted with me. I sent an invitation to Baron Bransburg and Mr Hamilton to dine which they accepted. They came early with a Mr Boardman[34] companion to the Baron. I was much pleased with their company and the evening passed off well. They remained until near night.

11th—I had pickets raised today which nearly completed a third side of the fort. And I had a House commenced for workmen, say Blacksmith & Carpenters Shop.

12th—I sent up the men to cut the remainder of the pickets, say 100. They cut 70 on this side the river. At night my Hunters all returned with 5 Deer and 2 Elk.

Two men arrived from the Gro Vonts with a letter from Mr Sublette bearing date 26th and 27th ult.[35] He had proceeded so far well and wrote for more goods and men to be sent to Gro Vonts. He got there 114 Robes and 11 Beaver skins.

13th Sunday—The weather appears Stormy. Most of the men visited the other Fort. I had 2 mules crossed from the opposite side with the intention of sending up the Yellow Stone and have meat killed and brought down in a canoe of skins. When the men went to look for Buffalo on the opposite side they found none and were obliged to return in on the river for Elk & Deer. I am thus reduced to the necessity of again sending up the Yellow Stone but hope my water excursion will succeed.

14th—I again sent up after Logs but owing to 4 of my animals that ran off last night I could not send to haul them in until the middle of the day. I started off my hunters 4 men with 2 mules.

Mr Chadron came down early this morning in consequence of one of His men having a disagreement and refusing to work. He requested that I would not hire him which I assured him was not my intention. He proposed to enter into an agreement to not interfere with each others men which I told him I was perfectly willing to although he returned without my entering into any positive arrangement. He said McKenzie told him if any of our men deserted to not hire them but to afford them a place in the fort. He proposed to enter into a written contract to not hire any man without having a written discharge from their employer, but previously he said a good man they would not give a discharge to. I told him such arrangement I could not make as from his own observation he would not allow us to have any man in the country. He made some observation about entering &c to which I did not attend to. The man came and stopped with my men.

15th—I was about starting two canoes for the Gro Vonts with the men who came up and Joe Ruel[36] and Pierre Walsh.[37] The man who deserted from the other fort applied to go down. I had no objections provided his late employers did not stop him. Accordingly I wrote a note to Mr Hamilton (a copy of which with his answer I have) stating the circumstances. He replied very politely expressing his thanks for my conduct, and being thus apprised I considered I had done all necessary.

16—After Breakfast I started the 2 canoes with the 5 men, viz. Ruel, Walsh, Wash, Vanvalkenburgh,[38] and the dutchman[39] who left the other fort. I wrote Mr Dougherty and Mr Sebille, copies of which I retain. Yesterday morning we had snow which went off early. The weather is so disagreeable that we cannot raft although all the Pickets are cut. We are getting out House Logs. 5 Cree Indians came here today and fired off their guns on their arrival. They are with 40 Lodges of Assinabonn who are coming in but have no meat nor robes. Chardon & the Little Doctor hearing I presume of the arrival of the Indians came down. Their arrival surprised me but Chardon said he came by invitation of Almond to spend the evening and play a game of cards. I entertained them well and they left at 11. The Indians left on their arrival.

17—The Cree chief returned in the evening. Stopped all night and told that when he went to the other fort they would give him nothing because they had been here first. The weather cloudy & cold.

18th—The Indian started *Happy* with a little present I gave him. He gave me 1 Fox skins and a mink. 6 assinabons arrived and the village will come in 2 days—the Band de Filles.[40] One of them gave me a Letter from Dougherty dated Augt 20th. They went to the other Fort a part of day.

19th—More Indians arrived and one lodge came. I got down a raft of Pickets but did not get any hauled. The weather so cold as to have caused great detention. Chadron came to try to get the Indians to pass to their fort.

20th—The Indians came and encamped around the Fort. *Fils* De *Gro Francais*, his *son*, the *White Cow*, the wounded Leg, & The Foolish Bear were the chiefs.[41] I talked with them and gave them a present. They talked fair but had scarce any thing to trade—they were starving. After night I got a few dressed skins & five Robes. I also got a 2 year old Horse for 1½ Gallon. We were kept up all night.

21—The weather moderated and I got up the pickets to the gate and had all prepared for the Gate posts. The Indians started off to the other Fort.

22nd—The Gro Francais came to me for a credit of a Kettle and Gun Yesterday. I credited the kettle but thought both too much. This morning he came back with the kettle and made an excuse about not wishing to take credit not knowing when they would trade. I appeared displeased and he said his wish was for me to exchange his kettle for a Gun. I done this and charged him for it Eight Robes. They crossed the river to hunt up the Yellow Stone. They were crossed at the other Fort. I got down House logs. The Fool Bear who says he will be for us, he got a Gun on credit and wishes to go up the East Side the Yellow Stone.

23—I had a raft made of the last Logs for the Fort and expected to have had the door made today but the wind rose so extremely high that it was impossible. I gave to the men a feast[42] and a little wine in consequence of the fort being done. The two Dechamps[43] who had been hunting returned at the other fort and came down to me. I engaged both—the one Francois as Interpreter and Joseph as Hunter—the one for 500 (Francois) and Joseph 510$. I bought what beaver they had which was in the other fort and for which they were offered 5$. I gave them 6$—in order to have it brought out. They were offered each upwards of 500$ by the Am fur Co.

24th—The Dechamps brought 51½ @ beaver and came here today after flattery and quarrels of the others. The wind high. I got up the remainder of the Logs and the door on its Hinges in the fort and placed myself without guard.

25th—Duro and S. Holcomb[44] arrived from the Mandans with a letter from Mr Dougherty, who thought Wash had been lost or killed. I had sent all he required before hand. Duro contrived for to make a fight with Old Dechamp who came to the Fort and upon the whole acted so badly that I was about to discharge him.

26th—Duro was very penitent and laid his conduct on his being intoxicated. A war party arrived here and says Buffalo are 2 days march from here on this side. They left the village 6 days ago—there is about 100 Lodges. *Brechu*[45] at their head. A quarrel that originated with Chadron and one of their men induced the man to come down but he did not speak to me. I rode up and seen Mr Hamilton and told him I did not wish any of his men and was willing it should be so understood. He assured me his desire was the same and promised to observe the same rules. I engaged to dine with them on Monday previous to Baron Bransburgs leaving it. The weather rather pleasant.

27th—The weather took a total change and it snowed a good deal today. I started off Duro in the evening and in all my intercourse I never was so much annoyed by a man. The most barefaced beggary and open effrontery I ever seen. Several of the clerks and interpreters of the other fort came here but after a short interview they went to the interpreters House and shortly returned accompanied by my interpreters who remained until night and became pretty much intoxicated before their return.

Monday 28th—I started off Joseph Dechamp, Mr Almond and Tessant Demet[46] with 6 animals on this side after Buffalo. The two men I sent up to bring down meat returned without finding the Hunters. I dined at Fort Union and passed an agreeable evening. Last night Joseph Dechamp seduced from the Bed and board of Doctor McCrevee his own lawfully purchased wife which he obtained from her father for the sum of 280$ in merchandise to him in hand paid. This proves the instability of the dear angels—receive them all love and affection and in a week they leave your arms for something new. The little doctor was outrageous but today the fair damsel accompanied her paramour on a Buffalo hunt and thus left her late spouse time to forget her before they again meet.

29—Last night Michael Gravel[47] arrived at the other fort with 40 Beaver. I had long spoken to hire him and buy his beaver but at present with so many I don't care if he comes or not. I sent Tom Kipland and another man up the Yellow Stone after the hunters.

30th—Baron Bransburgh started in a Mackinaw Boat and halted at our landing to bid me good bye.[48] I gave him a Letter of introduction to Mr Dougherty at the Gro Vents as he intends passing the winter there. He is remarkably agreeable and I much regret his leaving. Michael Gravel came down to see me and spoke of forming some arrangement tomorrow or day after. Brazo[49] a clerk at the Fort was sent down as a Spy to see what Gravel was doing here.

Some assinaboins came from the N and report Buffalo abundant.

31—The men I sent up the Yellow Stone return with disastrous news. A party of Indians came on the Hunters and took the two Mules in the night. Manchester followed a little distance and saw them but it would have been imprudent in him to have gone to them. The Hunters had killed 12 cows and had the meat on a scaffold but owing to the laziness of the man Brazo who did not go far enough up when I sent him the hunters remained with the meat until the Indians came on them. They then made a canoe and came here.

November 1st—At the other Fort this was given as a holiday and many of the men came down here.[50] Not knowing that this was any thing particular I did not give our Boys a rest today. Indeed strange as it may appear this day and Christmas are the only two Holidays given to the men. The 4th of July is not kept nor newyearsday.

November 2—My hunters which went out on this side arrived today which relieved me of much anxiety as I had dreaded a loss of these also. Chardon came down here pretty drunk and got beastly drunk with the interpreters before night. He became so very unruly and troublesome that I could scarce avoid putting him out of the fort. He was lying out of doors amongst the Hogs[51] but in consideration of his being Drunk and a clerk to our opponents I determined to bear with him lest it might be construed into malice. My Hunters found Buffalo very scarce. They killed some Bulls and but one Cow, the meat however was acceptable.

November 3rd Sunday—Dr McCrever was sent down by Chardon to Beg excuse for his conduct last night. And in the course of the day Chardon came himself and begged to be excused. He said he was ashamed and sorry for his conduct and observed that I had treated him as a gentleman and he behaved badly. Two men who had been trapping up the Yellow Stone came down with 100 Beaver skins. They encamped above the mouth of the Yellow Stone on the Mo. Mr Janis and myself went to them and I requested them to come down with their beaver. However the other company owed them 600$ and I doubted much we could not get it.

4th—One of the men came to me and breakfasted. I offered 4$ in cash and a deduction of 25 per cent off the goods they purchased on; if they did not require the money for 12 mo. I would give 4.25, at 2 years 4.50—they went up to the other fort and I suppose have made some Bargain there.

5th—I had all the men employed getting punchions[52] and timber to line the fort between the pickets inside. The weather remarkably fine. Yesterday I sent off the hunters up the river with 5 men so that when they killed anything they could send in a skin canoe down and then load their animals and come in.

6th—The weather for a week past has been fine and I have now all my Logs rafted for Ice House Kitchen and an additional House for men. An Indian came from the camp of the Gro Francais requesting I should send to him for to trade meat. I accordingly sent Mr Almond & Pierre Garro[53] with a Horse and Cart and sent amtn., Tobacco, Verm, Knives, awls, &c.[54] The camp is up on the Yellow Stone nearly two days travel. I instructed Mr Almond to leave immediately on finishing his trade and that I would expect him by Saturday night should nothing occur to prevent. In the evening just at dark Mr Tebo arrived from the Gro Vents with a perrouge load of corn. The passage was favourable but for high winds. As it was too late to unload the Perrouge I sent two men to sleep there tonight.

7th—I unloaded the Canoe and found about 40 Bushels corn, a Hoe & 5 pr mockasons. A few Indians came in from the timbered mountain[55] and re- port Buffalo. I traded 2 of their Robes for a small blanket each. The Hunters that I sent below killed a Deer very fat and very large as it was a Buck.

8th—I started down my two hunters below to kill Deer and I would send after them on Monday. I raised the house for the men and covered the Indian House and set about making a chimney in my dining room. Mr McKenzie arrived from below and came opposite the fort.[56] The day was very windy and the river very low and I sent my Canoe across. He sent a man over to go up to his fort and get a Boat down to the Yellow Stone to cross him. He has 15 Horses and six or eight men.

9—I had another raft of punchions brought down. Michael Gravel came to me to hire but would sell his beaver to the Am fur Co. I would not engage him. I went up to see Mr McKenzie and met McCrevie with Letters from Mr Sublette & Andrew.[57] I went on to see McKenzie and sat a few minutes. Poor Mr Janis heard of the Death of his wife and I never saw a man so distracted. Nothing I could say would reconcile him. I let him remain so.

10th Sunday—Last night was very cold and some snow fell this morning. The day was bitter cold. My hunters from below could kill nothing and returned tonight. Mr Almond did not return.

11th—Mr Almond came this morning with a good load of meat from the Indian village. He got to the opposite side yesterday at mid-day but could not be seen from here. I went up to McKenzies fort to see him and had a conversation on the subject of Mr Sublettes Letter.[58] We agree to meet at our fort tomorrow.

12th—According to appointment Mr McKenzie came down to day. I offered him all the merchd at 80 per ct and 8c carriage, the mules & Horses 55$, cows 40$, to pay the mens wages from 1st September, and to fulfil our contracts with them. He would not accept it but said tomorrow he would send me a written proposition which I am well satisfied I cannot accept but I will see it and Judge.[59] I made a proviso that he would take any articles Mr Sublette contracted for and pay expenses attending. I offered to sell the Yanktoney, Mandan, Grovont, Mountain, and Yellow Stone outfit at these prices and to have such men as objected to pass into their employ to be under the command of our clark during their terms of service.

13th—About one o clock I was waked to witness a most extraordinary spectacle in the heavens. A number of Meteors or *falling stars* were seen shooting in all directions and 10, 15, and 20 visible at a time.[60] They continued without intermission until morning and became larger, some remaining suspended as it were two minutes, beautiful and bright. The Am fur Co are about starting an outfit up the Mo[61] and I shall start one also with Mr Janis to establish wherever they do. I suppose it will be some 2 days march above here to keep the Indians from this fort, but I shall establish wherever they do. My Hunters have been out now 10 days and no news of them. I am very uneasy lest something befal them—after night two Squaws came and said they left 2 men with a skin Canoe loaded—and the animals would be here in a day or two.

14th—A party of 12 Lodges of Indians came here today. They are connexions of Francois Dechamps wife. I *treated* them and after night they gave me as present 3 Robes, Fox & Wolf Skins, meat, &c. and in all I traded of them 10 Robes. My Hunters came by land but those in the canoe sunk it so as it is probable I may get it again. The son of the Gro Francais came after night and was so insupportably disagreeable that but for policy I would have turned him out of the fort.

15th—The Ice for the first time began to run in the river and continued during the day. I had the Perrouge hauled out. Manchester came across from the opposite side having killed an Elk & Deer & scaffolded the meat but I cannot cross a Horse after it. I sent up after the meat in the canoe by Kipland and others. I commenced digging my well yesterday, and after sinking 8 feet in sand I came to the alluvial soil of the Missouri where the river has at one time evidently held its course.

16th—Kipland returned with the meat which although rather indifferent adds considerably to our stock of provisions.

17th—Sabbath. The Indians that were encamped here crossed over their Lodges at this place to hunt leaving six of their Lodges here and most of their women. Legreii,[62] a freeman, came to purchase of me a Dog that I brought down the Yellowstone which had left the Boats of the Am fur Co. I had kept him since then. I would not sell him as I required him for use. I had bought 2 dogs of the Assinaboins for each of which I gave a Blanket.

18th—My Dog was missing[63] and I sent up Joseph Dechamp to ascertain if he were in the other Fort, and if he were to bring him down. He went there and saw the Dog but McKenzie and Brazo & Legreii commenced fighting him. Dechamp, I believe, was a little intoxicated. When he came to me and reported the circumstances I wrote a note to McKenzie demanding the cause and sent Mr Almond to bear the letter. He wrote me in answer that Dechamp was drunk and abused them and that, that was the cause. He said he would send the Dog down tomorrow and the man with him.

19th—The Gro Francais sent his son to me to request me to go after meat but the Ice is running so in the river that it is impossible to cross the animals. Yesterday the Jamb blesse[64] came here (his daughter left the other Fort and came with one of my half Breeds). I talked with him and gave a little ½ Gallon Keg to him and he promises fair. The Ice appeared so in the evening that I ventured to cross the animals. I sent 2 mules and a cart by Mr Tebo and Pierre Garro. I sent the old fellow 100 charges amt, 10 plugs Tobacco, 1 Gallon Keg, and a Bottle and file for the meat. They crossed the animals swimming them safely. McKenzie did not send the Dog.

20th—Last night was remarkably mild and the weather seems a little cloudy. I sent off five men with five animals to go up the Missouri and three to kill Buffalo and bring in meat and two to follow the river and ascertain where Chadron has stopped so that I can send to build alongside. An Indian came from the Camp of *Du Foin*,[65] saying he and a part of his camp would come in a day or Two and trade with me. Another Indian came from Muddy[66] at which place he left 18 Lodges Crees and Assinaboines and came for amt. & tob. He saw Buffalo 15 miles from here.

21st—The Indian that came from the Camp of *Du Foin* wishes a white man to go back with him. I sent Brazo with a Bottle of whiskey and 2 twists tobacco and my little Colt for to bring him here. I sent Broken Arm, Laroche (crees) and little Ploo (assine)[67] each 20 charges amt and 2 twists Tob and requested them to send me word when they would have meat. Mr McKenzie wrote me that he could not prevail on Legris to come as he promised but said if I would go up he would hear and Judge the case and concluded hoping our personal feelings were too good to be interupted by a Dog. I wrote him in answer that I had a right to the Dog and valued him more from my attachment for him than for his services and refered him to McCrevie. I don't expect to get him. One of my chickens died today and my Turkey cock died two days ago. Both had internal injuries, and had been ailing for some time. An Indian came to the Forks and I sent for him. I got Robes of him and some meat. I had to give him a present of a Keg, indeed two, before he left.

22nd—The old Foin arrived with only 8 Lodges. His Brother to[ok] the rest to McKenzies Fort. I gave a old Filly on his arrival and a little Barrel. He gave meat, tallow, and Four Robes as present. I gave an Iron bound Keg. His son a fine looking Indian amused me laughing he said it made his bones feel good and he could not avoid laughing. A chief from the Band of Gauche[68] came to me. I treated him well and gave a Looking Glass, & Knife, tob, & amt. He engaged to work for me and exert his influence. Tom[69] came and saw Chardon 50 miles above.

23rd—Today Mr Tebo arrived on the opposite but the river was so full of Ice that I could not bring him across. The weather moderated and the men were employed making a chimney.

24 Sunday—I learned that Legris and Carrier[70] had found a packet of beaver that I lost last Summer[71] and had sold it to McKenzie which was kept secret until Chardon let it out. I went up to McKenzies to see them. McKenzie called them in and in their presence sided with them. Old Hamilton was his ECHO—what McKenzie said Hamilton said. When the men were not present they agreed my side was just. I offered the fellows ½ the Beaver for finding it but they refused. I then told McKenzie I made a demand of him to retain the amount in his hands as we should most certainly sue for it. I dined with McKenzie.

25 Monday—I learned from some of the men who were at the other fort that the Indians had come in to give up the mules stolen from me, but that McKenzie did not allow them. I sent for an Indian to learn the truth. I found it was correct and sent Tom Kipland and Joseph Dechamp to go to Jacksons Camp and endeavour to get them. Three of the 8 Lodges went off to go to the hunt. The Indian that was first here when Mr Sublette was here sent his pipe handle requesting a knife tobacco & amt. I kept the pipe handle & sent the articles by the men. He is called Black Tomoh Handle.[72] In the evening the old Foin gave me two Buffalo Robes. At night the men asked for something to Drink which I gave them as they would probably not meet for some time again. I sent a Letter from Chardon to McKenzie.

26th—Last night the men got very high and I was obliged to stop them. Francois Dechamp came and asked for some—I told him he could have it but that I wished the men to start tomorrow and that they should not drink nor could he get any more. A little while after He came for more which I denied him. He then packed up and prepared to start off. I did not let him but gave him some Liquor and he stopped. We have three Brothers of them and they are the only assinaboine Interpreters and the greatest rascals in the world. This morning Dechamp without assigning any reason went off. Mr Janis started with 8 men and 545.45c worth of goods first cost. He is to build near Chardon.[73] I sent Chas Dechamp with him—he took 2 carts. An Express reached me from the Gro vonts with letters from Sebille and Dougherty requesting more goods. The man on passing white river was met by Assinaboines who took his Horse and ammunition from him but did not further threaten him nor disarm him. One brave who came up took his part. Dougherty writes me the Gro vonts took my mules and would not give them up. He writes me to send the little Colt stolen by the Assinaboines of the Gro vonts and that he would get 10 robes for him. I have reason to believe Francois Dechamp was bought over by McKenzie as on passing there McKenzie gave him a Hat, Waistcoat, and a Keg of whiskey. And what further convinces me, Francois put a robe around him and went up to McKenzie the night previous. I shall meet that rascal McKenzie for this ere long.

27—The weather is remarkably fine and warm. This morning the Broken Arm came to me before I got up and said his Camp was coming and would be here today. I sent two Horses with him for a load of meat which they brought me. The camp in the mean while arrived and I gave them the usual present. I had to give double on a/c of the Assinaboines and Crees. I find the Crees troublesome as they must have what they drink stronger than the Assiniboins and more trouble. I found one of the Crees who speaks pretty good French who answered me as an interpreter. I got a Beaver skin 5 robes and Two Horses the latter 1½ gallon each. McKenzie sent liquor to them and had four men with them to take them off. I started off Pierre Walsh on the opposite side the river with the little Horse but from the danger sent no goods. I wrote to Mr Dougherty as per copy. I have a coal Pit about being burned and am making Chimneys sawing plank and covering Houses.

28th—This morning Wash and Holcomb came from the Gro Vonts and missed Pierre Walsh on the way. They had a letter from Sebille & one from Dougherty. Sebilles letter mentioned that the Am fur Co had arrived and were about to trade at two places with the Yanktonys and wished to know if he could hire a man for a few months who spoke Sioux. I told him to do so if at a moderate price. Some of the Indians came to the opposite side the river, and I crossed them. Tom & Joseph came from the camp where they went for the mules but of course were unsuccessful as the information was false, the Gro vonts having taken them. Mr Hamilton & Doct McKinney[74] came to visit me from the other fort. They took Tea and returned after passing a pleasant evening.

29th [November, 1833] I am now at this place Three months and I can safely say more trouble and less pleasure I never experienced in turn that length of time. What is worse my troubles are but commencing as all the low unprincipled means of annoyance McKenzie can give he is throwing in my way. I fear much the result of our business and as I have cast my fortunes on this die, all my future happiness depends on the turn. Would to God I Was free from it with my loss of time—but reflections are useless. I must only try my best in my present case. Six men of the Am fur Co came here from the Gro vonts and I crossed them over. They had been longer than the express I had and consequently no news later than I had received. It was their sign Wash seen coming up.

30th—This morning I started Wash & Holcomb with goods as per Invoice and a Horse in order to facilitate the trade below. An Indian came in from the band Canoe who says 44 will be here tomorrow but I know not what truth may be in it. I have had the men bring coal and daubing [RW/MC: white washing] the Houses.

December 1st Sunday—The sabbath seems to have been a day that I have not yet abstained from Worldly employments although I hoped to have done so. Yet the arrival of 15 Lodges of the band of 44 (the others went to McKenzies fort) engaged me during the day. I treated them and gave a little barrel as is customary. They then gave me a present of a little Mare and 3 robes 16 Bladders Grease and some meat—all of which they would drink for as that is all they think of. The Crees and assinaboines that were here a few days back left this morning. I found they very troublesome and unprofitable besides. Every man wanted credit to the value of from 3 to 15 robes. I gave but a small credit and loaned them 9 Beaver traps to Hunt with the understanding if they lost them they would pay a large beaver skin for each trap. The calculation of the payment is pretty certain but how much of their trade we may reckon for is more than I can determine.

Monday 2nd—The Brechu sent to me this morning that he was coming with his camp and I sent Tom Kipland to meet him. He brought 40 Lodges. I gave them 2 little kegs and some corn. I then gave the Brechu a chief coat a calico shirt and Breech cloth with an understanding that he was to work for me. How it may succeed I know not, it may be well or otherwise. After night he gave me only 24 Bladders grease a bad commencement. Another Indian the brother to Gro Francais gave me some meat and 1 robe. The old Sonnant[75] came on trade and I got 49 Bladders grease and 32 ps meat besides 3 robes. He traded nothing but Liquor. I have refused in many instances trading for meat of that article which much displeases the Indians. Francois Dechamp returned today but I doubt much how we shall make it. McKenzie has done his best to corrupt him and I expect he has succeeded. McKenzie gives as much whiskey as the Indians can drink for nothing. Barrel after Barrel he sends all around amongst the Indians and these will not trade otherwise.

Tuesday 3 Decr—The Brechu with his camp started today and went to the other fort to cross the Missouri and hunt between the Mo & Y Stone. He promised fair. The Sonnant left dissatisfied that I did not give him 3 or 4 Galloon liqr at parting. He went to McKenzie. The Sonnant wished me to go out to Mouse River[76] to build and trade there but I cannot send as it is 5 days journey and the season too far advanced. Besides I could only expect Muskrat and all land transportation and I have no man I could depend upon to send.

Wednesday 4th—The old Sonnant came back in better humour. He is certainly the greatest rascal I ever met—so troublesome that I could scarce mnge him. I credited him for 6 robes. Night before last the Indians were in liquor and one of them killed the Horse of another a not very unusual occurence amongst them. The one who sustained the loss came for me and offered me his saddle and aparatus which I declined. I gave him a few loads amunition and a piece of Tobacco which seemed to satisfy him.

Thursday 5th Dec.—Last night Joseph Dechamp came to ascertain the amt of his a/c and finding it large he requested to be sent off out of the way of temptation. I told him I would send him to Mr Janis. They then were for a frolic which I was obliged to let them have. McKenzie they say offer them their price to go to him and as there is very little principle amongst them if they be refused they are off. I sent Tom Kipland with him to meet Manchester and escort him past the Indians and return here. I wrote Mr Janis and told him the Horse of Joseph was not at our risk. The well that I am having dug is now so far advanced that we begin to find water. An accident was likely to have occurred but that I prevented it today. The man who digs was about going down in the Tub and entered it before any one had taken hold of the windlass—his weight of course caused a rapid descent which sent the Handle of the windlass with such velocity that the men ran from it. I saw the danger and pumped on it and succeeded in stopping it not however without being much hurt by the handle of the windlass. I nearly fainted but had secured the man from inevitable death as the depth is nearly 23 feet.

Friday 6th—Early this morning Manchester came with three mules loaded—he had killed 7 cows and left the rest of the meat with Mr Janis who had great abundance. Mr Janis had built 3 Houses and wrote me he thought the prospect fair. He said Manchester offered to hire to him but I know not what truth is in it as he denies it. The weather is lowering and appears as though we might soon expect snow. I had the men lining the fort inside with pickets and some preparing for a Boat.

Saturday 7th—The Indians from every direction report that no Buffalo are at hand and in consequence I sent up Manchester with Brazo and 4 animals to bring meat from Mr Janis. We consume an immense quantity of meat. A parcel of Lazy Indians hang about and do as I will they get meat. Pierre Garro asked me privlege to purchase a squaw by doing which he would overrun his account. I allowed him to do so as I am desirous of having him learn to speak the Assinaboin tounge.

Sunday 8th Decr.—This is the first Sunday that we have had without interuption for some time past. No Indians came today and devoted the time to reading the Bible and to writing my Brother preparedly to my sending by an express in a month.[77] Almond went up to McKenzies Fort but brought no news further than that Pierre Walsh was not robbed of the Horse by Indians but that the six men who came up were on the opposite side of the river and fired off their Guns whereupon Pierre left the Horse and ran off. It may be true.

Monday 9th—The water that I got in the well is a little brackish although better than I had expected. We can use use it very well for every purpose. I had 2 carts hauling rock to wall it up. Seven Indians came from the *Cappo Blue*[78] who is coming on trade. He says he will come here. I sent Francois and Tom Kipland to meet them—they are to be here tomorrow. I sent a few plugs tobacco, verm., and powder, and a Bottle. The Cappo Blue sent for a keg but I did not send it. Fasted.[79]

Tuesday Decr 10—This morning the squaws of Francois Dechamp and Tom Kipland ran off as soon as the gate was opened—what effect it may have with these mercurial fellows I cannot say. Jealousy was the cause on the part of the squaws. An Indian whose Lodge is in camp here went after Buffalo to the North but after an absence of 6 days he has returned having killed but one Bull. The Indians who went out on the other side have returned and I have to cross them over—they found Bulls. I commenced walling up my well. The Cappo Blue and some 20 men arrived. They have between 30 & 40 robes. I gave them a little keg and they expecting more I had to give another—after night they made some 6 of them presents. The Cappo Blue gave 5 robes and meat. I gave him a Blue chief coat shirt & breech cloth. He is well satisfied—they want Liquor & nothing else. An old fellow came down from McKenzie who he said had sent him. He said he was told to say our goods were mean, that they would give more and other such stuff. He then asked what I had to say. I told him *nothing* and sent him back.

Wednesday 11th—Last night Manchester was to have returned but he is not yet here today and I feel very uneasy about him. The Indians traded altogether about 30 robes. McKenzie sent down 6 men last night to talk to the Indians but as they were all in the Fort they did not see them nor did I know it until today. They threaten the Indians by saying they will kill their dogs if they come here. I shall notice them when they do something that I can get hold of. The weather most beautiful.

Thursday 12th—The Timber that the men have been sawing has too many Knots to build a Boat of. I have therefore moved them and am having the Logs 18 feet long. The Indians leave here today and I part on good terms with all. Credited Blue Capote 1 gun. I heard that five men with one Horse started up the river from McKenzies fort and I sent Tom and Pierre to overtake them and learn where they were going. Besides I am so uneasy for Manchester that I have sent them to learn the cause of the delay.

Friday 13th—The remainder of the Indians who have been encamped here started up the river today. I parted with all on good terms. Michael Gravel was here last night with Francois Dechamp—Drunk. I have the men working at the well and I expect tomorrow to have it finished. A man from McKenzies fort came here today and stated to me that he had quarreled with McKenzie and wished to know if I would allow him to remain here a few days. I told him he had better return to his employer as I did not wish to take any of his men. I told him he might remain but he had better return.

Saturday 14—The weather being so mild and clear for some time back I was surprised this morning on opening my window to see the ground covered with Snow 2 inches deep—but it is still more surprising that it was not so a month ago. I completed building my well having rock to the top. I covered my kitchen with dirt and have a new saw pit erected to go to sawing on Monday. The day was cold and it felt particularly so as it is unusual. At night it recommenced snowing and blowing. On Saturday night I always invite the clerks to take a Glass of wine and only then.

Sabbath December 15th—Last night two sides of McKenzies new fort was leveled with the ground.[80] He had built a stone and lime foundation and raised his pickets thereon but as it appears something more substantial is required in this country to brave the winds. The Black Tomohawk- handle who left 2 days ago stopped at McKenzies fort and this morning a child of his died. He sent to me to send for it and bring it here but this I would not. I told him he might come here and I would give him wherewith to bury it which he complied with. The Assinaboins envelope their dead in a Blanket or whatever else they have and place them up in a tree where they tie them securely with a cord. I gave a wrapper Blanket and sent some of the men to assist in arranging it. Tom and Pierre returned and much to my satisfaction informed me the Horses and Manchester were safe when he left Mr Janis. They brought a letter from Mr Janis saying he had trade 60 robes—had spent 1 keg and wished a supply which I intend sending. Brazo left Manchester and with Chas Dechamp went amongst the Indians and was gone 3 days. Manchester had not killed but was hunting.

Monday 16th—I raised a cow House in the comer of the fort and have the men getting the remainder of the rails to line the 4th side of the fort. Some getting out Cart timber which I intend to make up into 8 or 10 carts as they are very useful here. The day very cold yet the river not frozen across at this place. I now look with anxiety for the return of Mr Vasques as I think he had ample time to have reached here has he had no bad luck. All we have in this country is held by such a feeble tenure that a night may sweep the success of a hunt.

Tuesday 17th—I felt rather unwell today from a bad cold I have had for some two or three days past. The weather has again moderated a little and we continue our work, preparing to make a Boat and getting the fort regulated inside. I have devoted the House I built for Indians as a stable and Blacksmith shop for this winter and the second House for the men as an Indian House. All the Mud work done since the freezing weather is dropping off and will have to be renewed in the Spring.[81]

Wednesday 18th—This day I received bad news. Capt Stewart[82] writes me by the Am fur Co express that Fitzpatrick was robbed of everything by the Crows, and had started to find Bridger[83]—the Letter was dated 5th Sept.[84] Capt. Stewart draws on us for 99 dollars in favour McKenzie. The letters were accompanied by a note from McKenzie, stating he would in a few days call to see me. No news of Vasques and Glenday. Two of the men of the Am fur Co were killed by the Gros vonts of the Prairie in an engagement near the fort.

Tuesday 19th—Brazo came in the fort by climbing over the pickets last night. I was informed of his arrival and directed him to be watched but he got out again before day light. I sent Mr Almond up to McKenzies fort to get his gun which he obtained not without threatening him. I wrote a note to

McKenzie returning his compliments of yesterday. The articles of Brazo at a high valuation approach the amt he owes us. Brazo says Manchester arrived at Mr Janis camp having only killed one Bull and that we may expect him tomorrow. I am preparing to send Mr Almond up the Yellow Stone to trade.

Friday 20—I completed Mr Almonds preparations and sent his goods across at the mouth of Yellowstone. I sent the animals and had them crossed where the river was Frozen. I sent 8 men along and gave written instructions how to act. Manchester returned yesterday and brought only a Bull's meat along. By an Indian who came from the other Fort I learned some men with one or more Dog trains started last night he knew not where, but the men who went to cross the animals saw it going up the river.

Saturday 21st—Mr Almond started by day light and crossed to his party which proceeded immediately on. A party of assinaboines came in and crossed over to the other fort and traded there (the Fool Bear & White Cow). The river being still open is a great disadvantage to us. McKenzie started down two men to St Louis with an express. The weather still fine. The last of the Indians crossed over the river opposite here yesterday and one crossed back on the Ice which is froze across the river a little way below here.

Sunday Decr 22nd—A few of the men of the other fort came here today and amongst them two who had come from the Crows. I questioned one of them who had been in the Crow village when Fitz was robbed. He said the Crows took all his animals but returned inferior ones in their stead and returned a sack coffee and some Chocolate—about half their Traps and all the guns but one—that Fitz immediately started off for to join Bridger. I went to the Bute below to look at the country accompanied by Francois and David Herbert.[85]

Monday 23rd—Last night one of McKenzies men left him and came here but 5 men came after him and took him back at which I am much pleased. Jack Kipland[86] came down yesterday and not finding Francois returned immediately. Today he came again and after a conversation Francois came to me and asked permission to go to the other Fort which I have allowed although I know it is McKenzie that sent for him either to buy him in one way or other. What a misfortune to have a man so necessary in whom can be placed no dependence. On Saturday night the river froze across opposite this place. I sent Manchester below to hunt and get if possible fresh meat for Christmas. Mr McKenzie rode down to visit me and stopped a few Hours—our conversation was very general. Neither of us wished to come to particulars on any subject. He made me promise to return his visit. He told me the crows who came to Tullocks fort had said Charbone had arrived at their village but said nothing of Vasques or Glenday.

Tuesday 24th—Francois Dechamp returned this morning and said they had made him drunk which prevented his return last night. An Indian came from below and reports Sonnant on white earth[87] with 20 lodges — no Buffalo near. Manchester killed nothing consequently we pass our Christmas without fresh meat. Joseph Dechamp came from Mr Janis Establishment to spend his Christmas here—he met Brazo and another man going up. He brings no news but says there is about 20 Lodges Indians there.

Wednesday Christmas day 25th—At about 4 oclock the men all assembled with fife and Drum in front of my House and fired three salutes and played with great power. I got up and brought them all in and treated them. I then gave them about ½ Gallon wine, some flour, Sugar & Coffee and dried apples to celebrate the day. I went to bed again but they beat the drum so around and around my House that I got up and thus commenced an early Christmas. The day was very fine and as yet we have no snow. Jack Kipland came down from Francois and he got my permission to go up not without letting him understand that it was contrary to my wishes and that I believed they only wanted him to learn the news of our Fort. The men behaved very well although they drank pretty deeply. I had a better dinner than usual and after drinking absent friends and my friend Sublette's health I gave over for the day. The snow is not more than 1 inch deep and our cattle keep fat with what they eat during the day.

Thursday 26th—Francois Dechamp came down this morning and told me that Brazo (a/c Mr McKenzie) had started to go up the Yellow Stone and establish there but I could neither learn where nor what amt. of goods he took along. I prepared a small amt of goods which Mr. Janis wrote for and arranged to send it off tomorrow morning. Three or four of the men were sick and unable to work today owing to their dissipation of yesterday which is always the result.

Friday 27th—I started Mr Tebo Manchester and Joe Dechamp with 2 animals and some goods to Mr Janis and in order to guard against the machinations of the other company I sent them off two Hours before day light and instructed them to not pass in sight of the Fort.

Saturday 28th—The day was more moderate than yesterday. I had the men preparing to make a Mackinaw Boat. I expected Tom this evening but he did not return. We are now living on dried meat solely.

Sabbath 29th—This morning became very stormy high wind and snow which obliged me for the first time to keep up and feed the cows. If I had all our animals here I would be measurably happy—all that are here are snugly Housed. Nothing yet of Mr Vasques. The day continued stormy throughout. After night Francois Dechamp became drunk and threatened to leave. I was very near shooting him. I took back all his stuff and started him but after going to the gate he came back and solicited permission to remain. He said that McKenzie had already given him forty dollars for betraying and carrying the news—that he advised him to raise a quarrel with me and that he would hire him and give seven Hundred dollars per Annum—and that that was the reason he had tried to quarrel. He made a great many excuses and pardoned and so I allowed him to remain probably to leave in a day or two—but having three Brothers of them it will injure us if I send him off.

Monday 30th—I had reason to suspect Dechamp was acting the hypocrite and I directed three of the men to watch him but he started and got over the fort without their knowledge. He had bundled up his clothes which they told me but I desired them to watch close so that if he attempted to go out I could thus find him, and yet he got off without their perceiving him. This will be a severe blow to our trade and it was for this McKenzie debauched him. He stole my Spy Glass. Thermometer at 18 degrees below zero.

Tuesday Decr 31st 1833—This morning was more mild although at sun rise thermometer stood at 18 below zero, and mid day 8, and at sun down 8. I had the boys cutting fire wood but broke my cart wheel which I had repaired again. The Carpenters are preparing more timber for carts. Nothing of Mr Tebo who was to have returned tonight nor of Tom whom I expected back some time ago. The storm has no doubt detained him. And I feel a Hell upon earth on account of the uncertainty of all our affairs—the poorest beggar would scarce exchange situations with me at present and I have vowed if an offer arrives that I can leave this country I will do so forever, for even admitting that we made money (which is more than doubtful) I would not undergo the vexation which I now do for all that could be made here. Send out men and you know not but the property they have is stolen, or that they may be killed. While I was writing Mr Tebo arrived and brought Redmond and Leucot[88] along, and both the animals. Mr Janis had turned off Chas Dechamp and now we have only Joseph who I expect will join with the others, and I will thus be without any one who can speak even enough to trade at that post. I expect to have to recall Mr Almond immediately. Mr Janis had traded 75 robes and some Fox and Wolf skins—and had besides a quantity of meat on hand. Mr Tebo tells me that on Christmas day Doct McKenney and Chadrons men had made a man of straw and set up before Mr Janis Fort door and shot at it and then burned it, as an insult because he would not give them Liquor to drink. Janis says Chardon, Doct McKinney, Old Dechamp and all of them kept drunk all the time. If I had only the liquor they drank to trade to the Indians I would ask no more. It would seem as though all are a pack of rascals together. Another Year has now rolled around and I have much reason to be thankful to a bountiful providence who has preserved me through all the vicissitudes of the past year—and I may for the sake of curisoty make a review of the year bygone.[89] I was this day twelve month in New York at the City Hotel making preparations for this trip—I there enjoyed all the pleasures of the Season and was a few days after joined by my Brother and returned with him to Phila where I remained a short time. I took a farewell of my Brother 18th Jany proceeded to Pittsburgh—thence to St. Louis where I arrived on the 8th Feb and proceeded to make some arrangements for our starting there. On the 8th March I was joined by Mr Sublette and we set about fitting and hiring men. On the 14th April[90] I left with a company of 45 men for the Mountains and Mr Sublette by water with 68 men for this and immediate places with 2 keel boats loaded with merchandize—one remained at the Sioux and one came here. I proceeded directly to the mountains and fortunately sold out our equipment there and returned by the Yellowstone with our furs. In the Big Horn the skin Boat in which I was sunk and I had like to have perished.[91] Thrice I went under water and but for an all wise and all merciful God I should never have seen the termination of this Year. I got safe to shore and succeeded in recovering all but about 4 packs of Beaver and our arms. Besides I lost my saddle bags &c. I recovered again my boat and next day was joined by all the Crow Indians—and here again I must acknowledge my dependence on God who inclined those Indians to treat me kindly and return most of my beaver when they had us completely in their power. And I may here observe that these same Indians 17 days after at the instigation of the American fur Co robbed Mr Fitzpatrick of all he had with him,[92] but of themselves afterwards returned animals for nearly all they had taken.

I proceeded on down to this place where I arrived on the 30th of August and found Mr Sublette who had got here the day previous.[93] We took the next day to select a suitable place to build, and having pitched on this place we set to work. But to my mortification Mr Sublette was taken sick and barely recovered when he left me on the 20th Sept for St. Louis with the returns I had brought down—and I heard afterwards he had got as far as little Mo[94] and was much recovered. I may date my trouble from my arrival here. I had every thing to construct—I had to make a Fort build ten Houses dig a well and make an Ice House not yet built but all is in the fort to construct it. I have 5 carts made and the materials for six more. I have harness for as many—the stuff out for 2 mackinaw boats. I have made 4 canoes and a Perogue, and have established 50 miles above here where I made a Fort and 4 Houses and have sent up the Yellowstone to do the like there.[95] All this work requires much attention and is attended with immense troubles. Even the finding in provisions so many men, so badly provided with animals as we were, was enough trouble for one man. I can safely say as unhappy a time as this I have never before passed during my life. What is worst our prospects are not good for McKenzie has hired our interpreters and bribed them whilst they were here to betray us. But he must answer for this so soon as I get one to whom I can leave this business in charge. At the end of the Year I most gratefully return thanks to an Almighty and all powerful God for his gracious goodness in preserving me through all the dangers I have passed and implore his divine blessing and guidance in all my actions for the coming year. I implore his blessing in all my undertakings and pray his advice in my every action. Great Father grant me wisdom and understanding and judgment to perform my part in all things, and enable me to perform to those under my authority, the part of a lenient master. And do thou O God incline my heart to seek after thee as the one thing needful without which all worldly gain is but dross.

Notes

*This transcription of Campbell's journal, along with George S. Brooks's introduction and annotations, originally appeared in the *Bulletin of the Missouri Historical Society* 20 (Oct. 1963): 3–24 and (Jan. 1964): 107–18. The *Bulletin* divided the installments of the journal between the entries for 28 and 29 November. Brooks's brief introduction to the second installment has been omitted here. The statements in brackets are from Brooks's original. New editorial comments, also in brackets, are preceded by RW/MC. The Missouri Historical Society is now the Missouri History Museum.

1. Charles Larpenteur, *Forty Years a Fur Trader on the Upper Missouri: The Personal Narrative of Charles Larpenteur, 1833–1872*, Elliot Coues, ed., New York, 1898.

2. "*Fort Union Letter Book*, 1833–1835." Mss., Chouteau Collection, Missouri Historical Society (hereafter MoSHi).
3. Larpenteur, xxii.
4. In preparing the journal for publication, the original spellings, abbreviations, and word order were accurately preserved. It was necessary, however, to add punctuation—almost totally absent in the original—to separate sentences and enhance the readability of the text. Even this intrusion has been held to a minimum.
5. Coming upstream the keelboat had been towed from Lexington, Missouri, by the steamer *Otto*, probably as far as Fort Pierre, after which it proceeded on its own. The journey lasted from May 12 to August 29. On the return Sublette reached the Mandan villages on September 25, Fort Leavenworth by November 2, and St. Louis about two weeks later. (See John E. Sunder, *Bill Sublette: Mountain Man*, Norman, Okla., 1959, 236 ff.)
6. On October 9 Campbell refers to this man as "Joe Tebo"; even so his identity is difficult to establish. No record can be found of a Joseph Thibeau (or any variant of the name) in the area at the time, or of an appropriate age. Larpenteur (101-02) mentions "a Canadian named Tibeau" whom he met in 1836, but gives no hint of previous acquaintance. Annie H. Abel, editor of *Chardon's Journal at Fork Clark 1834–1839* (Pierre, S.D., 1932, 283, note 289) states: "There were two possibly of this name [Tibeau] on the Upper Missouri, Jean Baptiste and Alexis." Actually there were two named Alexis: see *List of Advances to Upper Missouri Outfit 1830*, Chouteau Collection, MoSHi, No. 60, Alexis Thibeau, boatman, and No. 61, Alexis Thibeau, steersman and patroon; and *American Fur Company Records*, Vol. "T" (Upper Missouri Outfit), Chouteau Collection, MoSHi: 57 Alexis Tibout, 58 Alexis Thibeau *St. Louis Church Records* show that a Jean Baptiste Thibault was baptized in St. Louis November 26, 1781, and his brother Joseph, age 17, on April 22, 1792, both sons of Joseph Thibault, Sr., and Marianne, an Indian, who were married September 16, 1776. This would make Joseph, Jr., about 58 years old in 1833, far too old a man to consider here. Apparently "Joe Tebo," like many other lesser men in the fur trade, must remain for the present unidentified.
7. Both William Sublette and his brother Milton were in need of medical attention at the time. William was "taken sick and barely recovered when he left" (see December 31 of this journal). Milton had injured his left foot, which, on his return to St. Louis, required daily visits by Dr. Farrar, who changed the dressings frequently and may have drained it; the leg was later amputated (see Dr. R. W. Gaul, "Death of the Thunderbolt: Some Notes on the Final Illness of Milton Sublette," *Bulletin of the Missouri Historical Society*, XVIII, No. 1 (October, 1961), 33-36). Since William's illness has generally been linked with his later tubercular condition, the "tub and sirringe" were more likely borrowed for use on Milton's leg.
8. Francois Auguste Chardon (Campbell sometimes spells it "Chadron") was a veteran employee of the American Fur Company, and a clerk at Fort Union. He was later at Fort Clark (1834–43); in charge of Fort McKenzie (1843); and at Fort F.A.C., which was named for him (1844). He died while in charge of Fort Berthold in 1848. (See Abel, xx, ff., for biographical details.)
9. Antoine Janis, Sr. (not to be confused with his sons Antoine II and Nicholas, who also played roles in the fur and Indian trade). Larpenteur calls him Johnesse (25) and Jeanisse (note, 52), and he therefore became confused with Francois LaJunesse (or Jeunesse) who is No. 46 in the American Fur Company lists of 1830 (Chouteau Collection, MoSHi). Janis appears in a letter of Kenneth McKenzie to Pierre Chouteau, Jr., December 16, 1833 (*Fort Union Letter Book*) as "Geness," and in a draft signed by Wm. Vanderburgh, July 15, 1832 (Chouteau Collection, MoSHi) as "Janice.' The Janis family appears frequently in Kaskaskia records.
10. Louis Vasquez, born in St. Louis October 3, 1798, the son of Benito and Julie Papin Vasquez. For a biography see Leroy R. Hafen, "Mountain Men—Louis Vasquez," *Colorado Magazine*, X (1933), 14-21.
11. James Archdale Hamilton (Palmer), bookkeeper at Fort Union, and in charge during McKenzie's absence. Born in England of good family, he left his native land and dropped his surname "Palmer" because of some unknown and often romanticized difficulties. After several years at Fort Union he came down to St. Louis as cashier for the American Fur Company, resumed his original name (*Missouri Republican*, April 20, 1839), and died in 1848 (see Estate Papers, MoSHi). He was about fifty in 1833; thus Campbell's reference to the "old man."
12. Thomas Glenday had been in the employ of the American Fur Company from August 1831 to June 1832 (*American Fur Company Records*, "T," Upper Missouri Outfit, 300, where he is listed as "Glendy," although on a draft signed by Kenneth McKenzie on

September 15, 1832, he appears as "Glenday." Both in Chouteau Collection, MoSHi). Vasquez and Glenday were to trade with the Crow Indians (see McKenzie to James Kipp, December 17, 1833, *Fort Union Letter Book*).

13. Called "Charbone" in the entry of December 23, this was probably Jean Baptiste Charbonneau, who had been sent by Jim Bridger to locate Campbell in August, 1833. ("The Correspondence and Journals of Captain Nathaniel J. Wyeth," *Sources of Oregon History*, I, parts 3–6, 207–08). and next appears at the summer rendezvous in 1834. He later settled in California. His obituary in the *Placer Herald* (Auburn, Calif., July 7, 1866, 2) gives a resumé of his life. As a youth he had been taken to Germany by Prince Paul of Württemberg for about five years, and it seems strange that Prince Maximilian, who later visited Fort William (see note 19 below) does not mention the presence there of this uniquely educated trapper, a fact which may possibly weigh on the identification in this case. J. B. Charbonneau is generally assumed to have been the son of Toussaint Charbonneau and Sacajawea of Lewis and Clark fame (Anne W. Hafen, "Baptiste Charbonneau, Son of Bird Woman," *Westerners' Brand Book, Denver Posse, 1949*, Denver, 1950, 39-66; W. A. Ferris. *Life in the Rocky Mountains, 1830-1835*, H. S. Auerbach, editor, Salt Lake City, 1940, 56). Toussaint Charbonneau was at this time employed as an interpreter at Sublette and Campbell's Gros Ventres camp.
14. Thomas Fitzpatrick (1799–1854), the famous trapper, trader, guide, and Indian agent.
15. Manchester, first name unknown, appears in *American Fur Company Records*, "V," 182, in the accounts of P. D. Papin. April 28, 1834 (Chouteau Collection. MoSHi). He was a free trader in the Upper Missouri area.
16. Fort Cass, an American Fur Company outpost at the confluence of the Yellowstone and Big Horn Rivers, established by Samuel Tulloch (or Tullock) on Kenneth McKenzie's orders in the fall of 1832.
17. Samuel P. Winter and James P. Beckwourth (whose memoirs were first published in 1856)—like Fitzpatrick and Bridger almost legendary figures in the West—were then associates of the American Fur Company as resident agents, living permanently with the Crows and traveling with their villages.
18. Jean Baptiste Moncrevier, a clerk at Fort Union, also listed in the journal as "McCrevee" (October 28); "McCrever" (November 3); and "McCrevie" (November 21). How he received the title of doctor is not clear. Larpenteur, 72–73, pictures him as a drunkard and libertine, an accusation Larpenteur, a teetotaler, was prone to make. In this case, however, he does not seem to have exaggerated, since Moncrevier was discharged by the American Fur Company in 1845 for alcoholism, and giving liquor to the Indians (*Fort Pierre Letter Book*, October 9, 1845: A. R. Bouis to Culbertson).
19. Campbell refers to Maximilian, Prince of Wied Neuwied, then on his tour of North America. The bears and fox had been obtained at Fort McKenzie a few weeks before. See Reuben Gold Thwaites, *Early Western Travels*, Cleveland, 1904–07, Vols. XXII–XXIV: "Maximilian's Travels in the Interior of North America 1832–34" (hereafter referred to as Thwaites), XXIII, 125.
20. Traveling as Baron Braunsberg, Maximilian landed in St. Louis March 24, 1833, accompanied by his secretary Dreidoppel and a young Swiss artist, Karl Bodmer. On April 10 he left by the American Fur Company steamboat *Yellowstone* for Fort Union, arriving, after a change of boats at Fort Pierre, on June 24. The Prince and his companions continued on to Fort McKenzie for the summer, and then returned downstream to Fort Union.
21. A thunderstorm had swamped his poorly constructed boat the afternoon of September 14, the day his party left Fort McKenzie (Thwaites, XXIII, 169–70).
22. Probably Le Brecheux (Strassaga), a Gens de Fille. For a lively description of his appearance in late June, 1833, see Maximilian in Thwaites, XXII, 370–71.
23. The *Gens de Canot*, a division of the Assiniboine. "Those Canoes were considered at that time the worst band of Assiniboines—great thieves and troublesome traders; they seldom came to the fort and left it without committing depredations..." (Larpenteur, 124, observation made in 1837).
24. Kipland was signed by the American Fur Company in July 1830 at St. Louis as a *voyageur* to be stationed at Fort Union (No. 172 on the 1830 roster, Chouteau Collection, MoSHi). His account in the Upper Missouri Outfit records lists employment through June 1833; he appears again in June 1834 (*American Fur Company Records*, "T," 66). In late 1837 he was employed as interpreter and trader by John B. Sarpy and Henry Fraeb (Chouteau Collection, MoSHi).
25. "You inform me that Bapte. Deguire is employed by you ... when he left Fort Cass in Sept. last he was indebted to A. F. C. $205.04 & engaged to deliver two horses he had to bring down. On his arrival here,

however, he sold his horses to Sublett Co. for $80 and never shewed himself here at all" (K. McKenzie to James Kipp, December 17, 1833, *Fort Union Letter Book*, 7–8).

26. Moses (Black) Harris, a familiar figure in the mountain trade and once one of General W. H. Ashley's employees. At this time he was engaged by the American Fur Company.

27. John Dougherty was Sublette and Campbell's agent at the Gros Ventres village and in charge of their post there, which opposed Fort Clark. Sublette had already instructed Dougherty "to buy 50 or 60 bushels of corn as you may send down for it soon …" (Sublette to Campbell, September 25–27, 1833, Risvold-Semsrott Collection, Minneapolis, Minn.). [RW/MC: The Dougherty in question here is not Indian Agent John Dougherty but in fact his younger brother Hannibal Dougherty, who had been a hunter on the Long Expedition. John E. Sunder appears to be the source of the original confusion over the Dougherty brothers, which modern historians have continued. Mark William Kelly, *Lost Voices on the Missouri: John Dougherty and the Indian Frontier* (Leavenworth, Kans.: Sam Clark, 2013), p. 809n47.]

28. P. Narcisse LeClerc, who had been a clerk at Fort Union (No. 254 in the 1830 Roster). Undoubtedly the LeClerc to whom McKenzie refers in his December 17, 1833, letter to James Kipp: "as he [Campbell] could not sell the Sioux outfit in which LeClerc had a share until Spring …" LeClerc seems to have left the American Fur Company's employ between 1832 and 1834, and then returned. "P. N. Leclerc" appears on Sublette's "Cash Receipts, Yellow Stone Outfit for 1833–4" (Sublette Papers, MoSHi).

29. "William B. Almond, a Virginian who had served as clerk in the Aull brothers' store at Lexington [Missouri], named a son after Sublette, and years later became a territorial judge in California" (Sunder, 102; Larpenteur mentions him, 52).

30. "Mr. Campbell happened to be out of luck this year, owing to the very warm fall of 1833, which kept the buffalo far north …" (Larpenteur, 59).

31. Campbell's party had brought four cows and two bulls along, but one bull died after being bitten by a mad wolf that invaded the camp in mid-August. The cows slowed travel, as their feet were tender and the men had to make raw buffalo-hide boots for them (*ibid.*, 35, 37, 48).

32. Rotten Belly (A-ra-poo-ash), perhaps the most important Crow chieftain of his day. For a biography, see Edwin T. Denig, *Five Indian Tribes of the Upper Missouri*, John C. Ewers, editor, Norman, Okla., 1961, 161–84. Gray Bull refers to the Greybull River.

33. "Burn" has not been identified; he was apparently an Indian chief.

34. The Swiss artist, Karl Bodmer. J. A. Hamilton in a letter to James Kipp, October 29, 1833, calls him "Bordmer" (*Fort Union Letter Book*).

35. The letter, in the Risvold-Semsrott collection, confirms the amount of robes and skins; the bearers were Joseph Wash and VanValkenburgh. Wash appears in Sublette's "Cash Receipts for the Sioux Outfit 1833–34" (Sublette Papers, MoSHi).

36. Joseph Ruel (or Ruelle) appears frequently in the *American Fur Company Records* (Vols. "X" and "GG") from 1836 to 1845, in the Upper Missouri area. He may also be the same Joseph Ruel who married Jeanne Pichereau on July 3, 1838 (*St. Louis Church Records*).

37. Walsh (sometimes listed "Welsh") first appears as a trader in the Upper Missouri Outfit (*American Fur Company Records*, "R" 417) in 1831. He was paid out in St. Louis in November 1832 (*ibid.*, "T," 217).

38. See note 36 above. The extra men were sent at Sublette's request: "You will have to send two or three men down as Ponto have been trying to kill himself so I am force to take him down and have got Van Vulkinburg to stay in his place which is a bad chance …" (Sublette to Campbell, *op. cit.*, Risvold-Semsrott Collection). The "Dutchman" in the entries immediately preceding is Peter Miller, hired by the American Fur Company in St. Louis in April 1831, and listed as a deserter from Fort Union October 13, 1833 (*American Fur Company Records*, "T," 220).

39. John Sebille appears in the American Fur Company Roster of 1830 (No. 260) as a clerk and trader. He apparently held a responsible position under Dougherty, and Sublette states: "I shall take Sabille with me to trade with the Yancktonians …" (Sublette to Campbell, Risvold-Semsrott Collection). He was later re-employed by the American Fur Company (*Records*, "X" 507, as "John Sibille").

40. *Gens des Filles*, a division of the Assiniboine. For a description see Thwaites, XVII, 387. The Dougherty letter cannot be located.

41. Maximilian records the visit of these Indians: "On the 20th of October several distinguished men of the Assiniboins arrived at the fort [Union], among them were Ajanjan (the Son of the Tall Frenchman), generally called General Jackson; Mantouit-katt (the Mad Bear); Huh Jiob (the wounded foot); all three tall, handsome men. Ajanjan, as we were told, was not

to be trusted.... All these people were Stone Indians (Gens de Roche)" (Thwaites, XXIII, 201). Le Fils du Gros Francais was "generally called General Jackson because he had made a journey to Washington (1832). He was a handsome man, in a fine dress; he wore a beautifuly embroidered black leather shirt, a new scarlet blanket, and a great medal around his neck" (*ibid.*, 21). "General Jackson" killed himself soon after this, and McKenzie had him buried at Fort Union [RW/MC: General Jackson (The Light) did not kill himself, but instead was killed in retaliation for another murder. *See* Denig, *Five Indian Tribes*, p. 87]. The White Cow (Pteh-Skah) was "characterized by a long nose, his hair smeared with clay, and his summer robe painted of varigated colours" (*ibid.*, 203). At the time that Denig visited Fort Union the ruling chief of the whole nation was The Foolish Bear (*Ours fou*), Mau-to-weet-ko.

42. The date of completion, and of the feast, differs from previous information, most of which owes its ultimate source to Larpenteur, who implies that these events occurred on November 15 (Larpenteur, 53). Much work must have remained to be done, for Maximilian described the fort as "yet unfinished" on October 30, 1833 (Thwaites, XXIII, 207).

43. The Dechamp (or Deschamp) family figures prominently in Larpenteur. Old Francois with his three sons, Francois, Jr., Charles, and Joseph, appear in this journal. There were also several female relatives, the whole group together being unsavory at best, leaving a long record of robbery and murder. The father, mother, and sons were killed in retaliation for a murder at Fort Union in 1836 (Larpenteur, 94 ff.). There is good reason to suspect that the three Deschamp brothers were spying on Campbell for McKenzie. As McKenzie wrote to Kipp, December 17, 1833 (*Fort Union Letter Book*), "Deschamp's three hopeful sons are in their employ, and are very active." Campbell, quite innocent at first, begins to be aware of the situation by November 26.

44. Probably "Duro" is "Durand," a clerk of Sublette and Campbell under Mr. Dougherty at the Gros Ventres camp, whom Maximilian mentions meeting on November 30 (Thwaites, XXIV, 35). Chardon's *Fort Clark Journal, 1834-1839* contains many references to "Durant"—probably Alexis Durand, who appears in the records of Pierre Chouteau, Jr., & Company as being on the Upper Missouri in 1834 (Abel, 275, note 276), and it would have been natural for Durand to enter the American Fur Company in 1834 through its nearest branch, Fort Clark. Listed in *American Fur Company Records*, "T," 531, is a James Durant who deserted on March 26, 1833, but he cannot be traced further. Samuel Holcomb appears in Sublette's "Cash Receipts of the Sioux Outfit 1833-4" (Sublette Papers, MoSHi).

45. Le Brecheux. See note 22 above.

46. Tessant DeMet cannot be identified either through the American Fur Company lists, or in records in the St. Louis area. A Francois Demay (or Desmay) appears at Fort Union in 1834 and 1835 (*American Fur Company Records*, "X," 155, 166).

47. Michael (Michel) Gravelle, a clerk at Fort Union, is No. 236 on the 1830 Roster. See also Abel, 297, note 360.

48. "On the 30th of October, the weather being fine, we left Fort Union, and stopped for a moment at Fort William, opposite the mouth of the Yellow Stone, to take leave of Mr. Campbell. The thicket of willows on the steep bank of the river had been cut down, in order to open a view to the yet unfinished fort, which is about 300 paces from the bank. Mr. Campbell presented me with some specimens of natural history, and furnished me with cigars, of which we had long been deprived; they really are a great comfort on a long voyage. We took charge of his letters, and having taken leave, proceeded on our voyage" (Maximilian in Thwaites, XXIII, 207).

49. There are two "Brazos" in Campbell's journal. This one is Joseph E. Brazeau, a clerk at Fort Union who appears frequently in American Fur Company Records. The other "Brazo," who appears in the entry of October 31 and thereafter, was in the service of Campbell until deserting on December 19. The identity of this man poses a considerable problem, since there were several Brazeaus in the fur trade at that time. A Baptiste Brazeau was on the Upper Missouri in 1831 (*American Fur Company Records*, "U," 289), with only that reference; Charles Brazeau does not appear until 1836 and was not as shiftless as Campbell's man; Edward Brazeau is also later. Antoine, Auguste, and a Louis Brazeau are all referred to much earlier. The choice seems to narrow down to Jean, Louis (not the same as above), or Nicholas. Jean (or John) Brazeau is probably the mulatto whom Larpenteur encountered in the late 1830's; he appears in *American Fur Company Records* ("U," 5) between July 1831 and August 1832, and again after 1838 ("AA," 330). Campbell's use of "the man Brazo" (October 31) might suggest a colored man of different status from his other employees, but on November 21, in answer to a request for a white man, he sends "Brazo." Larpenteur, furthermore, makes no

mention of having met the man previous to his later association. The American Fur Company engaged Louis Brazeau on August 23, 1831, and Nicholas Brazeau on August 25; both were hired as *voyageurs*, hunters, and winterers to work with Fontenelle & Drips on the Upper Missouri (Chouteau Papers, MoSHi). Nicholas appears to have been working out of Fort Union in the fall in 1833; he received payment on October 22 (*American Fur Company Records*, "U," 389), and is also listed in a long account: "Brazeau & Larente, Tavern Keeper" for the period (*ibid.*, 75), but not afterward. There can be no positive identification of Campbell's man.

50. All Saints' Day was a holiday for the large number of French-Canadian Catholics. On November I, 1836, Chardon also records: "This day being a Holliday with the French nothing in the way of work going on today—"(Abel, 87).

51. Whether there actually were hogs at Fort William, or whether this is a figure of speech, is debatable. Campbell had cattle, chickens, and turkeys—and possibly sheep (see Larpenteur, 17), but there is no other mention of swine.

52. Puncheons, split logs or slabs used as backing between the pickets.

53. Pierre Garreau the younger. Maximilian met the elder Garreau near Fort Clark on November 30: "Stopped at a hut, in which Garreau, an old trader of Messrs. Sublette and Campbell, resided" (Thwaites, XXIV, 35). The younger Garreau had previously worked for the American Fur Company (*Records*, "T," 274) and rejoined them after 1834.

54. "Amtn" (sometimes written "amt") is ammunition; "verm" is vermilion.

55. The Woody Mountains (*Les Montaignes des bois*).

56. McKenzie had been at Fort Pierre during September and October; he left there for Fort Union on October 24.

57. Andrew Sublette, a younger brother of William. For his biography, see Doyce B. Nunis, Jr., *Andrew Sublette, Rocky Mountain Prince, 1813-1853*, Los Angeles, 1960; also Leroy R. Hafen, "Mountain Men: Andrew Sublette," *The Colorado Magazine* (1933), 179-84.

58. The letter Campbell received on November 9 has not been located, but Sublette mentioned the subject to Campbell in a letter of September 25–27: "I shall propose to McKenzie what was talk of but I shall think he will not take yet. if you should succede with him try and get a division of the country" (Risvold-Semsrott Collection).

59. That letter, written on November 13, reads as follows: "On visiting you yesterday I was under the impression that you were disposed to negotiate with me for the transfer on equitable terms of your several establishments, mdze., stock, &c. I listened to your proposition and after I've reflected thereon am constrained to say our views differ so widely that as any offer I could make might to you have the appearance of under-rating the value of your property I decline submitting any proposal to your notice" (*Fort Union Letter Book*, 2). McKenzie wanted to drive out Campbell by cut-throat business competition, and so advised Chouteau, but the advice was not followed, and an agreement was reached in New York between the two firms.

60. The great shower of the Leonids, a meteoric display seen throughout most of the North American continent that night, and well recorded. For another description of the Leonid shower in the West, see Zenas Leonard, *Narrative of the Adventures of Zenas Leonard*, W. F. Wagner, editor, Cleveland, 1904, 187.

61. Campbell refers to Chardon's establishment of Jackson's Camp (or "Fort Jackson") near the mouth of the Poplar River, then *the riviere au tremble* (see also the entry for November 25). The camp was named after Andrew Jackson because Chardon admired him. Its fort was about 80 feet square, complemented with a "snug equipment & 20 men" (K. McKenzie to James Kipp, December 17, 1833, *Fort Union Letter Book*, 3).

62. Pierre Legris, originally hired as a *voyageur* (No. 217 on the 1830 Roster) by the American Fur Company. He became a free hunter and is so listed in later Fur Company records. Campbell also spells his name "Legrici" (November 18), and finally "Legris" (November 21).

63. Campbell stood little chance of getting his dog back. The animals were extremely scarce that fall, since the short supply of buffalo had forced the Assiniboine to eat the dogs they might normally have traded to McKenzie, whose letter in the *Fort Union Letter Book* contains numerous references to his need for them. Later in the winter a shipment of dogs was even arranged from Fort Clark to relieve the situation at Fort Union.

64. *La Jamb Blesse*, an Assiniboin chieftain (See Abel, 286, note 306).

65. Du Foin has not been identified.

66. Fort William was thirty miles upstream from the Little Muddy River, and about the same distance below the Big Muddy, both of which empty into the Missouri.

Larpenteur (124) refers to the "Muddy River, 24 miles below," and this may be Campbell's reference also.

67. Broken Arm, among "the foremost and most renowned of their [the Cree] warriors" (George Catlin, *Illustrations of the Manners, Customs, and Condition of the North American Indians*, London, 1850, 57), was sketched by Catlin in 1832 (Plate 30). His Indian name is given as both "Maschkepiton" and "Bro-cas-sie." Maximilian met him on June 25, 1833: "The chief of the Crees was Maschkepiton (the broken arm), who had a medal with the effigy of the President hung around his neck, and which he had received on a visit to Washington" (Thwaites, XXIII, 13). "Laroche" was a lesser Cree chief; Little Ploo (Campbell's script is not clear here) cannot be located among contemporary Assiniboin records.
68. *Gens de Gauche*. Gauche was the Assiniboine chief who led the attack against Fort McKenzie which Maximilian witnessed in July, 1833. "His name had undergone several changes in the course of his lifetime, as is their custom when fortunate achievements entitle them to this distinction. The first name by which he was known was Chat-Kah or Left Handed, usually called "The Gauche" by the French traders or Indian interpreters. Afterwards this name gave way before that of Tah to'ka nah, or the Antelope, for some exploit in which he distinguished himself, and lastly Me'nah u hi'nah or "He Who Holds the Knife ..." (Denig, 73). Father Pierre Jean DeSmet has a long biography of him in Letter XIII of *Western Missions and Missionaries* (T. W. Strong, New York, 1859).
69. Tom Kipland.
70. Michel Carriere, a free trader on the Upper Missouri. "Legris, Carriere, and Vilandre leave me to hunt on their own a/c" (K. McKenzie to S. Tullock, January 1834, *Fort Union Letter Book*. 36).
71. Presumably some of the beaver lost when Campbell's boat overturned on the Bighorn in August; see also entry for December 31 of this journal.
72. Black Tomahawk Handle, an Assiniboin chief; see also entry for December 15 of this journal.
73. At Jackson's Camp.
74. Dr. George W. McKenney was the son of Thomas L. McKenney, Superintendent of Indian Affairs and co-author of *The History of the Indian Tribes of North America*. News of a cholera outbreak in St. Louis worried McKenzie, and "as there was too much reason to apprehend that it might extend so far, [he] had taken a young physician with him to Fort Union" (Thwaites, XXIV, 14); they arrived on November 8. McKenzie admired the doctor personally, but thought him ill-suited for the menial life of a clerk (K. McKenzie to William B. Astor, December 16, 1833, *Fort Union Letter Book*).
75. Le Sonnant (the Rattle). "Several Cree Indians arrived at Fort Union, among whom was the celebrated medicine man, or conjurer, Mahsette-Kuinab (le Sonnant) whose portrait Mr. Bodmer took with great difficulty because he could not get him to sit still." (Thwaites, XXIII, 200-01.) Nonetheless, the portrait is one of the handsomest and most sensitive in Maximilian's *Atlas*. Campbell, in a letter to his brother Hugh in Philadelphia, dated November 16, 1833, describes Sonnant's appearance and character at great length. The journal gives no hint of this earlier visit (*The Rocky Mountain Letters of Robert Campbell*, printed for Frederick W. Beinecke, New York, 1955, 14–16).
76. Now the Souris River.
77. This letter, largely a description of the Assiniboine, appears in the Beinecke publication, *op. cit.*, 17–20.
78. Le Capot Bleu, an Assiniboine chief mentioned frequently in American Fur Company correspondence.
79. The word "Fasted" appears in large script at the bottom of a page, somewhat apart from the rest of the text. The occasion for, or religious significance of the action is not known. Campbell was a Presbyterian.
80. Maximilian heard at Fort Clark that "the wind had blown down all the pickets at Fort Union" (Thwaites, XXIV, 49).
81. This also happened at Fort Clark (*ibid*, 12).
82. Sir William Drummond Stewart, who had left Lexington, Missouri, with Campbell and accompanied him most of the summer.
83. The renowned trapper, Jim Bridger (1804–81).
84. The famous robbery took place on September 5, the date of the letter, which is unfortunately lost. Whether or not it was instigated by the American Fur Company, Campbell's reference to "bad news" confirms McKenzie's opinion that "this has been a severe blow to Sublett and Campbell" (McKenzie to D. D. Mitchell, January 21, 1834, *Fort Union Letter Book*, 26).
85. David Hebert (voyageur) is No. 28 in the 1830 Roster, and is recorded through July 1832 (*American Fur Company Records*, "T," 33) at Fort Union. He reappears on the Upper Missouri Outfit Ledgers in 1835 as David "Hubert" (*ibid.* "X," 277).
86. John R. Kippland, a freeman, appears on the Upper Missouri Outfit accounts from August, 1831, to June,

1834 (*ibid.*, "T," 265). Larpenteur calls him "Kipling" and it was his murder that led to the eradication of the Deschamp clan (Larpenteur, 97–98).

87. The White Earth River, emptying into the Missouri about eighty miles downstream from Fort William.

88. Possibly the "Redman" to whom Larpenteur refers: "Myself and an individual by the name of Redman started in advance of Mr Campbell ..." (Larpenteur, 12), and "Mr. Redman among the rest, finally got so drunk that Mr. Fitzpatrick could do nothing with him ..." (*ibid.*, 33). Leucot is not identified.

89. Campbell and Sublette had left St. Louis about December 1, 1832, on a trip to the East where they hoped to establish credit and get supplies for the forthcoming enterprise. They spent Christmas with Campbell's brother Hugh, a Philadelphia merchant, arriving in New York on December 30; Campbell returned to Philadelphia the second week in January and then came almost directly back to St. Louis. Sublette continued his business on the east coast, returning by way of Pittsburgh and Louisville (see Sunder, 116–122. Sunder gives the date of March 4 for Sublette's return, not March 8).

90. The date would refer to Campbell's departure from St. Louis. Larpenteur had said he left St. Louis on April 7, two days in advance of Campbell, but Coues, using the original Larpenteur journal, thought it nearer April 13 (Larpenteur, 13 and note). This new date would suggest that Larpenteur must have left on the 11th or 12th. The "45 men" agrees with Larpenteur (*ibid.*, 15, note). Sunder puts Campbell's departure on the 9th, apparently using Larpenteur's reference (Sunder, 125). Campbell implies that Sublette left at the same time, but according to Sunder he departed on the *Otto* between April 16 and 19 (Sunder, 125). Sublette must have left between those dates, for he signed correspondence in St. Louis on the 16th, and Ashley wrote to him c/o Lexington, Missouri, on the 19th (Sublette Papers, MoSHi). He did not, however, go on the *Otto*, for that boat did not arrive in St. Louis from Independence until the 20th; it departed again on May 10 (*Missouri Republican*, April 23, May 14, 1833). It would have been impossible for Sublette to leave on the 16th on the *Otto* and for the boat to return to St. Louis by the 20th.

91. "... he had capsized in the Horn, lost two packs of beaver and been near losing his life" (Larpenteur, 49). See also entry for November 24.

92. This would make August 19 the date for Campbell's accident, and August 20 for his meeting with the Crows.

93. August 29 and 30 for the arrival of Sublette and Campbell respectively seem generally agreed upon by modern writers. Larpenteur had Sublette arriving five days before Campbell. For example, Sunder says, "on a day or two before August 29" (Sunder, 127).

94. The Bad River; at that time the Teton or "Little Missouri."

95. "We were obliged to erect our Posts one was about fifty miles up the Missouri and the other about 80 miles up the Yellow Stone, the former was managed by Mr. Antoine Jeanisse and the latter by Mr. Wm. Almond from Virginia" (Larpenteur, 52, note).

APPENDIX

Letters Concerning Fort William, 1833–1834

Robert Campbell to William Stewart, 25 September 1833

Fort William—mouth of Yellow Stone River
Sept 25 1833
Capt Wm Stewart
Dear Sir

Mr Vasques starts from this place tomorrow for the Crow Country and I take advantage of this conveyance to send you as much of your memorandum as we had at this place being a double barrel Shot Gun and ten pounds of shot which I hope will please—At least the Shot Gun is such as I should have selected for you had I been able to make a more extensive search

I was fortunate on my arrival here to meet Mr Sublette who had just got here the day previous. I have been busily employed since then building houses and preparing for a Fort. Mr Sublette started 20th inst. for St Louis. I sent your memorandum by him & shall be able in the Spring to learn the probability of getting the Red Marble Slabs—Mr Liebiri I have written to and desired him to use every endevour to obtain them—

I hope you will derive pleasure from your Hunt this fall

When it suits your convenience to come here I shall be happy to see you; and can promise you at least the luxury of a chair

I have been several times in company with Mr Hamilton and find him very agreeable. Mr. McKenzie was here on my arrival and was handed the letter you sent by me—he is now gone to the Sioux

Should you require any thing next spring and forward a mem" by Mr Vasques I will endevour to send it to you

Very respectfully
Your obt Serv
Robert Campbell

William Sublette to Robert Campbell, 25, 26, and 27 September 1833

Capt. Robt Campbell
Fort William
Grovent Villiage Sept 25th 1833
Mr. Robt Campbell
Dear Sir

I arrive here this Evening and found all well the Mandans and Grovonlers have just maid peace with the Yancklonain and two hundred Lodges left here to day I shall take Saville down with me to trade with the Yancktonians Mr. [Major?] Doughtery has traded upwards of one hundred Robes and nine Beaver they are in want of copper kettles here and wish you to send all down you think you can spare Some Chiefs coats say haf doz ten or fifteen pounds of stone white and blue beads small and 6 doz bright Red handle knives. Some 1 doz 6 inch flat and 3 square files 2 quire of paper 10 lbs Vermillion some small brass wire and some iron or large brass wire for Wrist bands some oval blue beads and while if you have them to spare 1 goose the largest fire steels a few pair of Striped Blankets the old man Chaibrno thinks he will want some powder and ball in the Spring. Mr. Dougherty has got all his pickets for the fort and the Indians are determined to have a fort here or they will be much dissatisfied. I think you had better send two more good working hands who understand Rafting down here that they may be getting out timber this winter and have all ready for the Spring they want a cross cut saw whip saw and Plow if you can have one made they are in great need of a Cart here and I think you had better send down a pair of wheels and two set of harness and they will have hauling to do if you could get a Bull Boat for those things to come down in it will be best John Ruhan talks of staying here in pontoes place if he does he will fetch you this letter the Indians appear in fine Spirits and have furnished the men with meat for nothing whilst they were getting out the pickets and say as soon as the timbers are ready they will help down with them (some of those articles I have written for Saville thinks he will want there were six of the Aspineoumes here a few days since and after some difficulty they smoke and made a treaty with the Grovonties Mr. McKenzie made a lengthy speech at the Mandans I have been informed and gave out the Big talk as they saying is, they have one trader here he has traded about thirty Robes while Dougherty has nearly tripled him they gave there goods at the same price we do accepting the ammunion and they give 70 Loads whilst we give 60 I stated above that a skin boat would be best but on Reflection those articles I expect will have to come down in a canoe and I can't see how the Cart wheels will be managed which is wanting here worst of any article Likely they can be arrainged on the canoe in some way and you will excuse this letter and try and make out its contents if you can it is now late at night my health is not of the best but I am better than when I left you I have instructed Mr. Dougherty to buy 50 or 60 bushels of corn as you may send down for it soon I think if you was to send down two more kegs of Powder and Ball it would not be a miss as Saville thinks he will want it as there is some of the Sowones with the Yancktonaies and intend wintering with them and he thinks his supplies will fall short.

Yours with Respect
Wm L. Sublette
Capt. Robt. Campbell

I have been thinking if you could send down a Mackinaw Boat here Early in the Spring that is as soon as the ice is out of the river it would be well to take the Robes from this place and those that Saville may have traded down as I think there will be a Mackinaw Boat Load down from those two places if you think best so to do you had better send down word by the Express Mr. Dougherty thinks if he does not get those articles down this fall his trade will fall much shorter as the Copper kettles are all out He is scarce of knives also as it takes a great many knives to trade corn you will have to send two or three men down as Ponto have been trying to kill him self and I am force to take him down and have got Van Vulkinburg to stay in his place which is a bad choice they want a machine for Gulering out posts Mr. Dougherty is placed here in rather an awkward situation the old man Charbino has become quite childish and has to be humored much which makes it very disagreeable and to turn him off it will offend the Indians as he has much influence and will have much his way in trade and he informed the Indians he was going which made considerable disturbance but I have settled the matter today and we must try and Rub out the year with the Old man in some way and likely there can be some changes made next year placing him in one village to him self with some goods. I think Dougherty will do all in his power and I feel in hopes they will make a good trade this year if the Buffalo comes in it would be well for you to come down here when the Yellow Stone returns come down or take a single horse and come down some time in the Spring if possible let them know here if the Mackinaw Boat will be down in the Spring early or so, that Saville may know how to make his arrangements as he will have to purchase some skins of the Indians for a bull Boat three men will fetch the Boat down empty or if you have a few packs to send down in the boat you might do so if they could not take all some might be left here Dougherty will know what Saville has done through the winter I will write by Mr. McKenzie from the teton or Little Missouri river.

Sept 27th

Old McKenzie has told them here that you brought down the yellow stone a boat load whisky and that our men was drunk all that time and that we had been selling it and the news certainly would go below I am now at the Mandans and wind Bound the Indains appear much pleased here and talk fair they talk of Brass Kettles and chief coats all the time Dougherty will be in search of Knives and a few doz of common ones would do well for to trade corn I shall propose to McKenzie what was talked of but I think he will not take yet if you should succeed with him try to get a division of the country Keep your eye skind about trading whisky only Wine

Robe acts Dougherty traded at the grovonty Villages–84

Deaver–11

Down at Mandan Robes–30

One of Dougherty's men said Holcom have made application to trap next year he will hire or take equip or hire for that purpose if you should send the Mackinaw Boat likely you had better send two men with it as I think some of those will wish to stay with Saville and Daugherty will want all with him until the last boat will come down

Wm L Sublette

Sept 25, 26 and 27, 1833

Received October 12 1833

Robert Campbell to Hugh Campbell, 16 November 1833

FORT WILLIAM, Nov. 16th, 1833.

(At the mouth of the Yellow Stone river.)

DEAR BROTHER,—

My time has been so much occupied during the last five weeks, preparing our winter quarters, that I have been obliged to omit my usual monthly letter. You have never built a fort? Then pray Heaven you never may; for of all the trouble and annoyance I have ever experienced, that gives the most. A few days more will enable me to complete the outside of our accommodations, with the exception of an ice house and provision store. We can finish the interior at our leisure. Our fort is 130 by 150 feet—strongly built, with only one well guarded entrance—and inclosing all our houses, stores, &c. The trade has scarcely commenced; but we, and our rivals, are electioneering hard for it;—a business that would puzzle one of your most noisy politicians. Intrigue, bribery and corruption are the order of the day. The Indians feel their importance and maintain it.

Amongst those who lately visited me," was a part of the tribe of Creek Indians, accompanied by their chief Sonnant (anglice "Rattle.") He is a man above the common size, and of very remarkable appearance. When you look at an Indian, you generally try to discover his character from his eye; but the optics of this chief defied scrutiny. They were so embedded between high cheek bones, a hawk nose that exceeds belief, and large shaggy eye brows; that no man, even in your frying and starring city, could tell their colour, without such a look as an Indian brooks not; while my new friend Sonnant could peer into your very soul, without appearing to be looking at you.

His forehead was prominent,—and such were the general developments of his cranium, that without being much of a phrenologist you would at once attribute to him, resolution, to sustain his purposes ; implacable hatred and deadly revenge on those who crossed him. His head surmounted by a huge mass of hair, tied in a knot before, not unlike the mode adopted by some belles among the "white folks," (bless them) but with this difference—the hair was all his own.—His full chest and brawny arms, were tattooed with blue stripes, very regularly laid on; and indeed handsome, after your eye became familiar with it; although at first sight, you would condemn the taste that could admire such horrible and disgusting ornaments. The easy, dignified and elastic step of this chief, proved that he was "born to command." His apparel was simple, but comfortable. A Buffalo robe enveloped him from head to knee. Leggins of Antelope skin ensconced his legs; and plain moccasins protected his feet. Sonnant—or "the

Rattle," as I shall call him, has seven brothers, all of whom are chiefs of subordinate rank in the nation. To their influence, no less than his own savage bravery, is he indebted for the great and powerful ascendancy he maintains among his people. He has several wives, the youngest of whom, scarcely fifteen years of age, was amongst the party who visited me, and evidently proud of her lord and master. He seems to be fully sensible of his important standing; but he has one fault which materially lessened his claims on my respect:—namely, a most sacreligeous contempt for the rules laid down by the temperance society; not one of which will he observe; shame on him!—In other words he is a beastly drunkard.

Such as he was, however, he came to see me; and we had a talk on politics—or trade; which with us are synonymous terms. When we advised peace between nations, it is with a view to our benefit, in traffic:—when we advise war (a thing by the way, we have never done) our motives would be equally selfish. I could make some handsome compliments to myself, on recommending sobriety, when I had no spirits to sell; and very strongly deprecating the use of the "fire water" by our friends the "red skins." The advice was certainly good, be the motive as it may. Indeed such is the world, with all its attempts to dissemble. Self interest predominates; and the only difference in its exercise, in savage and civilized life, is that in the former we acknowledge; in the latter you conceal your motives.

Our smoke and talk, ended like all of a similar character, by me giving him some tobacco, ammunition, and vermilion, in return for many fair promises. He then begged me for something to drink, which he said should be strong, as he was accustomed drinking like his "white fathers." I ordered a pint of wine for himself and suite (enough, of the description we have, to make you and I tipsy) when lo! the old sinner swallowed the whole at a single draught! It was amusing to see his companions looking at him imploringly during the act, and very significantly smelling the empty cup. "The Rattle" soon began to make a noise, and became very troublesome from his loquacity. I paced the apartment with some degree of impatience; and to his solicitations for more drink, gave a flat denial; at the same time leaving the house.—The old fellow (for he has seen nearly sixty snows) in great good humour, paced through the room with his hands on his sides (Buffaloe robes have no pockets) observing that he too was a chief and a "medicine man;" and that he would walk as his father (meaning me) had done. The old rascal had seen enough moons to be my grandfather. His conduct and remarks were irresistibly comic. Our clerks and men, were so highly amused that another bumper was allowed his majesty, who departed greatly pleased with his interview; vowing everlasting friendship; which being interpreted; means, as long as I had wine and goods to give, and he had robes and beaver to trade.

Robert Campbell to Hugh Campbell, 8 December 1833

Copy

Brother Hugh

Decr 8th 1833.

My Dear Hugh

You have often asked me for a description of the Indians that I have been amongst; and particularly my impressions at the first interview. I confess until now I was not sufficiently aware of the difference between the first impressions and those formed after we became familiar. You were right; first impressions are the only that can be satisfactory to one who wishes a correct idea of the appearance of Indians

After our arrival here Thirty Lodges of the Assiniboine Indians came in to the Am. Fur Co's Fort to trade dressed Buffalo Skins; and after finishing their trade, they came to our encampment and stopped a night with us. Their arrival being on the Sabbath I had the better opportunity of observing the difference between them and the Indians I had formerly been amongst, which resulted to the disadvantage of my new friends

At about a mile distant they first drove in sight issuing out of a little ravine where they had made a halt to paint themselves before appearing amongst "The Long Knives" as they term the Americans. They were in number about 60, all men capable of wielding the merciless tomahawk or sending the shaft of death; and woe to the retreating for they pursued—the deer is but little swifter and a hound not more durable than these sinewy sons of the North, who esteem a Horse fit only to pack the fruits of the chase

I might say their appearance was grand—'twas certainly imposing. Imagine to yourself sixty able warriors walking abreast, some with spears fantastically ornamented with scarlet cloth and the feathers of the War Eagle, others carrying the War Club not less beautiful (Horrid should I say?) and all armed with Guns or Bows and arrows.

When they advanced so near as to believe they could be heard by us; they commenced a song expressive of satisfaction at their arrival at the white man's camp—in these songs they generally make the words to suit the occasion which one chaunts and all the rest join in chorus. When they got within two hundred yards of us they swelled and ceased their song: the chief then advanced six paces in front of the war rank and at mid distance, immediately behind him stepped three or four braves who ranked next in authority. Their halt was the signal for me to approach (Mr Sublette was lying sick)—I took my interpreter along and went up to them; I gave my hand to the chief—he was a fine noble looking fellow, as large as Mr Sublette, and possessed of the easy manners common to an Indian chief who ranks himself as second to none that walks the earth—he took my hand and grasped it firmly, ejaculating How! I may here observe an Indian has no good morrow—How dy'r or any other nonsensical greeting such as we use but if you try you will find his How delivers the heart of that pleasing sensation we feel on meeting a friend, better than our salutations. I invited them to proceed and set the example—the march was resumed, every gun was discharged in the air, and the song recommenced which ended only when we stopped to form a circle to smoke; here the same respect to rank was observed as in the march—the plebians formed the outer ring, the braves an inner one and the Chief still nearer the centre—I entered the ring and took my seat vis a vis his Greatness, my interpreter sitting to my left. A glance at the motley group was amusing—a part of them had the face all painted vermillion except the tip of the nose, others painted with vermillion leaving little spots on the forehead and cheek which they painted lead colour; a few had their eyes painted white and the other part of the face red and others again were painted as black as a Nigger; these last having been to war and killed of the enemy, were privileged to thus paint themselves as an honorary mark of distinction between them and those who had not sought Glory in the paths of danger (-their wives and daughters have the same privilege and are more strict in its observance). Everyone paints according to his taste as you may any day see pretty girls dressed in Phila (pardon the comparison) each considering his complexion our dress. After we had lighted a few pipes of tobacco mixed with kinikinick, and had each taken a few ambrosial whiffs in dread silence, I commenced and made them a speech the substance of which was that we came here to build a Fort and trade with them, and the sole object we had in view was benefitting them (I had almost said ourselves) Yes that we came here our sole object to better their condition—that we had a large quantity of merchandise in our boat and hoped we would find them disposed to trade with us, and reciprocate our good feelings. I then presented them with 300 loads amunition 60 plugs tobacco a doz knives and other kickshaws, which I had brought forward as my discourse ended in order to produce effect—I told them this was a small present as ernest of our future conduct, and which I wished them to accept as such—

My plan succeeded—The chief sent forth a "murmur of applause" which was responded by his followers—he then said they were poor. He was grateful for the presents and the words I had spoken which should not enter in one ear and pass out at the other—No they would carry my words under their left arm (near the heart) and when they joined the balance of their nation they would let them hear what I had said; he then finished with fair promises. The present I gave was laid at his feet and now he commenced assisted by his commissary to distribute it amongst his followers according to their station but retained nothing for himself—thus a chief gains popularity and influence, and if they distinguish themselves in war and use sufficient liberality amongst their adherents there is no degree of eminence in their nation to which they may not aspire. Each having received his portion they all arose and went to their several lodges which by this time had arrived.

But how shall I describe their women and the appearance of their camp? Ye gods assist me! After their Lords at a respectful distance came the women in Indian file although between each family was a space of a few yards—The principal squaw took the lead and was followed by her joint partners in the affections of their Husband. And then their Dogs dragging along all the effects of their lodges.

They fasten together at one end 2 poles and lay them on the shoulders of the dog with a strap passing under his neck to pull by, the other end dragging the ground, and immediately behind the dog is a hoop worked like a sifter and fastened to the poles to keep them firm and apart; on this is placed 50–60 or 80 lb baggage which their poor animals haul a days march. What would you say to see a child two or three years old fastened on one of these drags enjoying his ride seemingly as much as one of our little urchins of the same age would ride in a gig or a carriage with us. The howling of the poor dogs and scolding of the women produced such a disagreeable noise that I was glad to see the place selected for the encampment and the squaws set about their several duties of unloading the dogs pitching the Lodges, collecting wood and carrying water and finally (all being arranged) sitting down on the sweet scented floors of their wigwams well arranged and provided in the short space of half an hour.

The dress of the women was well adapted to their situation - Short frocks of antelope skin reaching just below the knee (as best adapted for walking) worked with porcupine quills—Beaded leggings and plain mocassans comprise their dress with an envelope of Buffalo skin or a blanket

Their Lodges when erected looked really fine, and at once reminded me of days by-gone when I have seen on a handsome meadow bordering one of our enchanting mountain streams, a city (village) of Two Hundred Lodges, more gracefully proportioned than your finest houses spring up as it were by magic and one or two thousand horses feeding luxuriantly, where but an hour before the Deer startled by the tainted gale accompanying the approach of its enemy Man had fled from the pasture it had long occupied apparently secure form the stealthy step of the prowling Hunter—

An Assiniboine village although wanting in my eyes the greatest ornament—Fine Horses, is more beautiful than you can imagine and I am certain it would make a handsomer view for those magnifying glasses at the Museum, than the arrival of the pilgrims at Mecca (I don't know if I be right in the name of this [triumphant?] ode). Some of their Lodges have painted on them the likeness of Bears pretty well executed, others Dogs, some men painted them wanting the head or the blood issuing out of the wounds—You would avoid that Lodge I dare say—in short you might from their hieroglyphics write a history of the nation—

Robert Campbell to Hugh Campbell, 1 January 1834

Copy

Brother Hugh

Jany 1st 1834

Fort William January 1st 1834

My Dearest Brother,

As none amongst your numerous relations and friends has more reason to rejoice at the return of the anniversary of your birthday than myself permit me to offer congratulations on your continued happiness and good health which I hope this day finds you enjoying, and although I cannot join in the social circles who are in more than one place assembled to celebrate your birthday not one amongst them enters more heartily into the spirit of it nor with more sincerity wishes you many happy returns.

But what can a poor exile do towards enjoying it so far from home! On such days as this more than any others I return with a mixed feeling of pleasure and regret to the times when I enjoyed the society of you and my dearest mother brothers and sisters. Seated around the paternal hearth in domestic felicity and celebrating your birthday or some other less worthy occasion. And as often do I lament the day that I sacrificed all these pleasures for a wandering restless life when the very happiest moments we experience affords as but a negative enjoyment—Without friend or companion capable of rational conversation my days pass tediously and my nights seem at least 24 hours long with just enough of cares and of such a nature as to render the mind unfit for reaping society from books although I read to kill time and whilst thus employed sometimes a sentence of peculiar force strikes my wandering thoughts and I have to return a page or two to collect the discourse—but too much of this—

Many times do I take up the pen to write you

for no other purpose than to enjoy the pleasure of communicating to you my thoughts although without any intention of sending them to you— And I thus enjoy my happiest moments—By the medly sort of my letters you perceive I always write in the humour in which I may be at the time without any consideration whether they be acceptable or otherwise—I know they will be read and I even presume so far as to believe they will be read with pleasure no matter how uninteresting or undeserving—So much for this tirade—

I know not my Dear Hugh how many years (even providing we are both spared life) before we may meet again—Sometimes I entertain hopes that next New Years day may be passed by me in your society in Philadelphia and again I fear years too numerous to reckon upon may pass ere we meet—but in either case rest assured when once extricated from my present engagements I do not again enter into any that has any Indian connections; and should we meet and I express any inclination on this point I beg of you to remind me of this promise which will effectually deter any such project. It is very lately that in taking a retrospect of my past life that since 1822 I have not passed 2 New Years days in succession at the same place—frequently thousands of miles between—And this at a period of my life when I can only hope for enjoyment and when I might hope to form friendships and acquaintances that might be beneficial in after life—I have tried novelty and variety until I confess they satiate desire and willingly would I relinquish them for quiet domestic happiness and I look back on my past life as containing only days misspent—I now know the value of your advice of leaving off any wanderings and I will obey as soon as I can—

As you are so good at arranging all your friends affairs I wish you would plan out something that will suit me if ever I get off from this country and should I even die here your plans may answer for others—you perceive by this my mind is seriously bent on settling in a less changeable life than I have been heretofore disposed for and hope you will take for positive this my avowal—and I can assure you never did man more sincerely make one than I have done this.

I expect to leave this country worse than I have entered it and of course my ambition will not be so great as it was heretofore and that I will readily settle in some of your moderate plans such as a small country business or a return to Ireland—the latter only in case of some derangement in our affairs there.

Robert Campbell to Hugh Campbell, 19 January 1834

Copy

Fort William January 19th 1834

My dear Hugh

I have sent you a few letters written from time to time as the humour of the moment dictated and have therein confined myself to the Indians or something that created pleasing sensations for the moment, I send them in hopes they will with you produce the same effect. But it is also necessary that I should give you some idea how we progress here and I do it the more readily as you are my only confidant.

I cannot yet form any very sure calculation of the result of our business as much depends on the quantity of buffalo the Indians will kill at the different posts where we have established, and as yet I only know the prospects up to this time at this post. The Buffalo have been here unusually scarce here and the Indians have killed but very few indeed we find it difficult to obtain enough of meat for our consumption—the time is not long now that the buffalo skins will suit for robes (say scarce two months) and at best our trade must be small. These Indians are by no means ambitious in making robes and even now the men are going out to war and neglecting the time to kill buffalo in season and by this war?] our returns here must be small—this however although our largest Fort we expected would produce least robes. I have sent out two clerks in different directions about 50 & 60 miles from here where they have built houses to trade during the winter and the Indians have all gone there and I remain here to furnish their supplies and trade with any chance party that comes in—I sent out a party to the mountains to trap and trade with the Crow Indians but I have had no account from them yet.

At the time Mr. Sublette left here we spoke of selling out to the Am. Fur Co. but after we had made our proposals we failed in making a bargain—had this succeeded I think I should have entirely abandoned the Indian life and settled myself permanently in some stable business, but probably I may find it is all for the best. Yet if an opportunity offers I shall most undoubtably sell out and leave this country at anything that will possibly save me.

You find me express myself in a manner that you perceive I have less inclination to my present mode of life then to my former roving avocation, and I believe such is the case. I begin to find that spending the prime of my life in a savage country is sacrificing that time when I can only hope for enjoyment, and when in the course of years (should I be spared life) I leave here I must form new friends and enter the world as a youth, obliged to assimilate myself to the manners of those around me. Many reflections of this nature rush upon me in my solitude and stretch the tedious hours that I pass alone here; and many resolves do I make to place myself in a more fixed situation when an opportunity arrives, and in order to this to advantage it requires to make the best run of the present moment which affords no little thought nor few plans and calculating to overcome all that a new company has to encounter in the Indian country, as you may well judge from the class of interpreters (greater rascals than free Negroes) who have long enough with the Indians to have forgotten the ties of honor which binds the white man to his obligation and yet not long enough to acquire the good qualities of the Indians—in them are centered the vices of both classes—may other not much less aggravating matters serve to sour the homes of solitude and make the time irksome in the desert—admit that a man in seven years made a fortune in this life so there paid for it dearly.

If I can get off from this port in the month of May I shall descend the river as far as our post at the Sioux and then possibly await the arrival of Mr. Sublette, but as yet I cannot make any sure determination—in the spring we will have more insight into our affairs and you shall know them as they appear to me. Our capital employed in the business and requires a great expense to employ it say nearly 100 more all of whose wages are progressing day and duly, and the term of trade is but short—the country has proved profitable and it may be so now but in any case I would prefer leaving it soon as I can do so honourably.

Robert Campbell to James Bridger, 28 February 1834

Fort William Feb 28th 1834

Mr James Bridger

Dr Sir

Last Season whilst in the mountains it was not in my power to meet you but I had some conversation with Mr. Fitzpatrick respecting you in which I told him in Case of any change in your affairs it was my wish that you and him would come in here and join us, and that I had no doubt we would make some arrangement for your advantage. As Mr. Vasques is now going to meet you I thought better to address a few lines to yourself and to offer any thing in our power to do for you.

I hope your Hunt has resulted favorably.

Respectfully Your Obt. Servant

Robert Campbell.

Mr. James Bridger

Rocky Mountains.

Robert Campbell to William Sublette, 8 July 1834

Fort William July 8th 1834

Mr. William L. Sublette

Dear Sir

I was on my way down to meet you when I met the steam boat about a days travel above the little Missouri and found Andrew W. Sublette on board who handed me your letters on 8th June which gave me the first intelligence of your transactions with Pratte, Chouteau, & Co. I had taken a mackinaw boat down in which was 55 packs robes, 9 packs Beaver and some fox & wolf skins. Mr. Tebo steered it and had 4 hands at the oars—After perusing your letter I asked Mr. McKenzie what prices he was disposed to offer for our furs and peltries and he submitted to me a written offer of 250 for best robes, [1?] $ for yearlings, 25 c. for red calves, 375 c. per pound for Beaver and other peltries at similar prices.

These prices of course I rejected and next morning started down the Boat and Andrew and Glenday to go as far as little Missouri and there send down Solomon with Tebo and put in 10 packs of robes more at that place, and having done this for Andrew, Glenday & Sebille to come on to the mouth of the Yellowstone—I wrote the Messrs. Kerr to pay the hands and to receive the furs and peltries and retain them until my arrival—We were detained by low water and did not get the to the Mandans until the 19th; an express had gone up from the little Missouri and gave the news there and Mr. Doughterty had come down to Kipps Fort with all the merchandise etc. consequently I was not long delivering over what we had there. The Gro Vents [Gros Ventre] were displeased at our leaving there and at first made some noise with Doughterty but it soon was quelled and they permitted him to leave them in peace. Sandford made considerable presents to both Gro Vents and Mandans.

The evening of the same day we left the Mandans Andrew Glenday and Sebille arrived on the opposite side the river but while they were preparing to cross a party of Indians rushed on them and took the three Horses, and after exchanging a few shots with the Mandans they retired. We supposed that it was Yanktoneys but afterwards turned out to be Assinaboines and I have now Almond, Manchester, and Tom Kipland started 4 days pack in search of the village to endeavor to find them and if possible get the Horses although with little hopes of recovering them but I did not like the idea of leaving the country without making a trial—Andrew and the others came on board at the Gro Vent Old Village and continued on up here. I arrived here on the 25th June and immediately set to building a boat and preparing matters for going off. The men all wanted to go out to the Platte but not knowing your views at the present I preferred sending only a few and as I was obliged to send to raise the Cache at the Crow fort I was induced to send the party in that direction as I believe it to be as safe as the other route and we were compelled to send to the Crows to raise the Cache there. On the last day of June I commenced transferring the merchandise and in two days got pretty much through except some articles that have to be valued which at the commencement was to be left to disinterested persons. Sanford, Mitchel, Wheaton (from New York) and Capt. Bennett were proposed to me and I selected Bennett as being most likely to do us justice and act impartially, but owing to the low stage of water he has gone up to Buffalo on the Missouri and is about to remain until a run takes place—and I was in consequence obliged to leave some few articles to the valuation of Mitchel which have been taken so low that it would appear incredible. I shall send you a copy of the invoice here and at the Gro Vent as I calculate leaving here tomorrow or day after should Mr. Almond return in time. I endeavoured to get Pierre Garro to go out but could not prevail on him. He has remained at the Mandans.

I cannot yet make any calculation of what our business may turn out here but in any case you will know any of your actions meets with my approbation—indeed be it as it may I am pleased with the arrangement altogether and I think if we make nothing we will lose little.

Your trip to the mountians was I think the only way of saving our credits there and even after all, I have sme fears we will lose by that company who have certainly acted anything but honorably with us for whilst they made no scruple of drawing on us for money they were using their best efforts to injure us. You are well aware I made no engagement for either Christy or Harrison—on the contrary I showed them our arrangements with them and left it entirely with them how to act. Harrison was coming down with me until Fitzpatrick and Milton made the arrangements to sell mules and furnish men to him. With both Christy and Harrison I showed the letters we had from their friends and allowed Fitz and Milton to judge for themselves and you well know I took Christy's receipt to exonerate us altogether from any responsibility—and besides in selling out to the Rocky Mt. Fur Co. I had them bound to fulfill our contract with Christy if he preferred joining them—I write thus far to explain although unnecessary as you are well aware I settled with both Harrison & Christy and took Harrison's draft & Christy's note for the balance due us and settled finally with them. I assumed nothing for [them?]

As respects our continuation of the business in the section of the country reserved for us I shall leave it entirely to your better judgement as you are now at the place and can determine the prospects—if you think the prospects will justify us I am quite willing to continue it and if you think that it would be hazardous to the Capital invested far be it from me to wish you to risk it on my account, but I am ever ready to perform any part that is in my power. Do therefore as you consider most to our interest and make any calculations on me that I can perform.

I sent Andrew and Glenday out with Manchester, Tom Kipland, Redmond, Beckert, Vancourt, Julian, & Billy Maxwell all of whom are hired. With Manchester I entered into a new engagement for three Hundred Dollars to commence 1st Sept next he is the best hunter I have ever met with and very careful of animals and so far I have found him trustworthy—he is anxious to trap if you can so arrange it. Tom Kipland is the most faithful half breed I have ever found and is to either be furnished to trap on the shares or any other way you think proper—he speaks Sioux and is good amongst Indians. I had entered into a new engagement with him for 600$ per annum to commence 20th August but it is agreed that without your wish it that is to be of no effect. I have made no promises to any of the other men either as to equipping or anything else. Jno [John] Rusha has equipped Jock [Jacques] Bourdon and himself and is but very little indebted. Lajoness [Lajeunesse] is also equipped bound to reman with the company until paying his debt. Bob Manion has turned in 6 traps to me at this place and is to get of you 6 traps on the Platte he paying five dollars each difference and he running the risk of your having a supply. I send Billy & Julian as the only two men who know where the Cache is at the Crow.

I think Glenday might wish to take an equipment but I have tried him here and I think he is more desirous of his wages running on—but I believe it would be better to equip him should to hire him as he could in the latter case be of very little service to us. Andrew goes out to be governed by your views when he arrives.

Vancourt offers to make a good trapper but I think there is not much dependence to be placed there. Saddler is a good fellow—

[Robert Campbell = unsigned copy]

BIBLIOGRAPHY

Manuscript Collections and Unpublished Sources

Missouri Historical Society Archives. Saint Louis, Mo.
Chouteau Maffitt Collection.
E. V. Papin Collection.
Fur Trade Collection.

National Archives and Records Administration. Washington, D.C.
Record Group 41, Bureau of Marine Inspection and Navigation.
Custom House Records—Port of New Orleans. Enrollments, 1832–1834.

AFC Voyageur Contracts Database. Centre du Patrimoine, Saint Boniface, Manitoba. Used with permission by Nicole St-Onge and Robert Englebert.

UMO Employee Database. Created and used with permission by William J. Hunt, Jr.

Published Sources

Abel, Annie Heloise, ed. *Chardon's Journal at Fort Clark, 1834–1839*. By F. A. Chardon. Pierre: South Dakota Department of History, 1932.

Albers, Patricia C. "Plains Ojibwa." In *Handbook of North American Indians*. Vol. 13: *Plains*, pt. 1, pp. 652–60. Ed. Raymond J. DeMallie. Washington, D.C.: Smithsonian Press, 1998.

Athearn, Robert G. *Forts of the Upper Missouri*. Englewood Cliffs, N.J.: Prentice-Hall, 1967.

Barbour, Barton H. *Fort Union and the Upper Missouri Fur Trade*. Norman: University of Oklahoma Press, 2001.

Boller, Henry A. *Among the Indians, Four Years on the Upper Missouri, 1858–1862*. Norman: University of Oklahoma Press, 1965.

———. *Twilight of the Upper Missouri Fur Trade: The Journals of Henry A. Boller*. Ed. W. Raymond Wood. Bismarck: State Historical Society of North Dakota, 2008.

Bonner, T. D. *The Life and Adventures of James P. Beckwourth, Mountaineer, Scout, and Pioneer, and Chief of the Crow Tribe*. Minneapolis: Ross & Haines, 1965.

Brown, Mark H. *The Plainsmen of the Yellowstone: A History of the Yellowstone Basin*. Lincoln, Nebr.: Bison Books, 1969.

Brunton, Bill B. "Kootenai." In *Handbook of North American Indians*. Vol. 12: *Plateau*, pp. 223-37. Ed. Deward E. Walker Jr. Washington, D.C.: Smithsonian Press, 1998.

Buckley, Jay H. "Rocky Mountain Entrepreneur: Robert Campbell as a Fur Trade Capitalist." *Annals of Wyoming* 75 (Summer 2003): 8–23.

Campbell, Robert. "The Private Journal of Robert Campbell," ed. George R. Brooks. *Bulletin of the Missouri Historical Society* 20 (Oct. 1963/Jan. 1964): 3–24, 107–18.

_______. *The Rocky Mountain Letters of Robert Campbell*. New York: Frederick W. Beinecke, 1955.

Casler, Michael M. *Steamboats of the Fort Union Fur Trade*. Williston, N.Dak.: Fort Union Assoc., 1999.

_______. "Drayage Included: Steamboat Operations of the American Fur Company at St. Louis." In *Indians & Traders: Entrepreneurs of the Upper Missouri—Fort Union Fur Trade Symposium 2000 Proceedings*. Williston, N.Dak.: Fort Union Assoc., 2001.

———. "Letters from the Fur Trade: Kenneth McKenzie's Letters to Prince Maximilian at Fort Clark, 1833–1834." *Museum of the Fur Trade Quarterly* 41 (Spring 2005): 9–14.

———. "Fur Traders as Undertakers on the Upper Missouri." *Museum of the Fur Trade Quarterly* 43 (Fall/Winter, 2007): 107–14.

———. "'This Outrageous Desease': Charles Larpenteur's Observations of the 1837 Smallpox Epidemic." *Rocky Mountain Fur Trade Journal* 10 (2016): 18–35.

———, and W. Raymond Wood, eds. *Fort Tecumseh and Fort Pierre Chouteau: Journal and Letter Books 1830–1850*. Pierre: South Dakota Historical Society Press, 2017.

———. "The Rise and Fall of the Columbia Fur Company: Rethinking the Fur Trade on the Northern Great Plains." Paper presented at the 2018 National Fur Trade Symposium, Bismarck, N.Dak.

Catlin, George. *Letters and Notes on the Manners, Customs, and Condition of the North American Indians*. 2 vols. London: by the author, 1841.

Chamberlain, Andrew B. *Historic Furnishings Report: Indian Trade House and Strong Room, Fort Union Trading Post National Historic Site, Williston, North Dakota*. Harpers Ferry, W.V.: Harpers Ferry Center, National Park Service, 1993.

Chittenden, Hiram M. *A History of the American Fur Trade of the Far West*. 3 vols. New York: Francis P. Harper, 1902.

———. "List of Steamboat Wrecks on the Missouri." In *Annual Report of the Chief of Engineers for 1897*. Washington, D.C.: Government Printing Office, 1897.

Dale, Harrison Clifford. *The Ashley-Smith Explorations*

and Discovery of a Central Route to the Pacific, 1822–1829. Cleveland: Arthur H. Clark Company, 1918.

Darnell, Regna. "Plains Cree." In *Handbook of North American Indians*. Vol. 13: *Plains*, pt. 1, pp. 638–51. Ed. Raymond J. DeMallie. Washington, D.C.: Smithsonian Press, 2001.

DeLand, Charles E., ed. "Fort Tecumseh and Fort Pierre Journal and Letter Books." Notes by Doane Robinson. *South Dakota Historical Collection* 9 (1918): 69–239.

DeMallie, Raymond J. "Yankton and Yanktonai." In *Handbook of North American Indians*. Vol. 13: *Plains*, pt. 2, pp. 777–93. Ed. Raymond J. DeMallie. Washington, D.C.: Smithsonian Press, 2001.

———, and David Reed Miller. "Assiniboine." In *Handbook of North American Indians*. Vol. 13: *Plains*, pt. 1, pp. 572–95. Ed. Raymond J. DeMallie. Washington, D.C.: Smithsonian Press, 2001.

Dempsey, Hugh A. "Blackfoot." In *Handbook of North American Indians*. Vol. 13: *Plains*, pt. 1, pp. 604–28. Ed. Raymond J. DeMallie. Washington, D.C.: Smithsonian Press, 2001.

Denig, Edwin T. *Five Indian Tribes of the Upper Missouri: Sioux, Arickaras, Assiniboines, Crees, Crows*. Ed. John C. Ewers. Norman: University of Oklahoma Press, 1961.

DeVoto, Bernard. *Across the Wide Missouri*. Boston: Houghton Mifflin, 1975.

Ewers, John C. *Indian Life on the Upper Missouri*. Norman: University of Oklahoma Press, 1988.

———. "Jean Baptiste Moncravie: Fort Union's First White Artist." In *Fort Union Fur Trade Symposium Proceedings*. Williston, N.Dak.: Friends of Fort Union Trading Post, 1994.

Ferris, W. A. *Life in the Rocky Mountains, 1830–1835*. Ed. H. S. Auerbach and J. C. Alter. Salt Lake City: Rocky Mountain Bookshop, 1940.

Gaul, R. W. "Death of the Thunderbolt: Some Notes on the Final Illness of Milton Sublette." *Bulletin of the Missouri Historical Society* 18 (Oct. 1961): 33–36.

Gilman, Rhoda, Carolyn Gilman, and Deborah M. Stultz. *The Red River Trails, 1820–1870: Oxcart Routes Between St. Paul and the Selkirk Settlement*. Saint Paul: Minnesota Historical Society, 1979.

Goff, William A. "Pierre Didier Papin." In *French Fur Traders and Voyagers in the American West*. Ed. LeRoy R. Hafen, pp. 239–52. Lincoln, Nebr.: Bison Books, 1997.

Goosman, Mildred. "Karl Bodmer, Earliest Painter on the Upper Missouri." *Montana: The Magazine of Western History* 20 (July 1970): 36–41.

Gray, John S. "Honoré Picotte, Fur Trader." *South Dakota History* 6 (Spring 1976): 186–202.

Hafen, Anne W. "Baptiste Charbonneau, Son of Bird Woman." In *Westerners' Brand Book*, pp. 39–66. Denver: Denver Posse, 1949.

Hafen, Leroy R. "Mountain Men—Louis Vasquez." *Colorado Magazine* 10 (Jan. 1933): 14–21.

———. "Mountain Men: Andrew Sublette." *Colorado Magazine* 10 (Sept. 1933): 179–84.

———, ed. *The Mountain Men and the Fur Trade of the Far West*. 10 vols. Glendale, Calif.: Arthur H. Clark, 1965–1972.

Haines, Aubrey L. "Johnson Gardner." In *The Mountain Men and the Fur Trade of the Far West*. Ed. Leroy R. Hafen. Vol. 2, pp. 157–59. Glendale, Calif.: Arthur H. Clark, 1965.

Hanson, Charles E., Jr. *The Northwest Gun*. Lincoln: Nebraska State Historical Society, 1955.

———. "J. B. Moncravie." In *The Mountain Men and the Fur Trade of the Far West*. Ed. Leroy R. Hafen. Vol. 9, pp. 289–98. Glendale, Calif.: Arthur H. Clark, 1972.

———, ed. *The David Adams Journals*. Chadron, Nebr.: The Museum Association of the American Frontier, 1994.

———, ed. "A Letter to David Adams." *Museum of the Fur Trade Quarterly* 33 (Fall 1997): 2–5.

Hanson, James A. "The Amazing Journal of David Adams." *Museum of the Fur Trade Quarterly* 34 (Summer 1998): 1–2.

———, and Samantha Eickleberry. "Marginal Men: Lesser Lights of the Fur Trade in the American West, 1800–1865." *Museum of the Fur Trade Quarterly* 50 (Fall/Winter 2014): 1–80.

———, and Dick Harmon. *The Encyclopedia of Trade Goods*. Vol. 1: *Firearms of the Fur Trade*. Chadron, Nebr.: Museum of the Fur Trade, 2011.

Hardee, Jim. "An 1824–1825 Columbia Fur Company Ledger." *Rocky Mountain Fur Trade Journal* 5 (2011): 119–49.

Hunt, William J., Jr. "Fort Floyd: History and Archaeology of an Enigmatic 19th Century Trading Post." *North Dakota History* 61 (Summer 1994): 7–20.

———. "'At the Yellowstone.... to Build a Fort': Fort Union Trading Post, 1828–1833." In *Fort Union Fur Trade Symposium Proceedings*, pp. 7–23. Williston, N.Dak.: Friends of Fort Union Trading Post, 1994.

———. "Origins of Fort Union: Archaeology and History." In *Fur Trade Revisited: Selected Papers of the Sixth North American Fur Trade Conference, Mackinac Island, 1991*. Eds. Jennifer S. H. Brown, W. J. Eccles, and Donald P. Heldman. East Lansing/Mackinac Island: Michigan State University Press and Mackinac State Historic Parks, 1994.

Innis, Ben. *How t' Talk Trapper: 252 Words and Phrases*. Williston, N.Dak.: Sitting Bull Trading Post, 1983.

Jackson, Donald. *Voyages of the Steamboat Yellow Stone*. New York: Ticknor & Fields, 1985.

Kane, Paul. *Paul Kane's Frontier: Including Wanderings of an Artist Among the Indians of North America*. Ed. J. Russell Harper. Austin: University of Texas Press, 1971.

Kelly, Mark William. *Lost Voices on the Missouri: John Dougherty and the Indian Frontier.* Leavenworth, Kans.: Sam Clark, 2013.

Kline, Mary-Jo. *A Guide to Documentary Editing.* Baltimore, M.d.: Johns Hopkins University Press, 1987.

Kurz, Rudolf Friederich. *Journal of Rudolf Friederich Kurz.* Trans. Myrtis Jarrell. Ed. J. N. B. Hewitt. Washington, D.C.: Smithsonian Institution, 1937.

Landry, Clay J. "Hugh Glass: The Rest of the Story." *Rocky Mountain Fur Trade Journal* 10 (2016): 1–17.

Larpenteur, Charles. *Forty Years a Fur Trader on the Upper Missouri: The Personal Narrative of Charles Larpenteur.* Ed. Elliott Coues. 2 vols. New York: Francis P. Harper, 1898.

———. *The Original Journal of Charles Larpenteur: My Travels to the Rocky Mountains Between 1833 and 1872.* Ed. Michael M. Casler. Chadron, Nebr.: Museum Association of the American Frontier, 2007.

Lass, William E. *Navigating the Missouri: Steamboating on Nature's Highway, 1819–1935.* Norman, Okla.: Arthur H. Clark, 2008.

Lavender, David S. *The Fist in the Wilderness.* New York: Doubleday & Company, 1964.

Lecompte, Janet. "The Chouteaus and the St. Louis Fur Trade." In *Papers of the St. Louis Fur Trade*, pp. xiii-xxii. Ed. W. R. Swagerty. Bethesda, M.d.: University Publications of America for the Missouri Historical Society, 1991.

———. "Pierre Chouteau, Jr.," in *The Mountain Men and the Fur Trade of the Far West.* Ed. LeRoy R. Hafen. Vol. 9, pp. 92–123. Glendale, Calif.: Arthur H. Clark, 1972.

———. "Charles Autobees." In *Trappers of the Far West*, pp. 242–58. Ed. LeRoy R. Hafen. Lincoln, Nebr.: Bison Books, 1983.

Leonard, Zenas. *Narrative of the Adventures of Zenas Leonard.* Ed. W. F. Wagner. Cleveland: Burrows Brothers, 1904.

Lepley, John G. "The Prince and the Artist on the Upper Missouri." *Montana: The Magazine of Western History* 20 (Summer 1970): 42–53.

Lowie, Robert H. "The Assiniboines." In *Anthropological Papers of the American Museum of Natural History.* Vol. 4, pt. 1, p. 15. New York: American Museum of Natural History, 1909.

Luttig, John C. *Journal of a Fur-Trading Expedition on the Upper Missouri, 1812–1813.* Ed. Stella M. Drumm. New York: Argosy-Antiquarian, 1964.

Mattison, Ray H. "Kenneth McKenzie." In *The Mountain Men and the Fur Trade of the Far West.* Ed. Leroy H. Hafen. Vol. 2, pp. 217–24. Glendale, Calif.: Arthur H. Clark, 1965.

———. "David Dawson Mitchell." In *The Mountain Men and the Fur Trade of the Far West.* Ed. Leroy H. Hafen. Vol. 2, pp. 241–46. Glendale, Calif.: Arthur H. Clark, 1965.

———. "James A. Hamilton (Palmer)." *The Mountain Men and the Fur Trade of the Far West.* Ed. LeRoy R. Hafen. Vol. 3, pp. 163–66. Glendale, Calif.: Arthur H. Clark, 1966.

———. "William Laidlaw." *The Mountain Men and the Fur Trade of the Far West.* Ed. Leroy R. Hafen. Vol. 3, pp. 167–72. Glendale, Calif.: Arthur H. Clark Company, 1966.

———. "Alexander Harvey." *The Mountain Men and the Fur Trade of the Far West.* Ed. Leroy H. Hafen. Vol. 4, pp. 119–23. Glendale, Calif.: Arthur H. Clark, 1966.

———. "Joshua Pilcher." in *The Mountain Men and Fur Trade of the Far West.* Ed. LeRoy R. Hafen. Vol. 4, pp. 251–60. Glendale, Calif.: Arthur H. Clark, 1966.

———. "Alexander Culbertson." *Fur Traders and Mountain Men of the Upper Missouri*, pp. 253–56. Ed. Leroy R. Hafen. Lincoln: University of Nebraska Press, 1995.

Maximilian, Prince of Wied. *The North American Journals of Prince Maximilian of Wied.* Ed. Stephen S. Witte and Marsha V. Gallagher. 3 vols. Norman: University of Oklahoma Press, 2009–2012.

McDermott, John Francis, ed. *Up The Missouri With Audubon: The Journal of Edward Harris.* Norman: University of Oklahoma Press, 1951.

McLaird, James D. *Hugh Glass: Grizzly Survivor.* Pierre: South Dakota Historical Society Press, 2016.

Merritt, John I. *Baronets and Buffalo: British Sportsman in the American West, 1833–1881.* Missoula, Mont.: Mountain Press Publishing Company, 1985.

Morgan, Dale L. *Jedidiah Smith and the Opening of the West.* Lincoln: University of Nebraska Press, 1964.

Moulton, Gary E. "Editorial Procedures." In *The Journals of the Lewis and Clark Expedition.* Vol. 2: *August 30, 1803–August 24, 1804*, pp. 49–54. Lincoln: University of Nebraska Press, 1987.

Nester, William R. *From Mountain Man to Millionaire: The Bold and Dashing Life of Robert Campbell.* Columbia: University of Missouri Press, 2011.

Nunis, Doyce B., Jr. *Andrew Sublette, Rocky Mountain Prince, 1813–1853.* Los Angeles: Dawson's Book Shop, 1960.

———. "Milton G. Sublette." In *The Mountain Men and the Fur Trade of the Far West.* Ed. Leroy R. Hafen. Vol. 4, pp. 331–49. Glendale, Calif.: Arthur H. Clark, 1966.

Parsons, John E. "Gunmakers for the American Fur Company." *New York Historical Society Quarterly* 6 (Apr. 1952): 37–50.

Peterson, Lynelle A., and William Jefferson Hunt, Jr. *The 1987 Investigations at Fort Union Trading Post: Archeology and Architecture.* Lincoln, Nebr.: Midwest Archeological Center, National Park Service, 1990.

Peterson, Gary. "Antonio Montero and the Portuguese Houses: An Outpost on Powder River." *Rocky Mountain Fur Trade Journal* 2 (2008): 31–47.

Porter, Mae R., and Odessa Davenport. *Scotsman in Buckskin: Sir William Drummond Stewart and the Rocky Mountain Fur Trade*. New York: Hastings House, 1963.

Porter, Kenneth W. "Negroes and the Fur Trade." *Minnesota History* 15 (Dec. 1934): 421–34.

Potter, Gail DeBuse. "Trading Posts of the Central Plains." *Museum of the Fur Trade Quarterly* 43 (Fall/Winter 2007): 75–81.

Potter, Tracy. *Steamboats in Dakota Territory: Transforming the Northern Plains*. Charleston, S.C.: The History Press, 2017.

Prucha, Francis Paul. *Indian Peace Medals in American History*. Bluffton, S.C.: Rivilo Books, 1994.

Robertson, R. G. *Competitive Struggle: America's Western Fur Trading Posts, 1764–1965*. Boise, Ida.: Tamarack Books, 2012.

Ross, Alexander. *The Red River Settlement: Its Rise, Progress and Present State*. London: Smith, Elder, & Co., 1856.

Schiller, Friedrich. *Schiller's Poems and Ballads*, trans. Lord Lytton Edward. London: George Routledge & Sons, 1887.

Schuler, Harold H. *Fort Pierre Chouteau*. Vermillion: University of South Dakota Press, 1990.

Smyth, David. "Jacques Berger, Fur Trader." *The Beaver* 69 (June/July 1987): 39–50.

Stevens, Orin A. "Maximilian in North Dakota, 1833–34." *North Dakota History* 2 (October 1961): 163–69.

Stewart, Frank Henderson. "Hidatsa." In *Handbook of North American Indians*. Vol. 13: *Plains*, pt. 2, pp. 329–48. Ed. Raymond J. DeMallie. Washington, D.C.: Smithsonian Press, 2001.

Stewart, George R., Jr. "Popular Names for the Mountain Sheep." *American Speech* 10 (Dec. 1935): 283–88.

Swagerty, William R., ed. *Papers of the St. Louis Fur Trade, Part 1: The Chouteau Collection, 1752–1925*. Microfilm. Reel 22. Bethesda, M.d.: University Publications of America for the Missouri Historical Society, 1991.

———. "A View from the Bottom Up: The Work Force of the American Fur Company on the Upper Missouri in the 1830s." *Montana: The Magazine of Western History* 43 (Winter 1993): 18–33.

Thompson, Erwin N. *Fort Union Trading Post: Historic Structures Report, Part II, Historical Data Section*. Washington, D.C.: Department of the Interior, National Park Service, 1968.

———. *Fort Union Trading Post: Fur Trade Empire on the Upper Missouri*. Medora, N.Dak.: Theodore Roosevelt Nature and History Assoc., 1986.

Thomson, Robert W. "'This Wicked Family': A Biography of the Deschamps Family of Fort Union: Their Feuds, Fights, and Violent Demise." *Montana: The Magazine of Western History* 54 (Winter 2004): 2–15.

Thwaites, Rueben Gold, ed. *Early Western Travels, 1748–1846*. Vol. 24: "Part III of Maximilian, Prince of Wied's Travels in the Interior of North America, 1832–1834." Cleveland: Arthur P. Clark, 1906.

Trottman, Alan C. "Lucien Fontenelle." In *Trappers of the Far West*, pp. 123–41. Ed. LeRoy R. Hafen. Lincoln, Nebr.: Bison Books, 1983.

Utley, Robert M. *A Life Wild and Perilous: Mountain Men and the Paths to the Pacific*. New York: Henry Holt, 1997.

Voget, Fred W. "Crow." In *Handbook of North American Indians*. Vol. 13: *Plains*, pt. 2, pp. 695–717. Ed. Raymond J. DeMallie. Washington, D.C.: Smithsonian Press, 2001.

Wishart, David J. *The Fur Trade of the American West, 1807–1840*. Lincoln: University of Nebraska Press, 1979.

Wilson, Elinor. *Jim Beckwourth, Black Mountain Man and War Chief of the Crows*. Norman: University of Oklahoma Press, 1980.

Wischmann, Lesley. *Frontier Diplomats: The Life and Times of Alexander Culbertson and 'Natoyist-Siksina'*. Spokane, Wash.: Arthur H. Clark, 2000.

Wood, W. Raymond. "James Kipp: Upper Missouri River Fur Trader and Missouri Farmer." *North Dakota History* 77, Nos. 1–2 (2011): 2–35.

———, and Michael M. Casler. "A Revised History of Fort Floyd." *North Dakota History* 80 (Winter 2015): 3–13.

———, William J. Hunt, Jr., and Randy H. Williams. *Fort Clark and its Indian Neighbors: A Trading Post on the Upper Missouri River*. Norman: University of Oklahoma Press, 2011.

———, and Lee Irwin. "Mandan." In *Handbook of North American Indians*. Vol. 13: *Plains*, pt. 1, pp. 329–48. Ed., Raymond J. DeMallie. Washington, D.C.: Smithsonian Press, 2001.

Wyeth, Nathaniel J. *The Journals of Captain Nathaniel J. Wyeth's Expeditions to the Oregon Country 1831–1836*. Ed. Don Johnson. Fairfield, Wash.: Ye Galleon Press, 1984.

———. "The Correspondence and Journals of Captain Nathaniel J. Wyeth, 1831–6: A Record of Two Expeditions for the Occupation of the Oregon Country." Ed. F. G. Young. In *Sources of the History of Oregon*. Vol. 1, pts. 3–6. Eugene, Ore.: University Press, 1899.

INDEX

Spelling variations are shown in (parentheses). Unidentified individuals known only by their surnames have been marked (u/i). PS stands for Photo Section [with unnumbered page in brackets].

Abel, Annie Heloise, xii, 3, 77n98
Adams, David (trapper), 56, 80n248
African Americans, 25–26, 28, 39, 77n190, 92, 104n49, 106n86, 116. *See also* slaves/slavery
Alberta, 62, 67n48, 77n189
alcohol (whiskey, wine). *See* liquor
Almanza (u/i), 18, 21, 71n92
Almond, William B., 68n62, 88–93, 96–99, 103n29, 107n95, 117
American Fur Company (AFC): bison robe trade, 3n2; competition from Sublette and Campbell, 15, 85–86, 106n84; construction of trading posts, 67n48, 102n16; employees, 62n6, 63n12, 65n26, 78n214, 101n8–9, 101n11–12, 102n17–18, 102n24, 103n26–28, 103n38–39, 104n44–46, 104n49, 105n53, 105n62; employee database, xii; incorporation, 3n4; merger to form UMO, 66n41, 71n90; ownership, vii, 1–2, 69n75; partnership with Columbia Fur Company, vii–viii; trade with American Indians, 70n82, 70n84
American Indians. *See* individual tribes
ammunition/gunpowder, 10, 14, 36, 42–47, 50, 56–58, 96, 105n54, 110, 112
Andrews, James, 44, 78n207
animals. *See* bison; cattle; chickens; coypu; dogs; horses and mules; turkeys
annuities, 47. *See also* trade goods
Apple River (Apple Creek), 8, 10, 17, 19, 31, 55, 65n31, 75n165
Arikara (Aricara, Arriccarra, Ree) Indians, 23, 25, 65n32, 72n111
Arkansas River, 66n45
Ashley, William H., 63n12, 68n68, 72n103, 72n111, 85, 103n26, 107n90
Assiniboine (steamboat), 12, 14–15, 32–33, 36, 59, 67n55, 70n82, 75n148, 76n172–73, 77n186, 81n271
Assiniboine Indians, viii, 22–24, 32, 34–35, 37, 44, 65n23–24, 74n139, 76n179, 77n184, 79n221, 89, 93–94, 96–97, 102n23, 103n41, 105n63, 106n68, 106n72, 106n78, 112, 114, 117
Assiniboine trading post, viii
Astor, John Jacob, vii, 1–3
Astor, William Blackhouse, 3n1, 15, 69n75
Astor medals, 17, 70n83
Audubon, John James, viii, 74n139
August, Friedrich Paul Wilhelm (Prince of Württemberg), viii, xii, 78n207, 102n13
Austin, Brian, xi
Bacarapa, L., 54
Bad River (Teton River, Little Missouri), 66n39, 71n89, 107n94
Bank War of 1833, 40
Bare, J., 55
Battle of Seven Oaks, 75n158
beads, 14, 23, 35, 47, 50, 57, 110
Beauchamp, Joseph, 7, 21, 25–26, 62n6, 73n114
Beauchamp, Pierre, 73n114
Beaugard, Hugron, 7, 62n6, 99
Beaugard, J., 23, 27, 30–31, 60
beaver pelt trade: decline, 1, 3n1, 19, 37, 48, 51, 68n69; Indians and, 8, 18, 24–26, 32, 65n27, 69n74, 94–95, 110, 112; quantity gathered, ix, 1, 7, 19–20, 34, 43, 46, 52–53, 88, 100, 116; shipment, 25, 60, 86; trappers and, 19, 21, 23, 37, 44, 51, 54–55, 72n111, 74n134, 80n246, 80n248, 90–93
Beckwith (Beckwourth), James, 19, 23–24, 26, 28, 48, 72n103, 86, 102n17
Bellehumeur, Michel, 8–9, 55, 65n29
Bellevue (Belview) trading post, 68n67, 79n233
Bennett, Andrew, 77n184
Berger (Berjen), Jacques (Jacob), 12, 20–22, 40–42, 50, 67n53
Bernard Pratte and Company, vii–viii, 2, 66n41. *See also* Pratte, Bernard; Western Department
Berry, Martha E., 63n12
Berthold, Bartholomew, 63n8
Bighorn River, 65n27, 65n33, 68n65, 106n71
Big Sioux River (River Sioux), vii
Big Soldier (Yankton), 68n63
bison (buffalo): abundant supply, 114; disappearance, 12, 88, 91, 96, 98, 105n63, 115; hunting, 9, 21, 25, 55, 72n104, 80n244; locating the herds, 86, 90, 103n30, 103n31; trading and harvesting meat, 40, 90–91, 93
bison (buffalo) robes: as Indian apparel, 111–12; quantities gathered, ixn4; shipment, 54, 86; trade, 3n2, 50, 91, 94, 110, 112. *See also* fur trade
Bissonette (Bigeau, Bazille, Basil, Bissonet), Louis, 80n249
Blackfoot Indians, 34, 40, 46, 48, 51, 57–58, 64n13, 67n48, 70n88, 71n95, 76n176, 87
Black Hawk War of 1832, 74n129
Black Tomahawk Handle (Assiniboine), 106n72
blankets/cloth, 3n2, 8, 12, 17, 20, 46–47, 50, 57–58, 91, 93, 97, 103n41, 110, 114
Blechere, J., 54

Bledsoe (Bledsoy), A., 54, 79n235
boats: bateux (batteaux), 32, 52, 79n229; canoes, 17, 23, 30–31, 38, 44, 48, 75n165, 88–89, 91–92, 100, 110; construction/repairs, 26, 31, 72n108, 74n131, 99; mackinaws, 42, 62n7, 63n10, 75n148, 76n167, 90, 100, 110–11, 116; pirogues, 87–88, 100; skiffs, 31; yawls, 36. *See also* keelboats; steamboats
Bodmer (Bordman), Karl, viii, 7, 12, 27, 61–62, 102n20, 103n34, 106n75, PS [4–5, 10–11]
Boldeu, Urban, 21, 73n114
Bolingston, J., 54
Bonneville, Benjamin, 19, 48–49, 54, 71n93, 80n248
Bouché, R., 54
Boullé (Brullé) (u/i), 55–56
Bourbonnais (Bourbonnet, Bournet, Bourbinnais), Auguste, 35, 77n187
Bourdalow, B., 79n234
Bourke, John P., 29, 75n158
Braunsberg, Baron. *See* Maximilian, Alexander Philipp
Brazeau (Brazo) (u/i), 93, 96–99, 104n49
Brazeau (Brazo, Braseau, Brayeu), Joseph E. (J.B.), 34, 40, 42, 50, 52–54, 58, 90, 72n104, 74n145, 78n199, 104n49
Bridger, Jim, 68n69, 97–98, 102n13, 102n17, 116–17, PS [12]
Broken Arm (Maschkepiton, Bro-cas-sie, La Bras cassé) (Cree), 34, 39, 76n178, 93–94, 106n67
Brooks, George R., xi
Brulé, Jean Baptiste, 75n164
Buffalo Bull's Back Fat (Stu-mick-o-sucks) (Blackfoot), PS [8]
Bulletin of the Missouri Historical Society, 3

Calomel (u/i), 9, 16
Campbell, Colin, 56, 60, 81n269
Campbell, Hugh, 106n75, 107n89
Campbell, John, 55, 80n242
Campbell, Robert: competition with McKenzie, 72n104, 85, 94, 104n43, 105n58–59, 106n84; historical importance of journal, 1–2, 85–86; letters to/from Fort William, 108–19; loss of dog, 93, 105n63; loss of pelts, 93, 100, 106n71, 107n91–92; mentions in Fort Union letters, 7, 9–10, 12–13, 15, 19–20, 22–24, 27; mentions in McKenzie letters, 7–8, 31; publication of journal, xi, 3, 100n, 101n4; religion, 106n79; travel to Saint Louis, 107n89–90; PS [2]
Campbell House Museum, xi, 85
Cancellai (Carisalle, Carifell), Michel, 37, 77n191
Cantonment Leavenworth. *See* Fort Leavenworth
Carrier (Cassier), Michel, 74n134, 106n70
Carriera, Legrie (Legris), 26, 74n134, 93, 106n70
carts (charettes), 36, 38–39, 56, 93–94, 96–97, 99, 100
Cary, William de la Montagne, viii
Cass, Lewis, 63n12
Catlin, George, viii, 76n178, 77n183, 80n244, 106n67, PS [2, 8–9]
cattle, 3, 7–8, 11, 13, 34–35, 37, 52, 54, 59, 88, 105n51
Cerré (Ceré), Michael Sylvester ("Lami"), 19, 29–30, 71n93
Cerré, Gabriel Pascal, 71n93
Charbonneau (Charboneaux, Charboncais), Jean Baptiste, 102n13
Charbonneau ("Old" Charbonneau), Toussaint, 13, 31, 75n163, 102n13, PS [10]
Chardon, Francis Auguste, viii, 2–3, 63n8, 67n54
Chardon, Francis Bolivar, 69n72
Chardon, Francis T. (Osage), 69n72
Chardon's Journal, xii, 3
Charrin, Henry, 52
Cheyenne Indians, 59
Cheyenne River, 80n240, 81n269
chickens, 93, 105n51
Chippewa Indians, 77n185
Chouquette, Pierrot (Pierot), 78n193
Chouteau, Emilie, 76n182
Chouteau, Pierre, Jr.: role in Upper Missouri fur trade, vii, 3, 66n46; competition from Sublette and Campbell, 85; creation of Sioux Outfit, 81n272; mentions in letter book, 11, 27, 28; letters to, 13–15, 28–30, 32, 45, 54–55, 57–58; relationship with McKenzie, 81n272, 105n59; PS [5]. *See also* Pierre Chouteau, Jr., and Company; Pratte, Chouteau and Company
Clark, William, 69n77, 76n182, 80n250. *See also* Lewis and Clark Expedition
Columbia Fur Company (Tilton, Dudley and Co.): construction of Fort Floyd, viii; creation of, 62n5; employees/clerks, 63n13, 66n39, 66n45, 67n50, 69n80–81, 70n86, 71n98; ledger of accounts, 63n7; merger with AFC, 66n41, 71n90; role in fur trade, vii
Columbia River, 19
Compton (Contois), Baptiste, 46, 78n215
Coté, A., 55
Cotte (Coté, Cota, Cote), Jean Baptiste, 79n237
Coues, Elliott, 86
Council Bluffs, 11, 14–15, 19, 57, 59, 66n43–44, 68n67
coypu (fur-bearing rodent), 1
Crawford, Lewis: as clerk for UMO, 70n86, 77n188, 78n213; letters to, 36–38, 43; mentions in letter book, 8, 19, 33–38, 40, 44, 46–48; travel to Saint Louis, 79n229
Cree Indians, viii, 8, 37, 39, 46–47, 56, 58, 76n178, 77n189, 77n185–86, 87, 89, 93–95, 106n67, 106n75
Crooks, Ramsey, 3, 16, 37, 59, 66n41; role in upper Missouri fur trade, vii; acquisition of AFC Northern Department, 2
Croteau, François, 9, 12–13, 37, 65n38
Crow Camp (village/post), 10–11, 19, 23–24, 26, 34, 45, 55, 59, 98
Crow Indians, 13, 25, 32, 35, 48–50, 52–55, 65n26–27, 68n65, 69n74, 76n176, 88, 100, 102n12, 103n32, 109, 115

Culbertson, Alexander: as AFC clerk, 70n88; as UMO agent, 66n39; at Ft. McKenzie, 79n226; letters to, 33, 40–41, 44–45, 49–51, 55; mentions in letter book, 20, 22, 42, 49, 52–53, 58; role in Upper Missouri fur trade, 3; PS [9]
Culbertson, John Craighead, 71n90
Culbertson, Julia, 70n88
Culbertson, Thaddeus, viii

Daignaux (Diagneau, Daigneau), Narcisse, 26, 74n138, 78n201
Dauphin, Baptiste, 58, 81n260
Dauphin trading post, viii
Dechamp, François, Sr., 75n158
Dechamp family (François, Jr., Charles, Joseph), 7, 19, 34, 36, 53, 64n13, 90, 92
Degrai (Deargen, Degray, Degree), Charles, 55, 80n241
Deguire, Baptiste, 8–9, 11, 23, 65n32, 102n25
Delorme, François, 13, 16, 21, 60, 69n80
Demaray (Demarais, Demary), Louis, 43, 78n201
Demay (Desmay), Francois, 54, 104n46
Demet, Tessant, 90, 104n46
Denig, Edwin T., viii, 12, 74n139, 103n32, 106n68
Denoyer (Desnoyer), Cyprien, 16, 69n80
Derois (Dero, Deroy), Maxan, 55, 79n237
Diabreuille (u/i), 23
Diana (steamboat), 81n266
Dickson, Robert, 71n98
Dickson, Thomas, 19, 71n98
Disease/illness. *See* health
Dodge, Henry, 25, 74n129
dogs, 7, 12, 25, 60, 96, 105n63, 114
dog sleds/trains, 8–9, 16–17, 21–22, 55–56, 60, 64n20, 69n79, 98
Dorion, Martin Baptiste, 57–58, 80n254
Doucette (Douartte, Dousset, Doucet), Charles, 22, 73n121
Dougherty (Mr.), 88–90, 94, 103n39, 104n44, 110–11
Dougherty, Hannibal, 103n27
Dougherty, John (agent), 19, 79n233, 103n27
Dougherty, John, Jr. (clerk), 71n98
Dreidoppel (Drydoppel), David, 7, 62n2, 74n146, 102n20, PS [10]
Drips, Andrew, 68n67, 68n69, 105n49. *See also* Fontenelle and Drips & Co.
Duchaine (u/i), 7, 64n16
Dupuis, Baptiste, 80n259
Dupuis, Joseph, 37, 44, 46, 73n112, 77n192
Durand (Durant), Alexis, 8, 65n30, 104n44
Durant, James, 104n44
Durocher, Charles, 7, 12, 21, 23, 64n16

Ebert (u/i), 37, 77n190
engagés (employees): agent/*bourgeois*, viii, 2, 33, 57, 59, 62n5, 66n39, 66n43, 70n84, 70n88, 71n98, 76n182, 80n250, 102n14, 102n17, 103n27; blacksmiths, 42, 57, 88, 97; boatmen (*bateliers*, steersmen, patroon), 62n7, 64n17, 65n32, 69n80, 71n99, 72n107, 73n114, 77n191, 79n219, 79n228, 79n237, 101n6; carpenters, 42–43, 46, 49, 57–58, 64n17, 72n108, 88, 99; clerks, xi, 2, 9–11, 13, 15, 17–20, 58, 60, 62n5, 63n12–13, 64n19, 65n37, 66n41, 67n54, 68n59, 69n76, 69n81, 70n86, 70n88, 71n93, 71n98, 72n103–4, 73n117, 74n143, 75n156, 75n165, 76n179, 76n182, 77n188, 78n213–14, 79n223, 80n241–42, 80n246, 80n249, 90–91, 101n8, 102n18, 103n28–29, 103n39, 104n44, 104n47, 104n49, 106n74; competition for, 88; deserters, 7, 12, 21, 31, 78n207, 86, 88–89, 103n38, 104n44, 104n49; interpreters, 3, 8, 19–20, 42, 60, 63n13, 65n28–29, 67n53, 71n98, 76n179, 78n206, 80n241, 80n254, 90–91, 94, 100, 102n13, 102n24, 106n68, 116; tin smiths, 10, 59; traders, 1, 13, 15, 18, 29, 48, 63n8, 63n12, 65n28–29, 65n37, 66n39, 66n43, 67n54, 68n67, 70n82, 70n86, 71n90, 72n103–4, 74n139, 74n143, 75n165, 76n179, 78n213, 79n235, 80n242, 80n248, 80n249, 102n14–15, 102n24, 103n37, 103n39, 105n53, 106n70; voyagers, 62n7, 63n11, 64n16, 65n32, 65n38, 67n52, 68n57, 69n80, 73n112, 73n114–15, 73n119, 73n121, 73n126, 74n138, 74n141, 75n149, 75n155, 75n164, 77n192, 78n195, 78n201, 78n205, 78n207, 78n212, 79n220, 79n235, 79n237, 81n268
Englebert, Robert, xii
express (communications): from Crow Camp, 54–55; from Saint Louis, 8, 55; letters between forts, 64n20, 67n49, 94–97, 110, 117; to Fort Clark, 45; to Fort Union, 10, 18, 42–43; to Saint Louis, 9, 11–12, 56, 60, 98

Farrar, Barnard (Bernard) G. (Dr.), 68n69, 85, 101n7
Fecteau (Fetceau, Facts, Facto), Martin, 27, 30–31, 75n149
Filteau, James, 27, 30, 75n148
Fitzpatrick, Thomas, 13, 15, 19, 24, 27, 68n65, 86, 97, 100, 102n14, 102n17, 107n88, 116–17
Flourant, Louis, 32
Floyd, Charles, viii
Floyd, John, viii
Fontenelle, Fitzpatrick and Company, 68n59, 68n67, 68n69
Fontenelle, Lucien, 14, 68n67, 68n69
Fontenelle and Drips & Co., 105n49
Foolish (Fool) Bear (Ours fou, Mau-to-weet-ko, Assiniboine), 7, 43, 45, 89–90, 98, 103n41
Fort Alexander, viii
Fort Assiniboine, viii, 35–36, 38–40, 43, 58, 77n183, 77n185, 78n183, 78n213
Fort Benton, 70n88
Fort Berthold, 101n8
Fort Buford, ix
Fort Buford State Historic Site, 65n35
Fort Cass, 11, 22–28, 31–32, 35, 37, 39, 43, 46, 48, 53–55, 63n12–13, 65n32–33, 69n74, 71n98–99, 75n156, 78n202, 102n15, 102n25

Fort Clark: employees assigned to, 62n6–7, 63n13, 64n17, 65n28–30, 65n38, 68n57, 69n80, 70n86, 71n93, 71n98–99, 72n107, 73n112, 73n114–15, 73n121, 74n138, 74n143, 75n153, 77n188, 80n245–246, 80n249, 81n260, 101n8, 105n53; Halsey family departure, 69n81; keelboat traffic to, 72n104; Kipp departure, 69n79, 79n229; letters to, 7–9, 16, 27–28, 30–31, 35, 37–38, 47, 55–56, 60; Mandan villages near, 62n3–4; Maximilian stay at, 65n29, 75n147, 75n162, 106n80; mentions in letters, 10, 13–14, 33–34, 44–45, 53, 57, 59–60; shipping dogs from, 105n63; Sublette and Campbell post near, 103n27, 104n44; trading with Indians, 62n4; PS [9–10]
Fort Clark Outfit, 44, 57
Fort de Prairie, 26, 74n142
Fort Floyd, viii, ixn3, 63n8, 66n39
Fort Hall, 71n97
Fort Jackson (Poplar River Post), 8, 10–11, 13, 21, 65n25, 68n62, 76n166, 105n61. *See also* Poplar River
Fort Laramie, 70n88
Fort Leavenworth, 19, 21, 25, 70n81, 71n97, 101n5
Fort Lewis, 70n88
Fort McKenzie, viii; bison robe trade, 1; considered dangerous, 79n226; employees/directors, 68n59, 70n88, 71n98, 72n104, 73n114, 73n117–18, 73n126, 74n138, 77n187, 77n191, 78n193, 78n195, 78n200, 79n223, 101n8; keelboat traffic to, 79n224; letters, mentions in, 9, 18, 33–34, 36, 41–44, 53–54; letters to, 17–22, 37–38, 40–44, 49–52, 55; Maximilian visit to, 72n108, 73n114–15, 74n146, 102n20–21; relations with Indians, 67n48, 67n54, 71n96, 73n125, 76n176, 80n259, 106n68
Fort Peck Agency, 70n88
Fort Piegan, viii, 67n48
Fort Pierre Chouteau, 11–12, 28, 36–37, 44, 53, 58, 63n8, 64n21, 66n39, 66n42–43, 67n50, 69n81, 75n165, 77n184, 79n229, 80n246, 81n266; letter books and journal, 80n254
Fort Pierre Outfit, 44
Fort Snelling, 66n45, 71n90
Fort Tecumseh: Chardon as agent, ixn3, 63n8; construction, 66n39; *engagés* assigned to, 69n80, 70n86, 72n104, 73n126, 78n207, 80n254; Hamilton visit at, 63n9; Laidlaw as agent, 67n50; letter book and journal, 62n7, 63n9, 80n254
Fort Union: artist depictions, viii; competition from Sublette and Campbell, 10–15, 32; construction, viii, ixn3–4, 2, 10, 63n8; letter book and transcriptions, xi–xii, 85–86; role in fur trade, viii–ix, 1–4; serving as army post, ix; PS [2, 5–6, 11]
Fort Van Buren, viii, 63n12, 78n202, 80n239. *See also* Rosebud Creek
Fort Vermillion, 59
Fort Washington, 67n50, 71n98
Fort William: bison robe trade, 9; competition with Fort Union, 3, 10; construction, 19, 23, 78n214, 86–88; purchase by Fontenelle and Fitzpatrick, 68n67; Sublette departure for Saint Louis, 86, 109; PS [6]
Forty Years a Fur Trader on the Upper Missouri (Larpenteur), 78n214, 85–86
Fox (keelboat), 72n104
Frainier (Freniere, Funiet, Frenier, Fraiiere), Louison, 31, 75n165
Franchère, Gabriel, 67n51
Francis (u/i), 34–36, 45
French fur traders, 66n41
Freseau, A., 55
Fulkerson, William Neil, 56, 80n250
fur trade: American Indians and, 62n4, 67n48, 73n120, 77n189; Astor family and, vii, 69n75; Campbell journal, 1–3, 85–86; Chouteau family and, 66n46; McKenzie and, 70n82; notable individuals, 63n8–12, 66n39, 66n41, 66n43, 66n45, 67n50, 67n54, 68n59, 68n67, 71n90, 71n97, 80n249; upper Missouri trading posts, viii–ix. *See also* beaver pelt trade; bison robe trade

Gaboleau, Pierre, 16, 39, 69n78
Gardner (Gardeau), Johnson, 2–3, 21, 25, 28, 72n111, 74n127
Garreau, Pierre, 105n53
Garro, Pierre, 91, 93, 96, 117
Gauché, Jackson, 37
General Jackson (Le Fils du Gros Francais, Wah hé muzza, Lye-jan-jan, Ajanjan, The Light, the Shining Man) (Assiniboine), 34, 51, 77n183, 103n41
Gens de Canot (Assiniboine division), 7, 34, 37, 45–47, 56, 87, 95, 102n23
Gens de Filles (Assiniboine division), 45–46, 89, 103n40
Gens de Gauché (Assiniboine division), 47, 58, 106n68
Gens de Roches (Band of Rocks, Stone Band) (Assiniboine division), ixn2, 46, 77n183
Gens des filles (Assiniboine division), 7, 34, 37, 45–47, 58, 89, 93, 103n40, 106n68
Girard (Gerrard), Frederick, 26, 48, 74n138
Glass, Hugh, 71n98, 72n111
Glenday, Thomas, 8, 65n26, 86–87, 97–98, 101n12, 116–18
Gordon, Christopher, xi
Grand Peace Conference of 1825, 67n50
Gravelle, A., 44
Gravelle (Gravil), Michel (aka Jack Ram), 35, 46, 63n13, 78, 104n47
Grendhouse, B., 55
Greybull (Gray Bull) River, 103n32
Gro Francais (Assiniboine chief), 89, 91–93, 95
Grosclaude, Justin, 26, 74n141
Gros Ventre (Minniteree) Indians, 7, 9, 13, 16, 19–21, 26, 32, 39, 45–47, 55, 62n4, 102n13, 103n27, 104n44, 117
A Guide to Documentary Editing (Kline), xi
Guilliotte, Nobert, 48, 79n220
Guinnard, A., 54
Guinnard, C., 54

Guion, Antoine, 21, 73n115
Guisite, B., 55
guns, 17, 21–22, 36, 38–39, 41, 46, 57, 69n70, 70n84, 89–90, 109

Hahn, Andrew W., xi
Hainelle (u/i), 26
Halcrow (Halero, Alcrow, Acrow) Joseph, 34, 46–47, 76n179
Halsey, Jacob, 16, 19, 28, 36, 39, 44, 53, 58, 63n7, 64n17, 69n81, 74n127
Hamille, Auguste, 22, 73n119
Hamilton, James Archdale (JAH), 2, 7, 10, 14, 16, 18, 20–21, 27–28, 30, 33–56, 58, 60, 63n9, 64n17, 75n153, 79n222, 86–90, 93–94, 101n11, 109
Harper, Robert F., 54
Harris, Joseph, 54, 79n235
Harris, Moses (Black), 103n26
Harvey, Alexander (A., Mr.), 12, 21–22, 37–38, 39–41, 42–43, 50, 52, 55, 67n54, 68, 70n88, 73n117, 113
health: amputations, 68n69, 101n7; cholera, 19, 25, 71n98, 106n74; doctors, 15, 25, 28, 68n69, 69n76, 85, 101, 106n74; gout, 79n222; illness, 15, 54–55, 59, 86, 99–100, 101n7, 113; medicine, 25; medicine man, 106n75, 112; medicine pipe, 51; pleuresy, 21, 26; rheumatism, 21, 26; scurvy, 75n147; smallpox, 63, 69n81, 78n215; starvation, 21, 76n174, 89; tuberculosis, 101n7
Heart River, 56–57, 59
Hebert, David, 106n85
Helvish, M., 54
Henry, Andrew, 63n12
Hidatsa Indians, 62n4
Holmes, Thomas, 7, 28, 55, 64n18
horses and mules: American Indians and, 7–8, 12, 19–20, 34–35, 37, 44, 46–48, 50, 65n24, 77n183; as pack animals, 19, 49; buffalo ponies, 9, 21, 25, 55, 80n244; purchasing/selling/trading, 9, 11, 22–23, 25–26, 28, 37–41, 44, 49, 55, 59, 102n25; treatment of, 3, 56
Howard, Joseph, 22, 31, 43, 73n118, 78n201
Hudson's Bay Company, 19, 66n39, 67n53
Hugron (Hunot), Amable, 75n156
Huh Jiob (Wounded Foot) (Assiniboine), 103n41
Hunt, William J., Jr., xii

"The Immutable" (Schiller), 79n231
Indian Wars, ix

Jabotte, D. J., 58, 80n256
Jackson (Dr.), 47
Jackson (u/i), 36, 39, 53, 72n111
Jackson, Andrew, 74n129, 77n183, 105n61
Jackson, David, xii
Jackson Le Maitre du Parc, 46
Janis (Janice, Geness), Antoine, Sr., 13, 101n9
Janis, Antoine, II, 101n9
Janis, Nicholas, 101n9
The Journals of the Lewis and Clark Expedition (Moulton and Dunlay), xi

Kamming, P., 58
Kane, Paul, 76n178
Kansas Outfit, 65n32, 77n192
The Keelboat (Rockwood), PS [7]
keelboats: *Enterprize*, 54; *Fairmought*, 54; *Gallant*, 86; *Louis Vallé*, 64n17; *Maria*, 51, 79n224; *Otter*, viii, 63n8; replacement by steamboats, viii–ix; transport of furs, 86; transport of goods and supplies, 15, 32, 42–43, 48–49, 53, 57; transport of livestock, 21. *See also* boats
Kelly, Hall J., 71n97
Kelly, Mark William, 103n27
Kennedy (Kiffer, Keefer), Alexander ("AK"), 36–37, 43, 55, 77n188
Killeans, J., 30
Kilneuf, P., 55
Kipling, Jack Rem (Jack Ram), 35–36, 46, 63n13, 78, 104n47
Kipp, James: bourgeois at Fort Clark, 65n29, 69n79; letters to, 7–8, 16, 30–31, 37, 41–44; mentions in letters, 17, 21, 28, 33–36, 39–41, 45–47, 49–51, 60; trading post/fur trading, viii, 1, 2, 62n5, 67n50, 117; PS [1]
Kippland, John R. (freeman), 106n86
Kline, Mary-Jo, xi
Koeland, Frederic, 75n156
Kootenai (Cootenasha) Indians, 22, 40, 71n95–96
Kurz, Rudolph Friederich, viii

Labadiere, H., 54
Labonnharde (u/i), 25
Labursier, Etienne, 48, 79n219
Labusico, E., 54
Labusiere (Labussiere), Louis, 45, 78n212
Lacomptes (u/i), 21
La Couris qui Marches (Assiniboine), 34
Lacroix, Alexis, 54, 79n235
Ladéroute (Laderente, Laderonte), Louis, 25–26, 28, 73n126
Lafferrier (Lafiere, Laferriere, Laferiere), Marcelin P., 78n213
Lafleur, Joseph, 78n204
Lafontaine, J. B., 49–52, 79n224
Laidlaw, Mary Ann (Sioux), 67n50
Laidlaw, William: biographical sketch, 67n50; letters addressed to, 12, 28, 37, 53, 58; manager of Fort Tecumseh, 66n39, 71n99; mentions in letters, 27–28, 30, 59; partnership in Columbia Fur Company, 62n5, 81n272; partnership in UMO, viii, 66n45; role in upper Missouri fur trade, 3
Lajambe blessé (Assiniboine), 34
Lake Traverse (Lac Traverse), 67n50, 71n98

Lamont, Daniel: biographical sketch, 66n45; letters addressed to, 53–54; letters from, 43–45, 48–49, 51–52, 56; mentions in letters, 11, 13–14, 16, 19, 23, 40, 42–53, 59–60; partnership in Columbia Fur Company, 62n6, 67n50, 81n272; partnership in UMO, viii
Landry, Francois, 58, 80n256
L'Ange, François, 65n36
L'Anje Guerir (The Healing Angel), 9, 65n36
Laramie River, 59
Laroche (La Roche) (Cree), 39, 45, 93, 106n67
Larpenteur, Charles, 46, 64n18, 72n104, 78n214, 85–86, 101n9, 102n18, 104n43, 104n49, 106n86, 107n90
Latrace (Latress, Latross), John, 26, 74n138
Le Borgne (Le Gros Francais, Iron Arrow Point) (Assiniboine), 26, 74n139, 77n183, 79n221
Lebrun, Baptiste, 69n80
Le Capot Bleu (Blue Cape) (Assiniboine), 34, 96, 106n78
Le Chien (Assiniboine), 34
Leclair, Baptiste, 75n147
Leclerc (Le Clerc), P.(A.) N. (Narcisse), 9–10, 13–14, 65n37, 88, 103n28
Lecompte, Paul, 80n238
Le Fils du Gros Francais. *See* General Jackson
Le Grand Soldat (Assiniboine), 34
Legreii (freeman), 92–93
Legris (Legriei), Pierre, 44–45, 73n112, 75n153, 105n62
Legris (u/i), 21, 23, 37, 51, 93
L'Enfant (Le Enfant) du Fer (Cree), 34, 39, 46–47
Le Petit Francais (Little Frenchman) (Métis), 46, 64n13, 78n215
Le Sonnant (Le Sonant, the Rattle, Mahsette-Kuinab) (Cree), 34, 39, 45, 106n75, 112
Letup, Jean, 32, 76n171
Leucot (u/i), 99
Le Vache Blanche (Assiniboine), 7, 53
Leviathna Company of the North. *See* Hudson's Bay Company
Lewis and Clark Expedition, vii–viii, 66n44, 68n60, 77n183, 102n13. *See also* Clark, William; Sacajawea
liquor: American Indians and, 11, 15, 24, 29, 50, 57–58, 70n82, 94–96, 102n18; distillery at Fort Union, 12, 16, 29, 75n157,; drunkenness, 29–30, 65n28, 75n148, 91, 95, 99, 112; McKenzie supplying to Indians, 81n272, 94–95; trade goods, 10–12, 34, 38–39, 46, 55
livestock. *See* cattle; chickens; turkeys; horses and mules
LoBombarde, Alexis, 26, 74n139
Long Expedition, 66n43, 103n27
Losett (u/i), 26
L'Ours. *See* Fool (Foolish) Bear
Luiss (u/i), 26
Lureman, A., 55
Luteman, Antoine, 34, 45, 57, 72n108

McKenney, George W. (Dr.), 15–17, 25, 28–29, 99, 106n74
McKenney, Thomas L., 106n74
McKenzie, Kenneth, 80n240; as "King of the Upper Missouri," 2–3, 85; banned from upper Missouri, 81n272; *bourgeois* of Fort Union, 62n5; burial of General Jackson, 103n41; buying out Sublette and Campbell, 9, 11, 16, 20, 24, 33; competition with Campbell, 3, 72n104, 86, 104n43, 105n58–59, 106n84; construction of Fort Assiniboine, 76n173, 77n186; construction of Fort Cass, 102n16; construction of Fort Union, 2, 63n8, 77n183; leading bison hunt, 80n244; letter to Ortley, 61; letters from JAH, 2, 7, 34–35, 37, 39, 45–47; letters to Astor, 15; letters to Bellehumeur, 55–56, 60; letters to Berger, 21; letters to Cabanné, 56–57; letters to Campbell, 7–8, 31, 55; letters to C. Campbell, 60; letters to Carlisle, 33–34; letters to Chardon, 35; letters to Chouteau, 29–30, 32, 57–58; letters to Crooks, 16–17; letters to Culbertson, 17–18, 33; letters to Fulkerson, 56; letters to Groselaude, 32–33; letters to Kipp, 8–9, 16, 30–31; letters to Laidlaw, 12–15, 28–30; letters to Maxmilian, 9–10, 27–28, 60–61, 81n272; letters to Mitchell, 18–22; letters to Papin, 11; letters to Picotte, 10–11, 17, 31; letters to Pilcher, 11–12; letters to Tulloch, 23–27, 31–32; letters to Winter, 22–23; mentions in Campbell journal, 89, 91–100; mentions in Campbell letters, 109–11, 116; partnership in UMO, viii; retirement from fur trade, 70n88, 81n272; slave ownership, 80n255; supplying liquor to Indians, 57, 70n82, 71n97, 75n157–58; travel to Europe, 42–43, 61, 66n45, 80n243, 81n272, 101n11; travel to/from Saint Louis, 4n9, 33–34, 43, 56, 67n50; writing style, xi–xii; PS [2]
mackinaws. *See* boats
McKnight, John P., 26, 74n143
Mad Bear (Mantouit-katt) (Assiniboine), 103n41
mail service. *See* express
Mallioux, H., 55
Maloney, J., 7, 27, 30, 64n18, 75n148
Manager (Manger, Mangeur) du Lards (Canadian *engagés,* "pork eaters"), 28, 58, 67n51
Manchester (u/i), 86, 91–92, 95–99, 102n15
Mandan Indians, 9, 20–21, 27, 87, 110
Mandan villages/post: location, 62n3–4; change in agents, 33; competition with Fort Union, 66n41; construction of Fort Union, viii, 10, 63n8; Fort Union employees and, 58, 65n29, 74n143, 80, 117; Sublette arrival at, 101n5; trade with, 13–16, 56–57, 59, 67n50 92, 111; PS [1]. *See also* Fort Union
Manitoba, 73n120
Manta, Narcisse, 28, 34, 37, 75n153
map, upper Missouri forts, xiii
Marcevan (Marcereau?), L., 78n200
Marchand, Jean B., 22, 39, 73n119
Marechal (Marchall, Marchal), Louis, 37, 42–43, 77n191
Marion, C., 58, 80n256
Martin (u/i), 19
Martin, A., 23, 73n125

Martin, Jacque, 71n99
Martin, Lamant, 71n99
Martin, Michele, 71n99
Maxan, Francois, 44, 78n205
Maximilian, Alexander Philipp (Prince of Wied-Neuwied, Baron de Braunsberg): arrival in Saint Louis, 87; at Fort Clark, 7, 12; at Fort McKenzie, 68n59, 70n88, 71n96, 102n19–20; at Fort William, 87, 102n13; McKenzie aid to, 8–10, 13–14, 20–21, 27–28; McKenzie letters to, xii, 9–10, 27–28, 60–61, 81n272; natural history collection/loss of, 14, 60–61, 74n146, 81n271, 87; record of Assiniboines at Fort Union, 103n41; recovery from illness, 75n147; return to Saint Louis, 72n108, 75n148, 78n207; visit to American West, 61n2, 62n7, 67n55, 102n19; PS [10]
May, William P., 55–56, 60, 80n246, 80n248
medical care/medicine. *See* health
Menard, Hilain, 71n98
Mexican War of 1846, 63n12
Milk River (*River au Lait*), 13, 21, 63n13, 68n60
Miller (u/i), 7, 12, 37, 39, 45
Miller, Peter ("Dutchman"), 64n17, 80n247, 103n38
Minnesota River (Saint Peters River), 66n45, 67n50, 71n90
Minnesota Territory, vii
Missouri Fur Company (Saint Louis Fur Company), 3, 66n43, 68n67, 80n249
Missouri Historical Society, 85
Missouri History Museum, 3
Missouri Indians, 66n44
Missouri River: American Indian tribes and, 62n3–4, 68n63; Lewis and Clark Expedition and, 66n44, 68n60, 77n183; steamboats, viii–ix; trading posts and forts, vii, 65n35, 66n41, 66n45, 67n50; water contamination, 71n91
Mitchell (Mitchel), David Dawson: biographical sketch, 63n12; *bourgeois* at Fort Union, 70n81; director at Fort McKenzie, 68n59, 71n96; letters addressed to, 18–22; mentions in letters, 7, 18, 31, 33, 38, 41–43, 59
Moncravie (Moncrevie, Moncreve), Jean Baptiste, 50, 64n19, PS [6]
Montagne (Montaignis, Montaigne), Francois, 75n155
Montagne, William de la, viii
Moose Dung (Assiniboine), 43, 46–47
Moreau River, 19
Morgan, John, 32, 76n167
Morrin, C., 28, 58, 75n152
Morrin, H[enr]y (Hyacinthe), 7–9, 18, 20–22, 53, 55, 62n7
Moulton, Gary E., xi
Mulatto/Negro/freemen. *See* African Americans, slaves/slavery
Musselshell River, 76n176

The National Atlas and Tuesday Morning Mail, xi
Newman (u/i, trapper), 56, 80n248
North West Company, 62n5, 66n39, 71n98, 75n158
Northern Department (American Fur Company), vii, 2; acquisition by Crooks, 2
nutria. *See* coypu

Ogallala Indians, 60, 81n260
Ojibwa (Sautieux) Indians, 22, 73n120
Omaha, Nebr., 68n67
Onkpapa trading post, 11, 13
Oregon Colonization Society, 71n97
Ortubise (Urtubise), Pierre, 8, 64n18, 65n28
Otoe (Otto) Indians, 66n44
Otter (keelboat), viii, 63n8
Otto (steamboat), 101n5, 107n90

Palmer, James Archdale Hamilton. *See* Hamilton, James Archdale
Papiche, Vital, 60, 80n268
Papin, J., 16, 20–21
Papin, Joseph, 69n80, 72n107
Papin, Pierre Didier, 2, 74n146; biographical sketch, 66n41; letters to, 11; mentions in letters, 13, 19, 32; role in Upper Missouri fur trade, 2–3
Papin's House (P. D. Papin & Co.), 26
Parker, James, 74n134
Parker, Janus, 73n120, 74n134
Patton, E. L., 13–14, 19, 23, 68n59
Paul (Prince of Wüttemberg). *See* August, Friedrich Paul Wilhelm
Pellot, Joseph E., 20, 34–35, 46–47, 52–53, 72n104
Pichereau, Jeanne, 103n36
Picotte, Antoine, 66n39
Picotte (Pecotte), Honoré ("Henry"): arrival in Saint Louis, 62n5; departure from North West Company, 66n39; head of Sioux Outfit, 81n272; letters to, 10–11, 31; mentions in letters, 8–9, 19–20, 31, 54; role in Upper Missouri fur trade, 2–3
Picotte, Joseph (Henry), 66n39
Piegan (tribe), 67n48, 70n88. *See also* Blackfeet Indians
Pierre Chouteau, Jr., and Company, viii, 2, 61, 63n9. *See also* Chouteau, Pierre, Jr.; Pratte, Chouteau and Company
Pierrot (Pierot), Chouquette, 78n193
Pilcher, Joshua, 2–3, 11, 66n43, 68n67, 70n86
Pinian, Louis, 80n240
Platte River, viii, 59, 66n44, 70n88, 80n252, 117–18
Poplar River (La Riviere au Tremble), 7–8, 13, 20, 24, 35, 65n22, 67n55, 76n175, 77n186, 105n61. *See also* Fort Jackson
Powder River, 72n111
Powell, Joseph, 66n45
Powell, Lamont and Company, 66n45
Powell, Peter, 66n45
Praal (Pril), John, 54, 79n235
Prairie du Chien, 62n5, 67n50

Pratte, Bernard, 77n184. *See also* Bernard Pratte and Company
Pratte, Chouteau and Company, 2, 45, 54–55, 57, 68n67, 70n86, 76n182, 81n272, 116
Prennard, Baria, 37, 42, 77n191
Pressy, Modest, 54, 78n206
Prince (servant/slave), 58, 80n255

railroads, ix
Redmond (Redman) (u/i), 99, 107n88, 118
Red River Colony/Settlements. *See* Selkirk Colony
Red River of the North, 29, 34, 53, 65n23, 67n50, 68n63, 74n129
Red River trail, 62n5
La Riviere au Tremble. *See* Poplar River
Rivière Bois Blanc. *See* White River
Riviere Platte. *See* Platte River
Rivière que Appell (Qu'Appelle). *See* Apple River
Robert (Robar), Henry, 54, 79n235
Rocky Mountain Fur Company, 68n65–69, 71n97, 72n103, 85
Rondin (Rodin, Roundin), Charles, 38, 78n195
Rosebud Creek, 55, 58. *See also* Fort Van Buren
Rotten Belly (*A-ra-poo-ash*) (Crow), 76n176, 103n32
Rouelle (Ruel, Ruelle), Joseph, 54, 79n35, 89, 103n36
Roulette's Post, viii
Roy, Joseph, 55, 79n237
Ruhan, John, 110

Sacajawea (Shoshone), 102n13
Saint Louis: as fur trade center, vii, 2; Bellefontaine Cemetery, PS [12]; Campbell House Museum located in, xi; furs and robes sent to, 1, 68n59, 76n167, 77n184; Laidlaw arrival in, 67n50; Lamont arrival in, 66n44; letters to Chouteau at, 13–15, 32, 45, 54–55, 57–58; letters to Lamont at, 53–54; letters to Ortley at, 61; McKenzie arrival in, 62n5, 81n272; Maximilian return to, 75n148, 75n150, 78n207; Missouri History Museum, xi; Mitchell arrival in, 63n12; Papin arrival in, 66n41; Picotte arrival in, 66n39; Pilcher arrival in, 66n43; Sublette arrival in, 68n69; winter communications, 64n20
Saint Peter's River (Minn.). *See* Minnesota River
Sandoval, Isidore (Isodoro), 22, 37–39, 50, 67n54, 73n117
Sanford, Emilie Chouteau, 76n182
Sanford (Sanfords, Sandford), John Francis Alexander, 38, 44, 47, 56, 76n182, 80n250, 117
Sarpy, John B., 102n24
Sarpy, Peter A., 81n272
Saskatchewan, 62, 73n120, 74n142, 77n185
Saskatchewan River, 65n23
Saucier, Louis, 21, 39, 46, 72n108
Schiller, Friedrich, 79n231
Sebille, John, 94, 103n39
Selkirk Colony, 29, 62n5, 66n39, 67n50, 75n158, 78n125
Semple, Robert, 75n158
Sevaillen, J., 55
Sibeau (Sicanze), Arguistte, 26, 74n139, 75n155
Sioux Indians (Seven Council Fires, *Oceti Šakowiŋ*), 14–16, 20, 49, 57–59, 65n28, 66n43, 67n50, 68n63, 80n254
Sioux Outfit, 9–10, 13, 65n37, 66n39, 75n153, 81n272, 103n28
Sisseton Indians, 67n50
slaves/slavery, 72n103, 76n182, 80n255. *See also* African Americans
Smith, Asa, 54, 79n235
Smith, Jackson & Sublette, 72n111
Smith, Jedediah S., 72n111
Solomon, A., 54, 116
Stanley, John Mix, viii, PS [9]
steamboats: *Assiniboine*, 12, 14–15, 32–33, 36, 59, 67n55, 70n82, 75n148, 76n172–73, 77n186, 81n271; *Diana*, 81n266; *Otto*, 101n5, 107n90; *St. Peters*, 69n81; *Yellow Stone*, viii–ix, 77n183–84, 102n20, 110; PS [4]. *See also* boats; keelboats
Stensfeit, Thomas, 45, 78n211
Stevens, Isaac I., ix
Stone, Bostwick and Company, vii
St-Onge, Nicole, xii
Sublette (Sublett), Andrew W., 20, 33, 92, 105n57, 116–18
Sublette (Sublett), Milton Green, 14, 68n65, 68n69, 101n7
Sublette (Sublett), William: role in Upper Missouri fur trade, 3; illness, 101n7; in Campbell journal, 92, 94, 98, 100, 103n29, 103n38; letters from Campbell, 116–18; letters to Campbell, 109–11; mentions in letters, 13–14, 20; return to Saint Louis, 85–86, 101n5; trip to East Coast, 107n89–90
Sublette (Sublett) & Campbell, 19, 65n26, 65n37, 68n65, 78n214, 85, 102n13, 103n27, 104n44, 105n53, 106n84, 107n93
Sublette (Sublett) & Co., 10, 13–14, 16–18, 20, 23–24, 26, 32–33, 44, 59, 102n25
Sunder, John E., 103n27

Taney, Roger B., 76n182
Thibault, Jean Baptiste, 101n6
Thibault, Joseph, Sr., 101n6
Thibault, Joseph, Jr., 101n6
Thibeau, Alexis, 21, 73n114, 101n8
Thibeau (Tebo), Joseph, 86, 88, 91, 93, 99, 101n6, 116
Tilton, Dudley and Company, 67n50. *See also* Columbia Fur Company
Tilton, William P., 66n41
tobacco, 14, 23, 42–43, 46–47, 50, 56–58, 60, 87, 91, 93–96, 112–13
Touchette, Alexis, 55, 79n237
Traca, Jules, 32
trade goods. *See* ammunition/gunpowder; beads; blankets/cloth; guns; liquor; tobacco; vermillion
transcontinental railroad, ix

Traverse des Sioux, 67n50
Trudelle, Charles, 12, 67n52
Tulloch (Tullock), Samuel, 7, 11, 21, 23–27, 31–36, 43–49, 52–55, 58, 63n12, 65n33, 102n16
turkeys, 93, 105n51
Turlick, Louis, 51, 79n223

Upper Missouri Outfit (UMO): competition with AFC, 3; creation and operation, 4n9; employee database, xii; employees, 73n117, 102n24, 103n37, 106n85–86; located at Fort Union, 85; McKenzie as agent, 62n5; mergers and reorganization, 2, 4n9, 81n272; operations within AFC, vii–viii, 2, 81n272; trade with Indians, 67n53; transition to bison robe trade, 1
United States Constitution, 38
United States Government: alcohol restrictions for American Indians, 11, 50, 57, 70n82; disrupted trade relations with Indians, 70n83; presents/Indian annuities, 41, 46–47, 56–57, 113, 117; reimbursement for Indian burial, 53
United States Superintendent of Indian Affairs, 15, 63n12, 69n76–77, 76n182, 196n74
United States Supreme Court, 76n182

Vachard, Charles, 28, 75n165
Vachard, Louis, 7, 18, 21, 28, 62n7, 75n165
Vallee (Vallé), J., 46, 55–56, 78n215
VanValkenburgh (u/i), 103n35
Vasquez, Benito, 101n10
Vasquez, Julie Papin, 101n10
Vasquez, Pierre Louis ("Old Vaskiss"), 8, 23, 26, 65n26, 86–88, 97–99, 101n10, 101n12, 109, 116
vermillion (trade goods, gifts), 47, 59, 91, 96, 105n54, 110, 112–13
Villandré (Valandre), Pierre, 21, 26, 73n112
Vortefeuille (u/i), 21

Wahpeton Indians, 67n50
Walker, Joseph Reddeford, 71n93
Wayotte, L. V., 54
weather: viii, 8, 10, 12–13, 16, 27, 30, 46, 56–57, 59, 87–94, 96–98, 104n48, 110
Welsh (Walsh), Peter (Pierre), 37, 77n190, 103n37
Western Department (AFC): creation and operation, vii; operations of UMO within, vii–viii, 4n9, 81n272; sale to Pierre Chouteau, Jr., and Company, 1–2
Whetton (Whetten), John B., 17, 60, 70n85
whiskey/wine. *See* liquor
White Cow (Pteh-Skah, Assiniboine), 89, 98, 103n41
White Earth River, viii, ixn3, 63n8, 107n87
White River, 65n28, 66n42, 77n91, 94
Wilson, Daniel, 75n155
Wimar, Karl Ferdinand, viii
Wind River, 13, 19, 25, 49
Wind River Mountains, 65n27
Winter, Samuel P., 19, 22–24, 26, 58, 72n103, 102n17
women: as wives/mistresses, 35, 36, 39, 56, 67n50, 70n88, 73n112, 74n139, 90, 92, 96, 101n6; at forts, 1[illegible] 52; Campbell description of Indian women, 113–14; producing bison robes, 1; purchase of, 55
Wood Mountains (Les Mountagnis-des-Bois), 46, 77n1[illegible]
Wounded (Foot) Leg (Huh Jiob) (Assiniboine), 89, 103[illegible]
Wyeth, Nathaniel J., 68n65, 71n97

Yankton (Yancton, Yanctonna, Yanktonnai, Yanktonys) Sioux Indians, 13, 16, 20, 67n50, 68n63, 92, 94, 103[illegible] 110, 117
Yankton (Yanctona) trading post, 56–57, 71n98, 73n12[illegible] 74n138, 75n165, 77n187, 78n195, 78n205, 79n237, 80n241, 81n268, 94
Yellow Stone (steamboat), viii–ix, 77n183–84, 102n20, PS [4]
Yellowstone (Yellow Stone) River, 15, 47–49, 88–92, 98–99, 102n48, 107n95, 110–11
Young, Benjamin, 77n184